ADVANCES IN QUALITATIVE PSYCHOLOGY:
THEMES AND VARIATIONS

ADVANCES IN
QUALITATIVE PSYCHOLOGY:
THEMES AND VARIATIONS

edited by

Florence J. van Zuuren
Frederick J. Wertz
Bep Mook

SWETS & ZEITLINGER B.V./LISSE
SWETS NORTH AMERICA INC./BERWYN
1987

Library of Congress Cataloging-in-Publication Data

Advances in qualitative psychology.

Bibliography: p.
1. Psychology--Research. I. Zuuren, Florence J. van,
1950-   . II. Wertz, Frederick Joseph, 1951-
III. Mook, Bep, 1940-
BF76.5.A24   1986   150   87-10195
ISBN 90-265-0849-2

CIP-gegevens Koninklijke Bibliotheek, Den Haag

Advances

Advances in qualitative psychology : themes and variations
/ ed. by Florence J. van Zuuren, Frederick J. Wertz,
Bep Mook. - Lisse : Swets & Zeitlinger ; Berwyn [Pa.]
: Swets North America
Met lit. opg.
ISBN 90-265-0849-2
SISO 415 UDC 159.9 NUGI 716
Trefw.: psychologie.

Cover design: H. Veltman
Printed by: Offsetdrukkerij Kanters B.V., Alblasserdam

© Copyright 1987 Swets & Zeitlinger B.V., Lisse and F.J. van Zuuren

ISBN 90 265 0849 2
NUGI 716

CONTENTS

Acknowledgements   vii

Introduction   ix

PART ONE: METHODOLOGICAL ISSUES

1. Qualitative research: educational considerations   3
   Frederick J. Wertz & Florence J. van Zuuren
2. Interpretation of the qualitative research interview   25
   Steinar Kvale
3. Problems in self-descriptive research as exemplified in a   41
   phenomenological analysis of imaginative experiences
   Amedeo Giorgi
4. Methodology in evaluative research on teaching and learning   53
   Mariane Hedegaard
5. Creativity and the methodological debate: 79
   a mytho-historical reflection
   Mike Arons

PART TWO: QUALITATIVE RESEARCH STUDIES

6. An empirical phenomenological approach to dream research   101
   Diana Reed
7. Dreaming: reality and allusion;   115
   an existential-phenomenological inquiry
   P. Erik Craig
8. A descriptive phenomenology of the experience   137
   of being left out
   Christopher M. Aanstoos
9. How priests experience celibacy   157
   Anke M. Hoenkamp-Bisschops
10. Phenomenology and family therapy   177
    Bertha Mook
11. Verbal dispute and topic analysis: a methodological   193
    commentary on a drama case-study
    Karin Aronsson

About the authors   207

ACKNOWLEDGEMENTS

First of all, we thank the authors for preparing their papers as well as for writing and revising their chapter manuscripts. Also, we want to thank all participants of the Second International Symposium on Qualitative Research in Psychology for their part in discussing and thereby improving the papers. To the University of Amsterdam we are especially indebted. Its Department of Clinical Psychology was so kind to offer secretary help and Marian Buys has fulfilled her typing task with involvement and witty commentary. Its Andragology Department put their laser printer at our disposal and Gert Hulstein spent many hours juggling with the word processor in order to improve the lay-out of the manuscript. Our gratitude is great. Finally, we want to thank each other for our overseas co-operation to complete this book in times wherein for each of us many other urgent tasks were pressing.

the editors

INTRODUCTION

It is well known that psychology, in its quest for scientific status, adopted the models and methods of the natural sciences and applied them to its own subject matter. Despite the fact that the dangers and inappropriateness of using a natural scientific approach for the study of human beings were already pointed out before the turn of the century, the young science of psychology grew with tremendous leaps and dwarfed the countermovement into relative insignificance. In mainstream psychology today, where quantitative and experimental methods have become almost synonymous with science itself, we witness an unprecedented sophistication in natural scientific psychological research.

Simultaneously, however, with the explosion of highly specialized but fragmented knowledge seeming to contain so little personal and social relevance, a dissatisfaction is rising. A small but growing countermovement is intent upon exploring alternative research approaches which might do better justice to the richness and complexity of the human experience. Within this movement, there is a search for paradigms in psychological research oriented towards discovery and theory development in contrast to the verification of existing theories. Its proponents believe that psychology must formulate its own approach to research questions along with methods capable of greater fidelity to the unique nature of its subject matter, namely, the meaning of being human and living a human existence. While such paradigms have been found in such applied areas of psychology as the clinic and in such other disciplines as sociology and philosophy, they have proven fruitful for appropriation by a genuinely scientific, yet necessarily broadened psychology.

In the present volume, we offer the contributions of an international group of researchers who are resolutely committed to widening the spectrum of methods available to psychologists while maintaining the general ideal of rigorous science. The book is composed of a selection of papers presented and critically evaluated at the Second International Symposium for Qualitative Research in Psychology, held in Leusden, The Netherlands, August 1985. The symposium brought together thirty participants from eight countries, including The Netherlands, Western Germany, Denmark, Sweden, Finland, Great Britain, Canada, and The United States. It resembled a study group in that all papers were distributed among the participants and read beforehand, and all participants contributed as presenters and/or discussants of these works. The papers included in this volume were selected on the basis of merit, clarity of exposition, and lack of overlap with research published from the First

International Symposium. The latter was held in Perugia, Italy, August 1983, and led to the publication edited by Ashworth, Giorgi, and De Koning (1986), entitled *Qualitative Research in Psychology*. Therein the authors address theoretical and methodological issues in qualitative research and present studies on perception, learning, thinking, rule-governed behaviour, social attitudes, interviewing, and psychotherapy.

Advances in Qualitative Psychology follows in a similar spirit. Likewise, the volume attempts to move beyond polemic dialogue with more traditional methods and the defensive justification of alternative procedures and instead concentrates upon positive advances in the establishment of a new tradition. Accordingly, this work also includes discussions centering upon methodological as well as theoretical issues and illustrates the use of various qualitative procedures applicable to the study of psychological phenomena. In keeping with the commitment to an approach which is flexible and encourages innovation, these works leave the door open for their further development and for other methods within the context of human science. Although a rich array of findings have been born by the projects represented here, most are not seen as in themselves conclusive.

The chapters are divided in two sections. The first contains those which predominantly stress methodological issues, in particular educational considerations, the interpretation of interviews, the use of self-descriptions, theoretically based research on practical interventions, and the interactive encounter between the subject matter of creativity and the emerging research methods in psychology. The second section includes qualitative research studies focused upon dreams and such increasingly complex interpersonal phenomena as 'being left out', the dysfunctional family in therapy, and verbal dispute. To introduce the reader, a brief characterization of each chapter follows.

Drawing upon phenomenological and symbolic interactional research in the first chapter, Wertz and Van Zuuren provide an overview of methodology for educational purposes. Some of the key terminology, available textbooks, and teaching strategies in the area of qualitative research are discussed. After highlighting the limitations and advantages of methodological guidelines for researchers, the problems and some alternative solutions in the tasks of identifying the research problem, collecting data, analysing protocols, and presenting findings are outlined and exemplified by studies in this volume.

In many qualitative research studies, the interview plays a central role, and Chapter 2 attempts to clarify and re-evaluate the use of this misunderstood and much maligned form of data. After an illuminating description of the phases of interviewing, Kvale suggests that the standard objections against the use of interview data in psychology have arisen, in part, from an inadequate conception of validity which has been applied to the interview. He counters the paramount criticism of subjective bias by proposing a more appropriate, hermeneutical approach to the interpretation and evaluation of interviews.

Chapter 3 explores the process of discovery in research on imaginal experience. Here, Giorgi grapples with the alternatives of using his own self-descriptions versus those of others. This chapter well illustrates the carefulness and rigour which may be employed in piloting different sources of data as they bear upon the research problem. Giorgi shows that protocols may contain implicit and yet discoverable presuppositions about the demands of the descriptive task which significantly influence the data, and he offers fresh observations and problems in the psychology of the imagination.

Qualitative research may be undertaken not only with a well developed theoretical foundation, but with the intention of guiding effective practical action. In Chapter 4, Hedegaard employs her method of the teaching experiment both to investigate the learning process in a 3rd-5th grade history, biology, geography class and to evaluate the teaching interventions. This research provides a fine demonstration of the process of designing theoretically based, practical research, the procedure of participant observation, and the employment of interpretive strategies in protocol analysis.

The section on methodological issues is concluded by Arons' intriguing and thought provoking Chapter 5. He presents us with a mytho-historical account of the rise of the creativity research in American psychology with its challenge and clashing impact of traditional methodology. The author argues that the encounter between the creativity research movement and traditional research methodology was fated. Arons argues that the ensuing dialectical struggle gradually shaped a climate increasingly receptive to the alternative methods now being proposed in human science.

The second section, containing qualitative research studies, opens with two consecutive chapters on dream research. Reed's Chapter 6 illustrates the use of an empirical phenomenological approach to the study of dream phenomena. She is particularly interested in discovering the nature of the coherence characteristic of dream events and in the process through which the structure of the dream may become apparent to waking consciousness. She fluently describes her rationale and the method of "walking through the dream", and presents her analyses of the unfolding dream images of two adults.

Craig, in Chapter 7, shows how a sophisticated existential analysis of a single dream can provide profound insight into the dreamer's lifeworld, resolve problems still pervasive in dream theory, and pave the way for therapeutic emancipation. While Craig argues that the dream must be analysed according to its own manifest time, space and phenomena rather than considered unreal in contrast to waking life or supposed unconscious material, he shows how the dream, by virtue of homologous structures, alludes to waking life, ignored aspects of the dreamer's existence, and liberating possibilities of the dreamer.

The experience of being left out is the central theme of Chapter 8. Here, a variety of subjects were asked to provide written protocols, a selection of which has been placed in the Appendix. Aanstoos concludes that the experience of being left out presents itself as the absence of the hoped for reciprocity of mutual concern. Implications for the implicit structure of the everyday horizon of being-with-others are discussed, whereby an anti-Sartrean stand is taken.

In Chapter 9, not an experience as such, but a life-style is investigated, that of living in celibacy. Together with a confidant, Hoenkamp interviews many Roman catholic priests in The Netherlands. After discussing some problems about reliability, the author analyses her data following the grounded theory approach of Glaser and Strauss. Two contrasting styles of celibacy are presented in the form of case studies and a preliminary typology is developed.

In Chapter 10, Mook challenges the heuristic value of the formal-systemic model currently being used to explain events in family therapy. As an alternative, she proposes a phenomenological approach which simultaneously incorporates experiential, structural, and systemic features of these events. Her in-depth study of a masterful family therapy interview reveals a complex structure which sustained the identified patient's problematic behaviour in the family. Her research illustrates the potential meaningfulness of a phenomenological approach to family therapy.

In Chapter 11, Aronsson investigates the verbal dispute, using a rather extravagant source of data, a drama play by O'Neill. Abstaining from current notions of rationality and consensus in discourse, the author performs a close reading of the drama from a phenomenological perspective. Among other things she concludes that the lack of topic coherence in disputes is related to the fact that quarrellers, above all, try to deal blows at each other's self-esteem.

The subtitle of this volume, *themes and variations,* suggests that the advancing field of qualitative research in psychology is multifaceted and heterogenous. We hope that the present volume will evoke in its readers an appreciation for the diversity of interests, styles, and procedures which have developed out of a common dedication to finding more truthful ways of understanding human life. If, rather than being a final word, this volume encourages others to reflect critically on alternatives and to risk encountering ever more diverse subject matters with promising however unorthodox methods, it will have served a great purpose.

Bertha Mook, Frederick Wertz, Florence van Zuuren, May 1987

PART ONE

METHODOLOGICAL ISSUES

Chapter 1

QUALITATIVE RESEARCH: EDUCATIONAL CONSIDERATIONS

Frederick J. Wertz and Florence J. van Zuuren

In this chapter, we will provide an overview of qualitative psychology as it is manifest here in this volume, with a special emphasis on its research methodology. In this way we will attempt to address some of the basic concerns of teachers and students considering embarkation on qualitative research in psychology.

TERMINOLOGY AND SCOPE

In qualitative psychology, there are many overlapping concepts and distinctions, as is shown by the diversity of terms in the chapter titles that follow. In addition to 'qualitative', the following are also used: phenomenological, exploratory, field-, inductive, interpretive, reflective, and descriptive. Often mentioned as opposite poles are: quantitative, verificatory, laboratory, and logico-deductive. It should be noted that some of these characterizations of research in this volume might be considered generally applicable to qualitative research while other terms describe only one type of research under this broad heading. Let us first establish some order here.

The term 'phenomenological' often appears in this volume. Phenomenology originally developed as a school of philosophy which, from its inception as a science of experience (Husserl, 1900-1901), has had much to say about psychology. These ideas have implications for the definition and conceptualization of our object of study as well as for our research methods (Giorgi, 1984, p. 13-15). This approach has appealed to some researchers in the present volume by virtue of its emphasis on returning (e.g., from received theories, preconceptions, and methods) to the topics under investigation so as to achieve a fresh and rigorously faithful conceptualization of their *essences,* that is their distinct qualitative structures. For this approach, it is an understanding of the meaningful concrete relations constitutive of the subject matter that is the primary target of knowledge. To this extent, the phenomenological approach is consistent with qualitative psychology in general, often itself employing terms such as 'descriptive', 'reflective', and 'interpretive', which may also be used by researchers without an explicitly or more fully phenomenological orientation. However, one important peculiarity of the phenomenological brand of qualitative psychology may be found by contrasting it with other qualitative approaches such as the method of conceptual encounter (De Rivera, 1981) or in this volume, Hedegaard's work (chapter 4), which begin with preestablished theoretical commitments or models which shape the data as well as subsequent conceptualizations on the part of the researcher. Another divergence is that phenomenological analysis does not utilize abstract or inductive procedures, which may play roles in other forms of qualitative research.

For the beginning student of qualitative psychology, probably of greater importance than methodological variations are the commonalities. All qualitative research attempts in one way or another to be *descriptive* of the full complexity of its subject matter. In this sense it is a primary goal of qualitative psychology to express the constitutive features of its subject matter with great accuracy and even vividness. If the term 'description' by itself suggests merely a restatement of the obvious, then the terms *interpretive* and *reflective* tell us that qualitative psychology attempts to do more than merely call attention to the obvious or immediately given by a naive recounting procedure. In our view, the best qualitative research in psychology involves the adoption of a point of view that seeks *insight* into the meaning of the subject matter rather than a merely passive stock-taking of its pertinent facts. This illuminating explicitation of meaning involves a great deal of interpretive thinking and mulling over data contextually and, in the case of human experience and behaviour, reflection, an apprehension of what it is like to live through the matter under investigation.

Some of the dimensions along which qualitative psychology varies also arise in the above terminology. A study may be 'exploratory' or heuristic, as is Giorgi's (chapter 3), implying that the findings are not intended to be conclusive, final, or complete. On the other hand, qualitative research may fully satisfy the researcher's original aims rather than being a preliminary access to the phenomenon. As we mentioned above, qualitative research may be used either in the service of original discovery or as a means to verify previously crystallized postulates. The terminological pair laboratory/field concerns the artificiality of the research situation, and although most of the research contained in this volume takes up naturally occurring events, qualitative research has been conducted on true experimentally designed situations (e.g., Colaizzi, 1973). Hedegaard's research (chapter 4), which concerns classroom learning, is in some respects 'experimental' since it involves the study of a carefully planned intervention. Therefore we would conclude that qualitative psychology may utilize naturalistic data from the field or investigate situations which are influenced by the researcher. Qualitative research may also vary considerably with regard to the extent that it pertains to applied settings, as Hedegaard's (chapter 4) and Craig's (chapter 7) clearly does, or whether its context and motivation is more purely theoretical, as in the case of Aronsson (chapter 11) and Aanstoos (chapter 8).

In conclusion, then, we will use the term 'qualitative research' in a broad sense, implying a descriptive and reflective approach which aims at elaborating the meaning of the psychological phenomena in question. The qualitative analysis of numerical data has sometimes been considered to fall under its head (see Glaser & Strauss 1967, p. 185-223). However, since in the present volume there is no utilization of quantitative data, we will focus on a research process which is exclusively qualitative throughout.

TEXTBOOKS ON METHODOLOGY

In the area of quantitative methodology, many textbooks circulate. To name but a few: Noether (1976), Allen and Yen (1979), and Bellack and Hersen (1984). The directives they provide are clearcut and compelling. For the qualitative researcher, however, methodological directives are less articulated. For the student interested in attaining a systematic overview of the conceptual (metascientific) foundations of these received quantitative methods in contrast to those which undergird the work of qualitative psychologists, we recommend reading the book by Polkinghorne (1983), entitled *Research methods for the human sciences,* or though more difficult reading, Radnitzky's (1968) *Contemporary schools of metascience.* Apart from isolated studies (e.g., Henri, 1972), two lines of publication are to be distinguished here since it is these which have served as a central guide for the specific methods of research used in most of the studies in this volume.

THE SOCIOLOGICAL TRADITION

First, there is the Chicago tradition in sociology, starting with pragmatism and the social behaviourism of George Herbert Mead (1934), incidentally relabeled as symbolic interactionism by Blumer in 1937. "Taking the role of the other" is one of the central themes in this theoretical approach and participant observation is the preferred mode of data collection, as is amply shown in the work of Goffman (e.g., 1959; 1963). Some methodological writings in this tradition are to be found in Cicourel (1964), Glaser and Strauss (1967), Blumer (1969), Glaser (1978), Schwartz and Jacobs (1979), Miles and Huberman (1984), and Kirk and Miller (1986).

The textbook most often used in classes is *The discovery of grounded theory: strategies for qualitative research* (Glaser & Strauss, 1967). This book, however, is written in a rather loose and repetitious way, which reflects its didactic qualities. For this reason, Wester (1984) adapted some parts of it for a Dutch public. Another disadvantage of Glaser and

Strauss' book is that the procedures described are very analytic. The accent is more on unraveling the elements of experience rather than on 'grasping the whole'; relations between the analytically discriminated units are in our view somewhat neglected. Another disadvantage is that the object of study is not psychological per se but may be sociological as well. These limitations do not alter the fact that for many years *The discovery...* has been a relief for many researchers otherwise working isolated and in the dark. In the present book, Hoenkamp's study (chapter 9) in particular borrows its method from it.

THE PHENOMENOLOGICAL TRADITION

Another line of publication is the Duquesne tradition of phenomenological psychology as exemplified in the several volumes edited by Giorgi *et al.* (1971; 1975; 1979; 1983). Giorgi pays ample attention to the philosophical foundations of psychology, pleads for adapting a phenomenological approach to psychological research, and provides a theoretical justification for this (e.g., Giorgi 1970; 1978; 1984). Specific accounts of the research process and general guidelines for researchers have been provided by Colaizzi (1971), Giorgi (1975, 1985), Wertz (1984, 1985), and Von Eckartsberg (1986). A special volume of the *Journal of Phenomenological Psychology* (Volume 16 (2), 1986) has recently been devoted to problems in research methodology and reflects the state-of-the-art thinking in this area. Characteristic of this approach is its emphasis on the *psychological* in qualitative research. Based on the philosophy of Husserl (1913, 1925, 1935-1937), Heidegger (1927), Sartre (1939, 1943), and Merleau-Ponty (1942, 1945), this approach stresses the analysis and interpretation of an experience as a whole, conceived as a temporally unfolding network of relations between a person and his world. In the present volume, the studies of Reed (chapter 6) and Aanstoos (chapter 8) well illustrate this approach.

Until now, both traditions in qualitative methodology have proceeded separately. In the present chapter, however, ideas of both will be used in trying to make the field more accessible for those who want to learn more about it. First, however, we will discuss the limited usefulness of research directives.

LIMITATIONS OF RESEARCH DIRECTIVES

The researcher starting in the field of qualitative research may think he/she is in want of specific, step-by-step directives such as those to be found for other research methods, or, for instance, for cooking. Especially in the present kind of research, however, providing the researcher with directives is only of limited value.

As for the researcher, directives are welcome in only some phases of his/her methodological schooling. At other moments, he/she may not be receptive to them. When, for instance, he is a new-comer in the field and may not yet even have a subject matter in view, let alone a familiarity with its particular methodological problems to be solved, taking cognizance of directives at this stage would be a matter of 'swimming on land'. Once involved in a particular study, however, directives may come too late for him/her, crucial decisions having already been made. In addition, a particular researcher is only in need of some directives, while in other respects he/she may spontaneously proceed in the desired way.

As for the qualitative research process itself, not every aspect of it can be accomplished by simply following general rules. Such aspects belong to the class of operations that are not carried out by virtue of a rigidly preconceived plan. Erwin Straus (1980), the brilliant phenomenological psychiatrist, has been known for his conviction that the most essential ingredients of method cannot be taught. The only thing a methodologist can do in regard to such matters is to specify the general necessity for such processes as free exploration, innovation, creative insight, and critical self-reflection, hoping that the desired attitude and mental operations are encouraged and at least not stifled by methodological prescriptions and will then emerge 'spontaneously' (see also 'General research attitude').

Finally, each research project is, in important and perhaps many respects, unique. Every research aim and subject matter, and even each researcher's individual style, makes specific demands which could not be answered in generally programmatic terms. Any methodological directives intended to be placed above these particular aspects of each research project could do more harm than good. Along similar lines, some directives can be specified only after a good deal of the specific research has been done. These properly form part of the contribution of the research and cannot have preceded it. They depend upon the particular circumstances of the project and on the particular phenomenon or problem under study and might not be directly applicable to another research situation. This does not imply that they are elusive. For the careful researcher, the particular demands imposed by the domain of interest will become clear through the work itself.

Should we conclude, then, that no directives for qualitative research are to be given? We think not, but would emphasize that guidelines will work only if 1) methodological directives are accompanied by concrete examples which illustrate their realm of relevance, 2) actual engagement in research and the reading of methodological texts alternate, with no necessary priority given to the latter, 3) the context in which the research is carried out is taken into consideration in all decisions pertaining to method, and 4) one keeps in mind that it is the researcher who decides at which moment to consult the directives. Here, we will elaborate only the third point, leaving the first and second to the next paragraphs, and the fourth to the researcher himself.

General research conditions

Research, and qualitative research in particular, can only proceed on proper conditions. These are seldom mentioned in methodology textbooks, wrongly taken for granted.

One such condition is that the researcher is able to work uninterrupted by other obligations. Turbulent developments in his private life may interfere with the concentration required since great attention needs to be devoted to the research project. A further favourable circumstance in carrying out qualitative research is the opportunity to communicate about the research process with one or two other people, for example a person who has conducted qualitative research or one who is familiar with the subject matter under investigation, according to one's needs. In order to guide the developing research as much as possible, the researcher's reflections benefit from memos. Sudden insights and associations should be written down as well, for in our experience even what appears self evidently clear at the moment of its inception may be virtually unrecoverable at a later time. These memos may be consulted in various phases of the research and especially when the ongoing research process breaks down (Wester, 1984).

Also, some general aptitudes of the researcher are decisive for the succeeding of the project. Linguistic sensitivity and a feeling for word nuances are of paramount importance, especially in the data analysis and in the final presentation of findings. Of further importance are what might be called the more 'clinical' skills, particularly during the data collecting but also in analysing the data. These concern such qualities as being able to listen and interview in depth, being able to summarize and to take the whole context into consideration during interpretation, being sensitive to implicit aspects of human expression, and finally, being able to create a research situation of mutual trust and understanding. These aptitudes can be learned independently of courses in qualitative research *per se.* They can also be used as criteria in selecting qualitative researchers.

PRACTICAL TRAINING

We have engaged in the process of educating students in qualitative psychological research in university classes with groups of six up to fifteen students. Although we will focus on the process of original research here, we should mention that it is helpful to include two kinds of readings to supplement the 'hand on' activities. Besides the methodological texts indicated above, we often attempt to provide students with exemplary qualitative studies of particular phenomena which serve not only as interesting models of methodology but which are exciting, creative, and show the students the kind of achievements that are possible in this area. Some of the works we have found useful in this regard are Keen's (1975) *Primer in Phenomenological Psychology*, Van den Berg's (1947)

Psychology of the sickbed, Bachelard's (1947) *La psychoanalyse du feu* and Berger and Mohr's (1967) *A fortunate man.*

We have found that it is best if the student's first research project is one conducted by the class as a whole, so a cooperative effort is engaged along with the teachers guidance, in making choices and solving methodological problems. The first task is to choose a phenomenon or research problem, and it is best to select one that is of direct interest to the students. We have sometimes selected a subject matter ourselves and at other times solicited suggestions from the class along with preliminary discussions about the motivating interests and problems involved in specific topics. Some of the topics we have researched in this context are 'fire', 'guilt', 'friendship', 'lying', 'procrastination', 'laughter', 'sexual attraction', 'infidelity', 'feelings about living apart together' or (of interest in many European countries) 'future unemployment'.

Subsequently, students are asked to collect some data, e.g., by writing first person descriptions themselves, by interviewing each other or one or two college students or neighbours. The experience of being an interviewee may help them in empathizing with future subjects and in judging the validity of verbal data collected in an interview. Students are then asked to provide the whole class with copies of the data collected, which serves as a basis for discussion of the criteria of good qualitative data as well as the optimal practices for their collection.

Some protocols are chosen for analysis, which may be conducted by the group collectively through classroom discussion or by each class member on an individual basis then followed by a class discussion. Reference is made to written methodological recommendations such as those in the next section, and similarities and differences in various students' comments and analyses are investigated. Consensus in the final interpretation of the data is sought. When this is not feasible, different options with their apparent suppositions and bases are enumerated. Means of further investigation which would shed light on and possibly resolve remaining ambiguities suggested by divergent points of view may then be devised. It is also advisable to provide ample opportunity for general questions and personal reflections.

Such classroom activities may be left to stand on their own or used as a point of departure for further data collection, protocol analysis and/or formulation of findings in smaller groups or individually on the parts of students. With this common classroom research project as a background, students have proven quite capable of selecting subsequent topics for individual investigation and proceeding on their own in consultation with the instructor and class discussion.

Of course, several variations of the practical training just described are thinkable and worth trying. Our colleagues the sociologists, for example, put more emphasis on (participant) observation and on making field notes. In any case, the student is advised to start with this training early in his research career and to alternate practical training with the study of textbooks on qualitative research methods.

METHODOLOGICAL GUIDELINES

The precautions discussed above notwithstanding, we shall give a description of qualitative research processes and even provide some guidelines. Where possible, the empirical chapters of this book will be referred to. We discuss the research process under four headings: identifying the research problem, data collection, elaboration of the data, and the presentation of the findings. It should be stressed that these are only conceptual distinctions. In the practice of the research, they are intertwined and only partially subject to chronological order.

IDENTIFYING THE RESEARCH PROBLEM

Irrespective of its motivational origin, the first moment of research is a preliminary identification of the research phenomenon in light of the research interest. The phenomenon must be clearly nameable and describable. This research phenomenon should also be psychological in nature, or at least avail itself to an investigation of its meaning(s) as lived through by individual persons. In this present book, rather pure examples of such are 'the experience of being left out' (Aanstoos, chapter 8) and 'priest's experiences of being celibate' (Hoenkamp, chapter 9).

Often, the starting point for research is some sort of opacity (Giorgi, 1984, p. 18), or a discrepancy between the phenomenon as known by first hand, everyday acquaintance and what is asserted about it in the professional, psychological literature. This discrepancy may evoke specific questions concerning the research phenomenon itself or its relations to other phenomena, which questions can become the center of the research interest as well. In this case it is better to speak of the research *problem* than of the research phenomenon. For instance, instead of merely describing 'dreaming', the researcher can try to answer such questions as "What determines the coherency of a dream?" (Reed, chapter 6) or "How is the dream experience related to waking experience and to the individual's existence as a whole?" (Craig, chapter 7). Also Aronsson (chapter 11), in studying verbal dispute , asks more specific questions like "What are the typical actor- and turn-taking characteristics?", "What are the typical manifest and latent goals?", and "What determines topic boundaries?". A final example here is Mook's study (chapter 10), which does not focus on one family structure *per se* but on a particular family's structure in relation to the problematic behaviour of one of its members, the identified patient. In this context, Hedegaard (chapter 4) even argues for a qualitative psychology which goes one step further than obtaining valid descriptions, namely one that is able "...to explain and guide human living and development", thereby making a practical aim part and parcel of the very definition of the researcher's interest, topic and aim.

Also, especially in the developing field of qualitative research methods, the research problem can partly consist of a methodological question, as in Giorgi's study of the imaginative process (chapter 3), wherein the issue of self-description is explored. Mook (chapter 10) belongs to this category as well, putting one of her research goals as "to illustrate the nature and possible heuristic value of a phenomenological method of analysis applied to a live, structural family interview". It is also central to Hedegaard's study (chapter 4) to explore a complex methodological strategy for ascertaining children's learning process in the classroom.

At this first stage of the research, the explicitness with which the research phenomenon or problem is identified varies. While some research begins from a relatively open-ended standpoint, other projects are formulated on the basis of many reflections, observations, and pilot studies which are used to bring the matter to be investigated before the researcher. At the very least, though, the phenomenon or problem must be identified well enough for one to know where to look for it. This implies that the researcher is in an apparently paradoxical position of having to understand something of the phenomenon prior to carrying out the research. This paradox ceases to be insoluble when one realizes that research always involves a dialectical interplay of precomprehensions and fresh investigations (Heidegger, 1927).

DATA COLLECTION

Based on the preliminary identification of the phenomenon, the researcher tries to gain access to certain subjects and situations in order to obtain descriptions of the phenomenon. This inevitably falls to some extent short of the fullness, complexity, and diversity of phenomena in the lifeworld (Lebenswelt) which are potentially relevant to the research aim, but an implicit wisdom should attempt to preserve as much as possible the phenomenon and its important variations in the selection of data sources.

The rich diversity of subjects, situations, and data utilized in qualitative research testifies to the fortunate lack of a priori procedures. The research process may be relatively predetermined, for instance when the researcher is interested in more or less exact replication of previously conducted research or in extending the knowledge of a specific experiment. On the other hand, the researcher may turn to largely unstudied areas of the lifeworld and originate novel procedures. Here, we shall specify some general guidelines and possibilities.

Subjects
The most basic criterion for the choice of subjects is whether a potential subject already has or can develop some significant relationship with the phenomenon under study. Choices of subjects vary and may include: the

researcher (Giorgi, chapter 3), one or a few other persons (Craig, chapter 7; Reed, chapter 6), expert or professional witnesses such as literary or journalistic writers (Aronsson, chapter 11), a system or group of persons (Mook, chapter 10; Hedegaard, chapter 4), or a larger sampling of people of different ages, genders, socioeconomic classes, religions, etc. (Aanstoos, chapter 8). In general, the researcher considers the full spectrum of types of people in the lifeworld and evaluates their respective potentials for providing descriptions relevant to the research.

Next, the researcher reviews their specific ways of relating to (e.g., living through in the first person, observing as a friend, adversary, or stranger, avoiding, being incapable of) the research phenomenon. For instance, Hoenkamp (chapter 9) has committed herself to studying celibacy, so she chose subjects who lived in celibacy - Roman catholic priests. Because age was considered an important dimension in comparisons, she took care to include subjects of different ages. Of course, not all dimensions important for further comparisons are known in advance. It may be, on the contrary, one of the results of the developing research process that additional relevant dimensions become evident. Such findings form the basis for further subject selection in the present or future studies.

Another procedure that can be used in subject selection is to look for subjects who are expected to disclose the absence of or some opposition to the research phenomenon. In Hoenkamp's study this might have meant selecting priests with a steady, non-secret sexual relationship, individuals who have left the priesthood in order to marry, or even promiscuous priests.

Not only the *type* but also the *number* of subjects depends on the developing research process. For that reason, the number desired is difficult to specify in advance, as is often done in quantitative research. The lack of a rigid standard guaranteeing an assurance of propriety in this matter is one of the most unsettling uncertainties for the novice student. The general principle determining the proper number of subjects in qualitative research which defies standardization, is that data collection continues until the various aspects of the phenomenon have emerged and the variations of the phenomenon critical for achieving the desired level of generality have been mapped. It is time to stop recruiting new subjects when the analysis achieves a stable articulation of the phenomenon's constituents and variations, or, in terms of Glaser and Strauss (1967, p. 111) when the categories are saturated, that is, new instances of the phenomenon do not lead to new abstractions. Sometimes the researcher can use the psychological literature and previous identifications of the phenomenon in the lifeworld to facilitate a decision about the number of subjects. It is also possible to use pilot analyses of subject variability. However, it is not necessary to know or decide on the number of subjects before the research is complete.

Practical considerations enter in as well. In qualitative research, data analysis is time consuming and complex, whereas the researcher's resources are limited. For this reason, Kvale (chapter 2) recommends, for interview data at least, putting serious limitations on the number of subjects, a recommendation we like to underscore for other kinds of qualitative research as well. A deep and profound analysis of one case can be more informative and satisfying than relatively superficial observations of a large number of subjects when it is a question of discovering the *quality* of psychological life.

Perhaps some attention should be paid here to the issue of the desirability of highly articulate subjects. Of course it is nice in some respects to have a well-worded protocol. But as to its validity, one must realize that even, and sometimes especially, the speech of highly verbal people may be far from the heart of their preverbal experience. Also, it must not be assumed that the language of 'less articulate' people does not precisely express their own style of experiencing lived reality. And finally, emancipatory praxic interests may lead the researcher to choose subjects who have not previously and might not spontaneously give testimony to their experience (e.g., Hagan, 1986).

Situations

The researcher must choose or devise situations wherein the phenomenon will best manifest its complete structure and lend itself to data generation and analysis. The researcher has a finger in the pie most strongly when he/she actually constructs the situation. An example here is van Zuuren (1986), who gave volunteering subjects written assignments to violate specific norms in public situations. Also, the researcher may invite subjects to participate in already existing situations, as Wertz (1986) did in his research on taboo perception. Less directive than arranging situations, there is the possibility of asking subjects to choose and recall certain experiences of an only generally specified type, e.g., "describe a situation in which you felt 'left-out'" (Aanstoos, chapter 8), or even of asking for a description of a more embracing present state of affairs, as in Hoenkamp (chapter 9): "describe what it means for you to live in celibacy". These alternatives form a continuum from the researcher to the subject with regard to who is choosing the research situation.

In all these instances, a certain reactivity on the part of the subjects is to be expected, if alone because they are *asked* to direct their attention to specific experiences instead of letting the stream of events take its own course. The researcher can get around this difficulty by employing participant observation, the classic method of data collection in cultural anthropology and also in the more qualitatively oriented sociological traditions (Kirk & Miller, 1986). But now, another attentional problem raises its head, namely that of the subjects feeling watched. This has led to unobtrusive ways of observing. But in essence, the problem of feeling watched always plays a part, even, for instance, in written protocols about past experiences. Here the subject feels the eyes of the future reader, probably the researcher, on him/her. However, instead of defining these interactional consequences as distortions, the researcher can try to lay them on the table and consider them as data to be taken into consideration and analysed. In sociology, it is Cicourel (1964) who has taken this stance. Hagan (1986) and van Zuuren (1986) show its application in psychological research.

It is also possible to use combinations of the variants mentioned above. For instance, Wertz (1986) in his study on taboo perception, asked subjects to enter what would turn out to be a pornography shop and spend time there; at the same time he accompanied them in the shop in order to describe their behaviour as an observer and later conducted in-depth interviews. Hedegaard's research situation is a carefully devised instructional programme in a classroom; she calls her method of observing the pupils 'activity-based observation' (chapter 4).

A more emancipatory variant of the above devices is to invite the subject to be a co-researcher and enter into dialogue with him or her, individually or in groups, to explore many situations, often of relevance not anticipated by either the researcher or subject.

Procedures

In the preceding paragraph the transition has already been made to the procedures of data generation. These procedures are selective and in some ways even creative processes in which the researcher attempts to make manifest those aspects of the situation that are relevant to the research interest. The data to be gathered are descriptions, ultimately verbal. They may refer to many aspects of the situation under study (e.g., things, other people, the subject's goals, the past, behaviours, bodily sensations) and may be generated from various points of view (e.g., simultaneously and/or retrospectively, the subject's own and/or others').

The following are strategies which can be used to generate descriptive data: questionnaires containing open-ended questions (Reed, chapter 6; Aanstoos, chapter 8), eventually followed up by more specific questions; open-ended interviews (Mook, chapter 10), interviews based on questionnaires (Hoenkamp, chapter 9) or interviews referring to questionnaire responses already made by the subject (van Zuuren, 1986; Reed, chapter 6; Aanstoos, chapter 8); the recording of spontaneous dialogue, group discussions, or non-verbal behaviour; activity-based observation (Hedegaard, chapter 4); and the writing of a collaborative statement by both subject and researcher (Dijkstra, 1984).

The researcher may also look for descriptions already available in the library, for instance, in journalistic or literary sources (e.g., Aronsson, chapter 11; Craig's last description, chapter 7). Library sources are recommended by Glaser and Strauss (1967, p. 176-183) because of their time and effort saving character. But they have obvious disadvantages as well. The research interest and the preliminary identification of the phenomenon suggest which kind of data is most revelatory. Their ultimate value and limits, however, are disclosed only in the analysis and practical applications. Here as most everywhere in qualitative research, there is no substitute for sound intuition and critical reflection at key choice points.

ELABORATION OF THE DATA

The goal of this phase is the psychological findings. Operations of two types are to be performed: handling and interpretation.

Handling

Sometimes descriptions obtained are short and well-ordered, each sentence being highly informative. But often they are long, complex, and contain some irrelevant material. In those cases the data must be grouped and condensed. How the data is to be grouped depends on the specific aims of the research. The groupings in the case of a researcher interested in preserving each individual's mode of expression are different from those of one interested in typical themes shared by many individuals. Several operations, which may be enacted reflectively, in deliberate steps, or spontaneously and taken for granted are to be distinguished here.

One starts reading, or listening to the data openly, attending to and perhaps explicitly demarcating changes in meaning or specifying constituent unities of meaning. Repetition is often recognized and eliminated, although one should realize that in some cases repetition itself expresses an emphasis or a meaning that is crucial in understanding the phenomenon. Also, description not revelatory of the phenomenon or relevant to the research interest should be judged as such and discarded. However, a potential problem here is that what on the surface appears to be unconnected with the phenomenon may be revelatory of it upon deeper reflection. For this reason we recommend a conservative approach to the discarding operations while acknowledging the great practical importance of reducing the unwieldy bulk of data to a more manageable level.

Subsequently, there may be a preliminary naming of the theme of each constituent meaning and placing descriptive material pertaining to the same theme together however disparate this related material appears in the original description or transcript. One should be on one's guard here because an experience or realization that occurs later in hindsight should not be placed back in the original situation, incorrectly implying that it occurred sooner than it did. A final handling operation is ordering the material in the manner which best expresses the situation as originally lived, including its gaps, contradictions, and ambiguities.

The products of these operations are succinct, orderly descriptions made out of the subject's expressions, the researcher's alterations being limited at this stage of research to semantically trivial, grammatical changes.

Interpretation

Here, psychological significance based on structural understanding is sought. This phase consists of an open dialogue between the researcher's explicit psychological reflection and the subject's 'naive', prescientific description. We will discuss three aspects of the interpretive process: the researcher's attitude, psychological comprehension, and generalization.

General research attitude. The general stance of the researcher in this phase can be considered 'openness' (Giorgi, 1970). It might also be called fascination, wonder, respect or even love. It is precisely this kind of attitude one cannot conjure up in a student on command. One of the few guidelines to be followed here would be to abstain from interfering activities such as hypothesis testing, deductive or inferential reasoning, premature generalizing, and value judgments. Often only afterwards or with the help of others, can one determine if one has succeeded in 'being open' or not.

Nevertheless, to give the reader a better idea of what is meant here, we will do some further paraphrasing. Openness is related to the suspending of preconceptions ('bracketing') and a fresh, empathic immersion in the lived reality to which the description refers. The researcher slows down, spends time lingering in the described situation, and allows himself/herself full contact with each detail. He/she does not regard the situation described in its neutral facticity but rather in its immanent meanings, that is, in its significance for the subject. The researcher may then become interested in the genesis of these meanings, their relations, and overall structure. More generally one can say that the research attitude described here tallies with some of the skills needed in counseling and in several forms of psychotherapy, except that in this case there is a different goal, namely faithful (and not necessarily practical or transformative) knowledge.

Psychological comprehension. To achieve psychological comprehension, several alternative operations may be used. Usually, one starts by analysing the description of one individual, this sometimes being the sole purpose of the research. We will save our elaboration of procedures used in generalizing across individuals for the next section.

The most important operation here is to systematically explicate, in a psychological way, the phenomenon's constituents, which had already been placed together during the handling operations. Glaser and Strauss (1967) consider these to be operations of abstraction and call them 'coding operations'. Together with the consistent comparing of different meanings, they consider these to be the core of the research process. Their approach, however, is relatively atomistic compared to the one proposed in the phenomenological tradition, in which integrative understanding of the phenomenon as a whole is the top priority, followed up by an unrelenting interrogation of the relations among various constituents. This difference also shows in the use of the terms 'abstraction' and 'category' (Glaser &

Strauss) as opposed to 'explicitation' and 'constituent', which better imply a concern for the contextuality, relationality, and holism of the subject matter (see also Giorgi 1985, p. 14).

Although the achievement and expression of psychological insight is in essence a creative process which at its best occurs spontaneously, it may be of some help to specify several additional operations. First, to see the phenomenon's contours and limits more sharply, one may start by distinguishing the phenomenon of central interest from its 'before' and 'after' as given in the description as well as from other imagined situations in which it is not strikingly manifest. A good example here is to be found in Wertz' (1985) study on victimization, where he explored what was going on before and after the victimization and imagined how life would have proceeded if there had been no crime in order to focus on the essence of victimization.

Also very helpful in understanding a verbal description psychologically is searching for and putting on stage *implicit* meanings. These concern aspects of the situation which are suggested though not stated in the description, including those which are omitted or concealed. They may refer to the person's hidden assumptions and comparisons, subtly expressed emotional connotations and colourings, unacknowledged goals or aims, and perhaps even how he feels toward the researcher and the research project. Of course the accompanying non-verbal behaviour can also be very revealing, but researchers are not always in a position to take record of it. Goffman (1959, p. 8) makes the distinction here between "the impression one gives" and "the impression one gives off".

In psychotherapy hidden, verbal aspects of the client's behaviour are called 'cues' or 'covert components of the message' (Beier, 1966). Therapists are trained to develop a special sensitiveness to them. What the researcher can do in trying to grasp implicit meanings is to go over the text again and again, asking himself "What strikes me, what does it mean, what does it imply?", "How does this statement relate to what preceded and follows it?" and "How could it have been said or stated otherwise?".

We give two short examples of the discovery of implicit meanings from the protocols Aanstoos provides in the Appendix of chapter 8. Towards the end of the description of "feeling left out", Fred writes: "....with melancholy I went back to the tent and joined the other sleeping bodies". One cue for interpretation here is the use of the word 'bodies'. He could have used 'guys' or 'fellows'; in using 'bodies' he emphasizes their inertness and incommunicativity, which expresses an important aspect of his growing feeling of isolation, namely the impersonal way of perceiving other people.

In the next description, Glenda mentions toward the beginning "...I was already feeling uncomfortable". Here, the word 'already' could have been omitted; it serves as a cue disclosing her pessimistic expectation concerning the course of her Christmas holidays, which in her case play an essential role in the developing schism between herself and others prior to its full actualization in the subsequent social encounter.

The above mentioned question "How could it have been said otherwise?" can even be extended more systematically, as in the phenomenological technique of *imaginative variation* (Husserl, 1913). Here, the researcher imaginatively varies all constituents, implicit meanings, relations and themes composing the phenomenon from top to bottom in order to distinguish essential from non-essential features.

Also, more directively, the researcher may reflect on the situation according to previously articulated concepts and questions, so that they may illuminate, be modified by, or be negated by the individual case described.

Finally, all insights arising in this phase are languaged in the manner which best articulates the psychology of the individual case.

Generalization.   Often the aim of the research is to achieve general insights, the level of generality being related to data sampling. Assessing the limits of possible generality requires critical, reflective thought; the researcher should ascertain the bearing of the type of subjects he/she recruited and whether all dimensions relevant to the phenomenon have been taken into account. In this, the researcher draws on his informal knowledge of the total lifeworld and may benefit from consultation with others.

All of the above mentioned operations are of continued use, but now they are integrated within further interdependent explicitation procedures. Glaser and Strauss (1967) suggest the constant comparing of meaning units across individuals in order to re-name and consolidate already developed categories. In phenomenological analysis, there is emphasis on comparing the whole structures as well as each specific constituent of individual psychological cases, although for the researcher this means a much more complex operation. Divergences in these constituents and in their overall organization and meaning are discarded whereas convergences are retained in the revelation of generality.

In order to further extend general insights beyond the data collected and analysed, the researcher may also personally recollect and imagine new examples and counter-examples of the phenomenon. In this way, the essential constituents and boundaries of a given level of generality can be delineated more incisively.

Finally, the researcher formulates his general knowledge of the phenomenon in a language which describes the specified diversity of instances included in the general class under consideration, whether it be a specific group, type, or universality. It should be noted that designation of general qualitative findings entails no claim as to the empirical frequency of the referred-to matters from a quantitative standpoint, which would require further research with the appropriate methodology.

PRESENTATION AND IMPLEMENTATION OF FINDINGS

Presentation

It is sometimes difficult to get reports on qualitative studies published in the professional journals. One reason for this is the prevailing lack of familiarity with and distrust of the methodological soundness of such studies. Another, more down-to-earth reason is their lengths of presentation, making the printed text expensive and asking much time of the reader.

How are these drawbacks to be overcome? As to the distrust, more specifically the problem seems to be an inability to judge the soundness of a particular study. What are the criteria? How exactly has the research proceeded? To answer these questions, accounting for one's method should be a substantial part of the presentation, *not* in the sense of legitimizing it profusely but in the sense of showing, in a transparent and representative way, what data have been gathered and how these have been analysed. This implies that a general impression of the depth and the scope of data collection should be provided, together with one or two examples of the 'raw' data. It may be edifying to not only describe analysis of the data in general terms but to illustrate the process with one or two examples. In giving examples instead of the whole material, the problem of length is partly solved. Also, these examples may be printed in smaller characters and if necessary they may be located in an appendix (as is done by Aanstoos, chapter 8).

A characteristic strongly in favour of qualitative research is that its results are usually inherently attractive to the reader. They are psychologically relevant, understandable, and not too abstract. The researcher can add to this advantage by striving for vivid descriptions, or to use Glaser and Strauss' (1967) term, by searching for concepts that are 'sensitizing'.

In presenting the results, one can choose essay-form, as is usually done, or much shorter, the form of a set of propositions, diagrams, or tables specifying, for instance, types, constituents and variations. When the latter is relied upon without supporting prose text, the results become more pregnant and more vulnerable to misunderstanding and criticism at the same time. If perhaps the research includes quantitative data as well, these can be summarized (and analysed!) in inventive tables and graphic representations instead of in a numerical way.

Implementation

The research process does not end with the formulation and first publication of findings. A further moment of the research is required to relate the findings to the various sectors of the lifeworld.

One sector, although seldom considered as such, is the world of psychological theorizing and research methodology. Here, results of qualitative studies may be related to already existent theoretical notions.

The work of Aanstoos (1986) on thinking, for instance, bears relevance to information processing theories of thinking, as does Wertz' (1986) study on taboo perception to the experimental procedures of perceptual research. Another option here is to integrate the results of different qualitative studies. Although of course these differ in the concepts they have generated, they do share a psychological interest and consequently a psychological way of framing. Solid procedures, however, for integrating the results of several qualitative studies are still ahead of us.

Second, the results of qualitative studies may be applied in several relevant sectors of the lifeworld. A first possibility is their use by professionals in the field. Traditionally in psychology, there is a problematic gap between theory and practice, between basic and applied science (Giorgi, 1984, p. 11 & 26). The same holds true for sociology. By their very nature, the results of qualitative studies are easy to apply. They concern lived experiences, are meant to refer back to the lifeworld, and as is stressed by Glaser and Strauss (1967, p. 237), qualitative findings can be readily applied since they are derived from empirical data rather than being the outcome of preconceptions and logico-deductive reasoning. By these very characteristics, the results of qualitative studies are understandable and valuable for laypersons as well, or anybody with a relatedness to the phenomenon under consideration. Sometimes, some retranslating operations are necessary for different audiences (e.g., Fischer and Wertz, 1979).

Finally, there is the value qualitative studies may have for the subjects (and even for the researchers) who participated in the research. Although there is always the potential danger that participating is harmful to a subject, for instance by raking up radical experiences from the past without any follow-up care being offered, it must be said that usually subjects are rather enthusiastic about participating. Concentration on a specific experience can be stimulating and may be an incentive for further self-exploration, as for instance this was the case for Craig's subjects (chapter 7). Being a subject in a qualitative study may even be of help in integrating a particular experience from which one feels detached. Studies on being criminally victimized (Fischer and Wertz, 1979; Wertz, 1985) have aided in restoring crime victims' broken sense of community and also instigated public forums about police and courtroom policies and neighbourhood life. Participating may even bring an extension of one's possibilities in its train, as some subjects in the study by van Zuuren (1986) noticed concerning their behavioural repertoire. In this context one can wonder how Hoenkamp's priests (chapter 9) have continued their life of celibacy after having been interviewed.

SUMMARY

In this chapter, we tried to aid educators and students who are interested in engaging in qualitative psychological research. After spelling out some terminological distinctions and referring the reader to the literature on which the present chapter is based, the limitations and potential usefulness of written methodological guidelines was discussed. With these qualifications as a background, we suggested some approaches to educational practica and some general guidelines for the praxis of qualitative research in each of its four phases: identification of the phenomenon, data collection, data elaboration, and presentation of findings. These guidelines draw on the holistic approach of the school of phenomenological psychology and the more analytic procedures used in symbolic interactionist research. Where possible, examples were drawn from the present book.

REFERENCES

Aanstoos, C.M. (1986). Phenomenology and the psychology of thinking. In P.D. Ashworth, A. Giorgi and A.J.J. de Koning (Eds.), *Qualitative Research in Psychology*. Pittsburgh: Duquesne University Press.

Aanstoos, C.M. (Ed.) (1984). Exploring the lived world; readings in phenomenological psychology. West Georgia College: *Studies in the Social Sciences XXIII*.

Allen, N.J. & Yen, W.M. (1979). *Introduction to measurement theory*. Belmont, Cal.: Wadsworth.

Ashworth, P.D., Giorgi, A. & Koning, A.J.J. de (Eds.) (1986). *Qualitative research in psychology*. Pittsburgh: Duquesne University Press.

Bachelard, G. (1947). *La psychoanalyse du feu*. Paris: Gallimard.

Beier, E.G. (1966). *The silent language of psychotherapy; social reinforcement of unconscious processes*. Chicago: Aldine.

Bellack, A.S. & Hersen, M. (Eds.) (1984). *Research methods in clinical psychology*. New York: Pergamon Press.

Berger, J., & Mohr, J. (1967). *A fortunate man*. New York: Pantheon.

Blumer, H. (1969). *Symbolic interactionism: perspective and method*. Englewood Cliffs, N.J.: Prentice-Hall.

Cicourel, A. (1964). *Method and measurement in sociology*. New York: MacMillan.

Colaizzi, P. (1971). Analysis of the learner's perception of learning material at various phases of a learning process. In A. Giorgi, W. Fischer, & R. von Eckartzberg (Eds.), *Duquesne Studies in Phenomenological Psychology*, Vol. I. Atlantic Highlands: Humanities Press.

De Rivera, J. (Ed.) (1981). *Conceptual encounters: a method for the exploration of human experience*. Lanham, MD: University Press of America.

Dijkstra, C. (1984). *De cursus zelfkennis*. (A course in self-knowledge). Lisse (The Neth.): Swets & Zeitlinger.

Fischer, C.T., & Wertz, F.J. (1979). Empirical phenomenological analysis of being criminally victimized. In A. Giorgi, R. Knowles & D.L. Smith (Eds.), *Duquesne Studies in Phenomenological Psychology,* Vol. III.. Pittsburgh: Duquesne University Press.

Giorgi, A. (1970). *Psychology as a human science.* New York: Harper.

Giorgi, A. (1975). An application of phenomenological method in psychology. In A. Giorgi, C. Fischer, & E. Murray (Eds.), *Duquesne Studies in Phenomenological Psychology,* Vol. II. Pittsburgh: Duquesne University Press.

Giorgi, A. (1978). *Fenomenologie en de grondslagen van de psychologie.* (Phenomenology and the Foundations of Psychology). Meppel (The Neth.): Boom.

Giorgi, A. (1984). Towards a new paradigm for psychology. In C.M. Aanstoos, (Ed.), Exploring the lived world; readings in phenomenological psychology. West Georgia College: *Studies in the Social Sciences XXIII.*

Giorgi, A. (1985a). Sketch of a psychological phenomenological method. In A. Giorgi, (Ed.), *Phenomenology and Psychological Research.* Pittsburgh: Duquesne University Press.

Giorgi, A. (Ed.) (1985b). *Phenomenology and psychological research.* Pittsburgh: Duquesne University Press.

Giorgi, A., Fischer, W., & Von Eckartsberg, R. (Eds.) (1971). *Duquesne studies in phenomenological psychology,* Vol. I. Pittsburgh: Duquesne University Press.

Giorgi, A., Fischer, C., & Murray, E. (1975). *Duquesne studies in phenomenological psychology,* Vol. II. Pittsburgh: Humanities Press.

Giorgi, A., Knowles, R., & Smith, D. (1979). *Duquesne studies in phenomenological psychology,* Vol. III. Pittsburgh: Humanities Press.

Giorgi, A., Barton, A., & Maes, C. (1983). *Duquesne studies in phenomenological psychology,* Vol. IV. Pittsburgh: Humanities Press.

Glaser, B.G. (1978). *Theoretical sensitivity; advances in the methodology of grounded theory.* San Francisco: University of California.

Glaser, B.G. & Strauss, A.L. (1967). *The discovery of grounded theory; strategies for qualitative research.* Chicago: Aldine.

Goffman, E. (1959). *The presentation of self in everyday life.* New York: Doubleday.

Goffman, E. (1963). *Behavior in public places; notes on the social organization of gatherings.* New York: The Free Press.

Hagan, T. (1986). Interviewing the downtrodden. In P.D. Ashworth, A. Giorgi, & A.J.J. de Koning (Eds.), *Qualitative Research in Psychology.* Pittsburgh: Duquesne University Press.

Heidegger, M. (1927). *Being and time.* New York: Harper and Row.

Henri, J. (1972). *Pathways to madness.* New York: Random House.

Husserl, E. (1900/1901). *Logical investigations. (Trans. J. Findlay).* New York: Humanities Press (1970).

Husserl, E. (1913). *Ideas pertaining to a pure phenomenology and to a phenomenological philosophy: First book.* Boston: Martinus Nijhoff (1983).

Husserl, E. (1925). *Phenomenological psychology.* Boston: Martinus Nijhoff (1977).

Husserl, E. (1935-1937). *The crisis of European sciences and transcendental phenomenology.* Evanston, Ill.: Northwestern University Press (1954).

Keen, E. (1975). *A Primer in phenomenological psychology.* New York: Holt, Rinehart and Winston.

Kirk, J. & Miller, M.L. (1986). *Reliability and validity in qualitative research.* London: Sage.

Mead, G.H. (1934). *Mind, self and society, from the standpoint of a social behaviorist.* Chicago: Chicago University Press.

Merleau-Ponty, M. (1942). *The structure of behavior.* Boston: Beacon Press (1963).

Merleau-Ponty, M. (1945). *Phenomenology of perception.* London: Routledge and Kegan Paul (1962).

Miles, M.B., & Huberman, A.M. (1984). *Qualitative data-analysis; a sourcebook of new methods.* London: Sage.

Noether, G.E. (1976). *Introduction to statistics, a non-parametric approach.* Boston: Houghton Mifflin Company.

Polkinhorne, D. (1983). *Methodology for the human sciences: systems of inquiry.* Albany: Suny Press.

Radnitzky, G. (1968). *Contemporary schools of metascience.* Chicago: Henry Regnery.

Sartre, J.P. (1939). *The emotions: outline of a theory.* New York: Philosophical Library (1948).

Sartre, J.P. (1943). *Being and nothingness.* New York: Philosophical Library (1956).

Schwartz, H. & Jacobs, J. (1979). *Qualitative sociology; a method to the madness.* New York: The Free Press.

Straus, E.W. (1980). *Phenomenological psychology.* New York: Garland.

Van den Berg, J.H. (1966). *Psychology of the sickbed.* Pittsburgh: Duquesne University Press.

Von Eckartsberg, R. (1986). *Lifeworld experience: existential-phenomenological research approaches in psychology.* Lanham, MD: Center for Advanced Research in Phenomenology and University Press of America.

Wertz, F.J. (1984). Procedures in phenomenological research and the question of validity. In C.M. Aanstoos (Ed.), Exploring the lived world; readings in phenomenological psychology. West Georgia College: *Studies in the Social Sciences XXIII.*

Wertz, F.J. (1985). Method and findings in a phenomenological psychological study of a complex life-event: being criminally victimized. In A. Giorgi (Ed.), *Phenomenology and psychological research.* Pittsburgh: Duquesne University Press.

Wertz, F.J. (1986). Perception in a taboo situation. In P.D. Ashworth, A. Giorgi, & A.J.J. de Koning (Eds.), *Qualitative Research in Psychology.* Pittsburgh: Duquesne University Press.

Wester, F.P.J. (1984). *De gefundeerde theorie-benadering; een strategie voor kwalitatief onderzoek.* (The grounded theory approach: a strategy for qualitative research). Nijmegen University (The Neth.): Dissertation.

Zuuren, F.J. van (1986). The experience of breaking the rules. In P.D. Ashworth, A. Giorgi, & A.J.J. de Koning (Eds.). *Qualitative Research in Psychology.* Pittsburgh: Duquesne University Press.

Chapter 2

INTERPRETATION OF THE QUALITATIVE RESEARCH INTERVIEW[1]

Steinar Kvale

In recent years, the qualitative interview has become extensively used within psychological research. At the same time, earlier synonymizing of science and quantification is declining. When the qualitative research interview is used, specific problems appear both in the research process and in the communication of the results. I shall here argue that several of these problems are not due to the relative newness of the interview method nor to insufficiently developed techniques, but that they are the result of unclarified theoretical assumptions.

The objective of the qualitative research interview may be described as one of obtaining qualitative descriptions of the interviewee's life-world in order to interpret the meaning of the described phenomena. Contrary to the positivist philosophy of science, which has influenced so many discussions within the social sciences, the specific character of the interview method can best be understood on the basis of a phenomenological and hermeneutical philosophy (Kvale, 1983a). This is the point of departure for the following discussion.

In the first section, some practical problems in the research process and the communication of results from interview investigations will be described. Subsequently, some consequences of a re-interpretation of subjectivity through interpretations will be outlined. The empirical point of departure is my own experiences from an interview investigation of the influence of grades on high school pupils (Kvale, 1980).

SOME PRACTICAL PROBLEMS

THE FIVE PHASES OF THE RESEARCH PROCESS

Somewhat pushed to extremes, an interview investigation can be described by five characteristic phases:

The antipositivist enthusiasm. An interview project usually begins with enthusiasm and commitment. The researcher is intensively engaged in a problem and wants to carry out realistic natural life research. It has to be meaningful qualitative research of common people's lives and not a 'positivist' quantifying data gathering on the basis of some abstract theories.

The interview-quoting phase . By now the researcher will have recorded the initial interviews and is involved in what the interviewees have told him. Forming a contrast to the more ideological enthusiasm in the antipositivist phase, the second phase may be characterized by a personal engagement in and a solidary identification with the interviewees who have revealed so much of their often oppressing life situation to the interviewer. The researcher communicates to his colleagues a wealth of new quotations. Although exciting at first, it may, after a while, be difficult for his colleagues to fully share the interviewer's involvement in his interviewees' world.

The working phase of silence. After a while, silence falls upon the interview project. The researcher no longer brings up interview quotations. Should a colleague inquire about the project, he receives a laconic answer: the interviews are now being transcribed or the analysis has only recently started. This working phase is characterized by sobriety and patience.

The aggressive phase of silence. A long time has passed since the interviews were completed and still no results are presented. Should a colleague now inquire about the project, he would run the risk of being met with distinct annoyance. The researcher bristles up and more or less clearly signals "don't get too near to me". To the researcher himself, this phase may seem characterized by exceeded time limits, chaos and stress.

The final phase of resignation. There are several variants of this phase where the results of an interview investigation are to be written down in a scientific report. One version is that *"nothing is reported"*. The many hundred pages of typed interviews remain in the files. Another version, the *"lecture variant"*, reveals a little more of the results. The researcher may conjure up some interesting illustrative quotations in his lectures, while the final report remains postponed. The *"save what can possibly be saved"* termination is probably the most common. It is a report in which the interview results mainly appear as illuminating and exciting isolated quotations while no systematic analysis of the content of the large number of interviews is made. In cases where a methodical *"final report"* does appear, the researcher may feel distinctly resigned because he has not succeeded in passing on the original richness of the interview material in a methodologically justifiable way.

The intensity of the different phases may vary. Moments of enthusiasm can occur during the later phases of work and analysis. The five phases may also appear when other research methods are used. However, it seldom happens that the contrast between the initial enthusiasm and the rather common final resignation is as distinct as in interview investigations.

THREE STANDARD OBJECTIONS TO INTERVIEW RESULTS

If an interview researcher succeeds in escaping unhurt through the five research phases, his problems are not yet over. The results of an interview investigation tend to be rejected by three standard objections.

The small number of interviewees. The results from interview investigations are dismissed by the objection that they are based on a too small number of interviewees and, accordingly, they cannot be generalized to larger groups. They constitute a too slender basis for a scientific investigation.

The leading questions. The interviewees' statements are rejected as unreliable. The question is put forward whether they are not simply the result of the interviewer's leading questions. The interview material does not reflect the opinion of the interviewees but, on the contrary, the answers which the interviewer's leading questions have put into their mouths.

The subjective interpretations. The interpretations of the interviews are rejected as random and subjective; they totally depend upon the analyser of the interviews. The interpreter will find the answers he expects to find. Another reader of the interviews would come to quite different interpretations and the interview investigation has thus no scientific value.

There is no doubt that interview investigations do exist where these three standard objections are to the point. However, the general, almost automatic, wording of the objections raises the question whether the three standard objections reflect an inadequate understanding of the nature of the qualitative research interview.

A RE-INTERPRETATION OF THE THREE STANDARD OBJECTIONS

An attempt to re-evaluate the three standard objections to interview results will now be made on the basis of an alternative understanding of the qualitative research interview. The two first objections, i.e., the small number of interviewees and the leading questions, are dealt with in a rather brief and postulating manner. A re-evaluation of the third objection, i.e., subjective interpretations, will be thoroughly treated in the last part of the paper.

Too many interviewees. - Interview investigations are often based on too many interviewees and therefore the individual interviews cannot be properly interpreted. Within the social sciences, in general, there has been for a long time a quantitative hegemony where quantitative analyses of data from a large number of persons have been the criterion for acquiring scientific status (Kvale, 1983b). The fact that creative research has often been based on intensive analyses of few persons' relations to their surroundings is hereby neglected. This applies to qualitative research, e.g. psychoanalysis, as well as to pioneer work within a quantitative natural science psychology. One example is Ebbinghaus' experimental-statistical investigations of one person's memory activities (his own), and another is Skinner's critique against the use of large groups which hamper a systematic analysis of how behaviour is controlled by the surroundings (Kvale, 1986). By thoroughly analysing a small number of individuals' relations to their environment, it becomes possible to bring out general relations. By explicitly describing the procedure, it becomes possible for others to re-examine the results.

Current interview projects are, however, often characterized by a large number of subjects and a general text-inflation. For instance, my own interview investigation on grading in high school involving 30 pupils and 6 teachers resulted in more than 1,000 pages of interview protocols (Kvale, 1980). A German interview investigation among unemployed school teachers ended with 20,000 pages (Mayring, 1983).

As a contrast, systematic text analysis which penetrates deeply into the texts and also explicates the presuppositions of the analysis, often result in reports where the analysis by far exceeds the original text in number of pages, e.g. Giorgi's (1975) phenomenological analysis of an interview on learning. A quantitatively limited text is a condition for a profound and systematic analysis of the content and structure of the text as well as for an analysis of one's own presuppositions and of one's questions to the text.

Too few leading questions. - In interview investigations the interviewer often asks too few deliberately leading questions, and therefore the analysis of the completed interviews is often made difficult. As a result of a general demand for neutrality within the social sciences, a non-directive interview form has become widely used resulting in inordinately long interviews and lack of elaboration of the interviewees' answers in the interview situation itself.

A research interview is unavoidably leading in a formal sense. The interviewer leads the interviewees to talk about specific topics and, more or less, in a particular order. As to the content, the interviewer has the possibility of clarifying the meaning of the answers and of testing hypotheses by deliberately asking leading questions. When analysing the question-answer sequences in the interview transcriptions, it is possible to evaluate whether and to what extent the interviewee is led by the interviewer's wording of the questions.

A deliberate use of leading questions in a hypothesis-testing interview is not new. It is well illustrated in a famous quotation from Shakespeare:

Hamlet: Do you see yonder cloud that's almost in shape of a camel?
Polonius: By th' mass, and 'tis like a camel indeed.
Hamlet: Me thinks it is like a weasel.
Polonius: It is back'd like a weasel.
Hamlet: Or like a whale ?
Polonius: Very like a whale.
Hamlet: ....(aside) They fool me to the top of my bent.
(Hamlet, Act III, scene 2)

Too few subjective interpretations. - Interview investigations often contain too few reflected subjective interpretations. In social research, there may be an implicit demand for objectivity in the sense that statements have only one correct meaning and the task of the interpretation is to find this one and only meaning. Contrary to this demand, a hermeneutical mode of understanding implies a legitimate plurality of interpretations. Neither author, nor reader may fully know the content of a text. What meaning a reader finds in a text depends upon the questions he poses to the text. When different readers reach different interpretations of the same text it is not necessarily due to a subjective haphazardness in interpreting the meaning, but may be a consequence of the fact that readers pose different questions to the text and thus get different answers. The subjective arbitrary character of interpretation appears because the questions asked to a text are not explicitly stated, i.e., the 'spectacles' through which the text is read are not specified. Hereto comes the lack of recognition of how the questions asked to the text co-constitute the resulting answers.

In an application of a phenomenological method to interview analysis, Giorgi (1975) acknowledges that another researcher, who would read the interview he is analysing, could quite well reach another interpretation. The decisive criterion in this kind of qualitative research, according to Giorgi, is whether a reader who adopts the same viewpoint as articulated by the researcher can also see what the researcher saw, whether or not he agrees with it. When the researchers' different perspectives on a text are made explicit, the different interpretations should also become comprehensible.

The main problem in an interview analysis is not the variety of interpretations of the same statement but a lack of clarification of the questions asked to the text which co-constitute the different interpretations. The decisive issue in interpretation is then to explicate the questions asked to the interview text, and to account for the general perspective adopted towards a text. With such a perspective explication, several interpretations of the same text will not be a weakness but a richness and strength in the qualitative research interview.

ON THE RELATION BETWEEN STANDARD OBJECTIONS AND PHASE PROBLEMS

It is now possible to see an intrinsic relation between the earlier mentioned phase problems of the research process and the standard objections against the interview results. In the research process the planning and interviewing phases were characterized by enthusiasm and involvement; quietness, aggression and resignation became conspicuous in the later analysis phase. It is possible that the initial enthusiasm may have contributed to the later problems in the phase of analysis. A general anti-positivism may have contributed to an anti-methodological attitude whereby problems of method do not become visible until the interpretation of the completed interviews. The analysis may then easily end up in a subjective interview quoting impressionism or in a formalistic quantifying straitjacket, neither coming to grips with the wealth of meanings in the interview text. A solidary identification with the interviewees may further hamper the necessary theoretical distance in the interview analysis.

Despite a verbal anti-positivism, interviewers may have been caught in the research process by the three standard objections against interview results. The pressure for quantity may have resulted in a far too extensive text material, making a systematic and thorough text analysis difficult. The demand for neutrality, with the critique of leading questions, may have implied that a clarification of the meaning of the statements does not take place in the interview itself, but has to be made on an unnecessarily slender basis in the following interview analysis. The fear of subjectivity may have implied that the researcher's perspective, the basis for the questions he asks to a text, and also for the resulting answers often remain implicit, whereby different interpretations may appear haphazard and subjective. Paradoxically, a fixation on the leading questions in the interview phase has taken place parallel to a neglect of the influence of the questions asked to the text in the phase of analysis.

SOME QUESTIONS TO AN INTERVIEW TEXT

The relation between questions to and answers from an interview text will now be discussed in connection with different types of questions to interview texts on grading. One type of question concerns the context and level of interpretation. Another type of question is whether the interviewee is considered an informant or a representative. The last type of question refers to statements which, from the perspective of an informant, turn out to be empirically invalid. From the perspective of a representative, they may be questioned with respect to the consequences as well as the origin of the invalid understanding.

THREE LEVELS OF INTERPRETATION

I know that somebody will say that it is wheedling ("apple polishing") if one seems to be more interested in a subject than is usual and says: "This is really interesting", asks a lot of questions, wanting explanations. I don't think it is...

In religious instruction, where we get grades, but do not have an examination at the end ofthe school year, there is plenty of time to talk about anything else. Well, people do their homework during these lessons, and then we sometimes, perhaps two or three of us, discuss something interesting with the teacher. And then, afterwards, it sometimes happens that someone remarks: "Well, well, somebody seems to be wheedling".

(About other pupils, later on in the interview): "Sometimes we don't know whether they do it in order to wheedle or not, but at other times it seems very opportunistic. (In a tense voice): It's rather unpleasant... It isn't easy to figure out whether people wheedle or whether they're just interested (Kvale, 1980, p. 67).

This pupil's statement is rich in information about the grades' influence on the relation between teachers and pupils. However, it is not quite clear what the separate statements mean. As an attempt to explicate the meaning of the statement several types of questions will be asked to the text. One approach is to question the meaning of the text on three levels, or in three interpretation contexts: self-understanding, common sense, and theory.

Self-understanding. On this level the interpreter attempts to condense what the interviewee himself understands as the meaning of his statement. The interpretation is here, more or less, limited to the self-understanding of the interviewee. It is a summing up of the meaning of the interviewee's statement from the interviewee's own viewpoint as this is understood by the researcher.

This pupil is interested in the subject of religious instruction and enjoys discussing it with the teacher, but he experiences that other pupils may regard it as wheedling. In other situations, the pupil may have difficulties in finding out whether the other pupils wheedle or whether they are sincerely interested in the subject. This is experienced as rather unpleasant.

Common sense. A second level of interpretation goes beyond what the interviewee himself experiences and means about a topic, while remaining within a broad context of common sense understanding. The interpretation may include a wider frame of understanding than the interviewee himself does. By including more general knowledge about the *content* of the statement, it is possible to amplify and enrich the interpretation of a statement. A common sense interpretation may also refer to the *form*, and the wording of the statement, exceeding what is directly stated and including how the statement is made, i.e. "reading between the lines" of the text. For example:

Hamlet: Madam, how like you this play?
Queen: The lady doth protest too much, methinks.

(*Hamlet,* Act III, scene 2)

The questions to the text may be *content-centered*, i.e., what the statement expresses about a phenomenon or the question may be *person-centered*, i.e., what the statement expresses about the interviewee. Thus the question 'behind' Hamlet's questions to Polonius may not concern the content (the shape of a cloud), but the person (Polonius' trustworthiness).

To the question "What does it express about the wheedling phenomenon?" the pupil statement quoted earlier may be interpreted as a manifestation of the basic ambiguity in the teacher-pupil relation created through grading. Within a dominating grade perspective, the subject matter and the human relations in school are 'instrumentalized'; they become mere means to an end which is the highest possible grade point average. In the everyday life at school, it may appear ambiguous as to whether an expressed personal interest in a particular subject is genuine, or whether it is just a means to manipulate the teacher. To the question: "What does it express about the pupil's own attitude towards wheedling?", the statement may be interpreted as if the pupil has a double standard, meaning that the same activity is evaluated more positively when conducted by oneself than when conducted by others. The topic involves a conflict for the pupil; the voice is tense and a speculative interpretation might be that this pupil belongs to a group of pupils whom the others believe to wheedle.

Theoretical interpretation. On a third level, a theoretical frame for interpreting the meaning of a statement is applied. This may be a Marxist theory about society or a psychoanalytic theory about the individual. The theoretical interpretations will then probably go beyond the interviewee's self-understanding and also exceed a common sense understanding.

If the question of the meaning of the statement is asked within a Marxist theory about the school as a socializing agent for wage labour, the statements may be interpreted as an expression of learning at school having a 'commodity character'. The pupils learn how to distinguish between the use value and the exchange value of their work. Their questions to the teacher may be led by a utility interest in the knowledge acquired. The questions may also be part of an exchange relation; the knowledge about which they ask interested questions has no use value for the pupils. The question serves only to make a positive impression on the teacher in exchange for a higher grade. At school the pupils learn how to subordinate the use value of their work to its exchange value.

In a somewhat speculative interpretation, the psychoanalytical concept 'projection' may be used: at an unconscious level the pupil projects his own non-acceptable wheedling behaviour onto other pupils.

Interrelatedness of levels of interpretation. The three levels of interpretation are explications of the researcher's perspective. They are abstractions from a continuum of levels, they may shade into each other, and they may be further differentiated. The instrumental attitude towards learning, discussed above at a common sense level, also follows from sociological and Marxist theories about education. At the same time, this kind of ends-means thinking may constitute a more or less common part of the everyday consciousness of school. To some pupils an instrumental attitude may be an open part of their self-understanding:

"My interests have taken me very far from that which takes place at high school. I go here with the explicit purpose of getting as good an examination as possible, with the least possible effort" (Kvale, 1980, p.12).

The depicted levels of interpretation serve the purpose of explicating the context prior to interpretation. The abovementioned statement of a pupil on wheedling has given rise to a number of interpretations. The various interpretations are, according to this perspective, not haphazard or subjective, but follow as answers to different questions to the text. Not only the questions in the interview situation, but also the questions in the analysis of the interview text co-constitute the answers. The validity of the interpretation of meanings given must be evaluated differently for each level.

VALIDITY AND LEVEL OF INTERPRETATION

Validity means whether a method investigates what it intends to investigate. The three levels of interpretation - where the meaning of a statement is asked within three different contexts - involve three different explicitations of what is asked, of what is to be investigated. The three ways of asking do not only result in different answers, but also imply different ways of judging the validity of the answers given.

Self-understanding. At this level the question about the interviewee's own understanding of the statement is asked, and, in principle, the validity of the interviewer's interpretation must be decided by the interviewee herself. The pupil's "yes" or "no" to the interpretation that she does not wheedle herself, but believes that other pupils do, is here the criterion for validity. In practice, it is seldom possible to present every single interpretation to the interviewee for confirmation or disconfirmation. The researcher must try to keep his interpretations within the interviewee's context of understanding as he sees it.

Common sense. Here the interpretation is directed towards a more general understanding. The criterion for validity is then whether the interpretation of the statement is reasonably documented and logically coherent; whether there is a consensus of interpretation in a wider context. The aforementioned statement on wheedling was interpreted as an expression of a basic ambiguity in the teacher-pupil relation through grading. It is here up to ordinary readers to judge whether the interpretation is fairly documented and argued. The validity of interpretation does not, in this case, depend upon the acceptance of the interview subject interpreted, but upon whether it is generally intersubjectively acceptable.

The intersubjectivity by interpretations at this level may be illustrated by Hamlet's 'interview' of Polonius. Hamlet here leads Polonius to agree that the one and the same cloud looks like a camel, a weasel and a whale, respectively. The spectator will then probably have interpreted the 'interview' as showing Polonius to be an unreliable weathercock before Hamlet, suspecting a conspiracy against him, puts forward his interpretation: "They fool me to the top of my bent".

Hamlet's interpretation is hardly acceptable to Polonius himself, but there will probably be an intersubjective consensus among the audience. A reservation to this interpretation should be made. Earlier in the play Polonius has himself given a lesson in interview technique, a demonstration of a 'funnel-shaped' interview where questions are asked in a way that the interrogated person will not know the purpose of the questions; where one "by indirections find(s) directions out" (act II, scene 1). Taking into account Polonius' sophisticated knowledge on interview technique, the question could be put forward whether Polonius is deliberately naive in this scene.

Theory. When a statement is interpreted in the context of a theory, the validity of the interpretation will depend on whether the theory is valid for the area studied, and whether the specific interpretation made follows logically from the theory. An evaluation of the validity of the theoretical interpretation implies a specific theoretical competence.

The validity of the theoretical interpretation of the statement on wheedling as an expression of the commodity character of schoolwork, will thus depend on a judgment whether the economic commodity theory is valid within the area of education, and whether the specific interpretation involves a reasonable use of the commodity categories. In this case, the validity of the interpretation will depend on an intersubjective consensus among theoretically competent persons.

Communicative and pragmatic validation. The discussion of interpretative validity has been limited to a situation where the researcher analyses his interview protocols all by himself or together with other researchers. Thereby two important forms of validation have not been included. These are: *communicative validation* where the researcher enters a dialogue with the interviewee and presents his interpretations to him, not only in the interview situation but also in the later interview analysis. The validation of the interpretation thus takes place in a dialogue between researcher and interviewee. A therapy may also imply a dialogue, but in this case there may be limits to the communicative validation of interpretations. In psychoanalysis, *pragmatic validation* may be most important; the interpretations' effects are decisive for the therapy. Freud assigned a limited value to the patients' "yes" or "no" to the therapist's interpretations. Both answers could be expressions of resistance. The decisive validation of the therapist's interpretation took place through their influence on the therapeutic process as instigating the memory of forgotten episodes and the change in neurotic symptoms. Somewhat pushed to extremes, it may be said that in psychoanalysis, a pragmatic validation of the therapist's interpretations through a successful termination of a therapeutic process, is a pre-condition for the dialogue in which a communicative validation can take place.

It is part of the therapeutic 'contract' that the therapist interprets the patient's statement by exceeding his/her self-understanding through involving critical analysis and theory. This kind of critical and deeper interpretation of ordinary interviewees' statements may, however, imply a number of ethical problems.

THE INTERVIEWEE AS AN INFORMANT OR AS A REPRESENTATIVE

Until now, the question of validity has focused on the validity of *the researcher's interpretation of the interviewee's statement*. Validity has been discussed in relation to three frames of interpretation (self-understanding, common sense, and the use of theory) and the three forms of validity involved have been mentioned (the subject's acceptance, a general intersubjective consensus and a consensus among theoretically competent persons). The question of validity can also be raised in connection with *the content of the interviewee's statement*. The interviewee's statement may be true or false, the interviewee can be a reliable or an unreliable witness.

As one approach to the question of validity of an interviewee's statement, a distinction between two perspectives towards the interviewee will be made: as an *informant*, a subject, a witness; and as a *representative*, an object, an object of analysis. Hamlet's interview of Polonius may again be used. To Hamlet, an informant perspective on the content of Polonius' statements - what the cloud actually looks like - is irrelevant; from a representative perspective, the indirect message in the statements about Polonius' attitude and personality may be a matter of life or death.

In the investigation on grading, the pupils interviewed were, from one viewpoint, considered as informants about whether the learning and work situation at high school is influenced by grading. Here the pupils were, in a sense, witnesses, 'observer substitutes'; they were to report as reliably as possible what they had experienced about the grades' influence on their own as well as on the other pupils' schoolwork. From the other viewpoint, the interviewed pupils were themselves considered as representatives of the pupils, as objects who were themselves, subject to the effects of grading. In this approach the pupils' attitudes, as expressed in the interviews, could be important in themselves, be it in the form of resistance towards talking about grading, a general understatement of grades' influence on the school situation, or a distinct exaggeration of the grades' influence. In the first perspective, the focus is upon the interviewee's observations and experiences. In the second perspective, the interviewee's personal attitudes are the theme of interest. That which from an informant perspective may be sources of error, reducing the reliability of information from the interviews, may from a representative perspective be essential information about how the pupils are influenced by grades.

The different questions of validity raised by the informant and the representative perspective on interview statements may be illustrated in connection with the following statements.

"Grades are often unjust, because they very often are only a measure for how much you talk and for how much you agree with the teacher's opinion" (Kvale, 1980, p. 59).

In this statement the pupil gives an exact formulation of two assertions: grades are very often only a measure for 1) how much you talk, and 2) how much you agree with the teacher's opinion.

The validity of both assertions may, in principle, be empirically verified or falsified. A 'triangulation' may be used for the purpose; the same phenomenon is investigated, 'approached', by different informants and different methods. Concerning *'informant-triangulation'*, other pupils also pointed to the amount of speech and a teacher adaptation hypothesis for high grades while both hypotheses were generally rejected by the interviewed teachers. One, or both, hypotheses have earlier been put forward by another 'informant'. Holberg, in a rector speech in Copenhagen in 1736, criticized the examinations of those days for primarily rewarding the pupils' verbal fluency. Concerning *'method-triangulation'*, an indirect support for the amount of speech hypothesis was found; for the 30 interviewed pupils there was a connection between how much they talked during the interview and their grade point average (correlation 0.65, $p < .001$). Concerning the teacher adaptation hypothesis, a small number of investigations exist which show a slight connection between the pupils' use of adaptation tactics and their grade point average (Kvale, 1980). Thus, the pupil statement quoted above on the influence of the amount of speech and teacher adaptation on grade level is somewhat supported by a number of other sources of information, but clearly not to the same extent as the assertion is put forward.

From an *informant perspective*, the pupil's statement then has a certain, although limited, validity. If a *representative perspective* is used on the statement, two other questions are raised: What are the consequences of a partly invalid understanding of the basis for grading for the everyday life at school? How does a partly invalid understanding of the basis for grading arise, how is it 'produced'?

THE CONSEQUENCES OF AN INVALID UNDERSTANDING - The Thomas theorem of sociology.

"You might take "8" as the average grade in a class. And then, if you want more than "8", you have to make yourself more noticed by the teacher than the other pupils. So, in order to deserve a higher grade, it almost unavoidably has to be done at the expense of others" (Kvale, 1980, p. 80).

This pupil, and several others, are convinced that there has to be a certain grade average in a class and that the teacher thus only has a limited number of high grades to distribute in the class. If one pupil gets a higher grade, then another pupil in the class must get a lower grade. This pupil's belief is invalid according to the official regulations on grading and according to interviews with teachers.

While the pupils' belief - that there has to be a given grade average in a class - in all likelihood is empirically false, the invalid notion is part of their social reality and may have consequences for their actions at school. Several pupils report that the belief in a fixed grade average in a class contributes to a destructive competition ranging from passive omission of helping others (for fear that if others improve their grades, one's own position on the grade scale will deteriorate) to active attempts at obstructing other pupils.

While the statement about a fixed grade average is invalid from an informant perspective, it contains, from a representative perspective, valid knowledge about the motives for the pupils' actions by referring to one condition among several for the grade competition that the pupils describe. In sociology, the phenomenon that empirical misconceptions may have real social consequences, is termed the Thomas-theorem. "If men believe ideas are real, they are real in their consequences".

PRODUCTION OF AN INVALID UNDERSTANDING - Freud's Copernican reversal of psychoanalysis.

The origin of an invalid understanding may be essential to the understanding of the phenomenon in question. The question then concerns those conditions in the interviewee's life-world which produce and sustain an incorrect conception of reality.

In his development of psychoanalysis, Freud was shocked at discovering that a number of the patients' stories about being exposed to sexual seduction in childhood, which Freud had regarded as valid, turned out to be imaginary according to new information. The invalid stories about sexual seductions had been an important part of the basis of a sexual theory on the origin of neuroses. The discovery that many of the patients' stories were empirically false, led to a crisis in the development of psychoanalysis, until Freud performed a "Copernican reversal": the decisive point for the development of a neurosis were not the sexual events but the phantasies about the sexual events of the child and, later on, of the adult.

A related reversal from an informant viewpoint to a representative viewpoint on conditions which produce distorted stories can be found in an English interview investigation by Hagan (1986). Mothers, living in slum areas, were interviewed about their experiences with the social welfare system. They had many strongly negative accounts of experiences with the social workers. According to the interviewer, many of the episodes about harsh and degrading treatment by the staff clearly had to be exaggerated and tendentious. The first reaction could be to reject the interview method, as it led to unreliable information about the staff's behaviour. Hagan took on another approach by regarding the distorted statements as expressions of the mothers' generally degrading life situations. Their self-respect was strongly threatened because they had to be on social welfare. The distortion of these situations, as it appears in the interviews, could be regarded as a means of sustaining the welfare clients' self-respect.

In the grade interviews, statements also occurred which had to be incorrect in content, but which were important for the understanding of the situation the pupils are placed in by grading. In the quoted statement on wheedling, the other pupils, and not the interviewee, wheedled. Of the 30 pupils interviewed, no one said that they wheedled themselves, while 16 pupils told that others wheedled. From an informant viewpoint, the pupils' reliability as witnesses on the presence of wheedling must be rejected, because a large part of the statements on wheedling were obviously invalid.

From a representative viewpoint, the empirically incorrect statements on wheedling may, however, provide important knowledge about the psychological situation in which the pupils are placed by the grading system, i.e., why they have to 'produce' a distorted understanding. Wheedling appears to be a taboo behaviour which the pupils would rather not recognize in themselves but which some of them may feel impelled to undertake in order to achieve the necessary high grades. Wheedling refers to a basic ambiguity in the teacher-pupil relation; the pupils may experience the same activities in themselves as a genuine interest in the subject matter and in the others as a deliberately calculating exchange attitude in order to maximize grades. In the present 'situation analysis' grade behaviour is 'de-individualized' and interpreted as the pupils' subjective attempts at solving the objective and conflicting demands they are confronted with by the grading situation.

In summary, interview statements which, from an informant perspective, are empirically invalid, need not be useless. From a representative perspective, with regard to social consequences as well as to psychological origin, the distorted and more or less empirically incorrect conceptions may contain important knowledge.

SUMMARY

In this article some characteristic problems of interview investigations and some standard objections to interview results have been traced to an inadequate understanding of the nature of the qualitative research interview. The issue of subjectivity in interpretation has been dealt with and the primacy of the question has been argued. The questions asked to an interview text co-constitute the answers given by the text and decide how the validity of the answers given can be evaluated. The occurrence of different meanings in the interpretation of interview statements is, from this perspective, not primarily a practical problem, or a principal methodological objection, but - on the assumption that the different questions to the text and their basis are clarified - a strength of the qualitative research interview.

The types of questions which have here been put to interview texts about grading, may also be relevant to other interview texts. They do not, however, constitute a general formal scheme of interview analysis. The question asked to a text will depend on the purpose of investigation and upon the content of a text. Interviews on grading involve partly taboo phenomena, which has involved an interpretative attitude of suspicion. Therefore, interpretation of empirically problematic statements has been more thoroughly dealt with than the analysis of interview texts, which contain generally empirically valid information.

The above emphasis on the questions put to an interview text is inspired by the hermeneutic tradition of interpretation. There are two issues in contemporary hermeneutics which have not been sufficiently included in the present understanding of the interview as a text (Gadamer, 1975; Palmer, 1969). One is the attempt to trace the literary text understanding to an original understanding of the spoken dialogue. The second is the development of a question-answer dialectic, where it is not only a matter of the questions the reader poses to a text, but also an awareness of the questions with which the text confronts the reader.

NOTES

[1] An earlier version of this paper has appeared in *Tidskrift för Nordisk Förening för Pedagogisk Forskning*, no. 3-4, <u>4</u>, 1984, 55-66. The translation into English was conducted by Annie Dolmer Nielsen.

REFERENCES

Giorgi, A. (1975). An application of phenomenological method in psychology. In A. Giorgi, C. Fisher, E.E. Murray (Eds.), *Duquesne Studies in Phenomenological Psychology*, II, 82-103. Pittsburgh: Duquesne University Press.

Gadamer, H.G. (1975). *Truth and method*. New York: Seabury Press.

Hagan, T. (1986). Interviewing the downtrodden. In P.D. Ashworth, A. Giorgi & A.J.J. de Koning (Eds.), *Qualitative Research in Psychology*, 332-360. Pittsburgh: Duquesne University Press.

Kvale, S. (1980). *Spillet om karakterer i gymnasiet - elev-interviews om bivirkninger af adgangsbegrænsning*. København: Munksgaard.

Kvale, S. (1983a). The qualitative research interview - a phenomenological and hermeneutical mode of understanding. *Journal of Phenomenological Psychology*, 14, 171-196.

Kvale, S. (1983b). The quantification of knowledge in education - on resistance towards qualitative evaluation and research. In B. Bain (Ed.), *The Sociogenesis of Language and Human Conduct*, 422-447. New York: Plenum Press.

Kvale, S. (1986). Psychoanalytic therapy as qualitative research. In P.D. Ashworth, A. Giorgi, & A.J.J. de Koning (Eds.), *Qualitative Research in Psychology*, 155-184. Pittsburgh: Duquesne University Press.

Mayring, P. (1983). *Qualitative Inhaltsanalyse*. Weinheim: Beltz.

Palmer, R.E. (1969). *Hermeneutics*. Evanston: Northwestern University Press.

Shakespeare, W. (1964). *Hamlet*. Complete Works, Tudor Edition. London: Collins.

Chapter 3

PROBLEMS IN SELF-DESCRIPTIVE RESEARCH AS EXEMPLIFIED IN A PHENOMENOLOGICAL ANALYSIS OF IMAGINATIVE EXPERIENCES

Amedeo Giorgi

Kuhn (1970) has observed that textbooks give a false image of the praxis of science because everything seems neat, clean and precise. The same may be true of the polished article. Since it is written retrospectively, the problems encountered are usually skirted and only the interesting results are given. Obviously, such polished articles will have to be continued to be written since most people are interested in the results of research. However, an article descriptive of the research process itself still has some value, especially since descriptive research and qualitative analyses are going back to the beginnings in order to try to initiate a new tradition.

The purpose of this article is to describe some of the problems that arise in analysing descriptions of a phenomenon by the researcher himself as well as to present some findings regarding the experience of imagining objects and scenes. Since space is limited, the article will emphasize the problems that arise despite the maintenance of a critical attitude by the 'researcher-subject'. On the other hand, it is equally important to note that certain hidden assumptions are discoverable by subsequent analytic processes and thus it is possible to contextualize properly the interpretation of the findings.

Most descriptive studies in the experimental psychology of the imagination can be found in the older literature (Lay, 1898; Dearborn, 1898; Weil & Nellen, 1910; Barlett, 1916) but none were 'self-descriptive'. Self-description of experiences as data are found more frequently in philosophical literature (e.g. Sartre, 1962/1936), but such descriptions are used primarily as part of a philosophical argument rather than analyzed totally in their own right (Casey, 1976 is an exception). The descriptions by myself presented in this article were meant to be analyzed as a whole and from a psychological perspective. The context is as follows.

Recently, I had the occasion to do some research on the description of imaginative experiences on the part of others (Giorgi, in press). In this research, the description of the content of the imaginative experience was fairly complete but the contextual factors were often only implicitly and haphazardly given. I reasoned that perhaps descriptions by oneself would be more complete regarding contextual matters of the contents of the imaginative experience since this could easily be posited as a goal. Casey (1976) refers to contextual factors in his analyses, but he does not make them part of his primary data. It seemed to me important to do so.

I first attempted some self-descriptions of imaginary scenes, but then soon realized that in order to make the findings of the imaginative experience more vivid, the contrasting perceptual situation in which I was located ought also be at least partially described. This would enable a comparative analysis that would be helpful in trying to understand the imaginative process itself.

PROCEDURE

In order to be sure that I would be describing an imaginative experience and not a memorial one, I tried to imagine experiences I knew I never had. However, while doing the first two descriptions I experienced certain problems (to be described below) and that made me decide to try to contrast those descriptions with descriptions of imaginative experiences of places with which I was familiar. Therefore, in addition to brief descriptions of my actual perceptual surroundings plus reflections on the processes of imagining to the extent to which I became aware of them, the primary data also includes descriptions of familiar and unfamiliar images. These four descriptions were written during September 1985 and the resport is being written up five months later. There was a gap of about one week between the first two descriptions and the last two.

RESULTS

With descriptive resesearch, there is no substitute for actual presentation of the concrete descriptions provided by subjects. Sometimes the results have to be placed in an appendix because of their length, but in this case it will not be necessary to do so because of the modest length of the actual descriptions. They are as follows.

FIRST DESCRIPTION: UNKNOWN SITUATION

Imagined presence: first perceptions of Rio de Janeiro. I see an airplane circling around the mountains of Rio (which I quickly recognize as scenes from photos I've seen) (I stop now to pick up the scene again. - For many seconds, nothing happens, I feel an urge to get the scene moving and I try to thrust a logical sequence in it - e.g., if I'm flying, I need an airport and a landing strip, etc.). Next, I see myself walking boldly through an airport with lots of busy people around; I seem to have a coat slung over my arm and I'm carrying an attache case. I seem to be smiling as I search for someone familiar. I notice that I have a brown suit on and the scene seems to be frozen for me as I attempt to describe it. Suddenly, I see the person who is to meet me. She has black hair and is wearing a white blouse. I suddenly become aware that the scene is soundless and that I have barely described Rio.

Actual conditions: I'm sitting in an airplane in Pittsburgh waiting for take-off to New York and Kennedy Airport. There is a delay due to air traffic. It is noisy and busy as people walk up and down and back-ground music is playing. I feel tired and sleepy as I try to do this description.

Reflection on Process: I'm aware of controlling the images in terms of 'realistic possibilities' - e.g. I know 'airports in general' and the parameters afforded by that knowledge 'control' what can possibly appear. It seems that only things within that boundary can 'surprise' me.

SECOND DESCRIPTION: UNKNOWN SITUATION

Imagined presence: perceiving my host's apartment. I see a tall, European-style block of apartments with balconies. I pick a corner out as belonging to my host. It is somewhere in the middle of the building - like 5th or 6th floor - and the walls are brown and the balconies have opaque glass, but transparent sides. I see myself going up an elevator and then I turn to the apartment door - a solid, green door. My host lets me in and I am surrounded by a light, neat, simple apartment with modern furniture in front of me - Scandinavian type - it is light coloured wood and tan cloth - and somehow the kitchen has white painted wood. I stand looking around - admiring the apartment, with my luggage still in my hands. I notice a rough-hewn type light-tan carpet on the floor. There are vague pictures on the wall and I'm aware of lots of corners and bends in the apartment that suggest more space and more things to see.

Actual conditions. I'm sitting in Kennedy Airport, waiting for Flight Time. I'm sitting on a blue, leather chair and with a stream of people constantly going by me, with Muzak playing in background, interrupted by pages and announcements regarding flight departures. The light is dim here, the floor is marble and the walls are brick with posts covered with tiles.

Reflection on process. Previously, I was aware of controlling 'images' in terms of 'realistic possibilities' but now I try to use obviously recollected scenes even if I'm not sure where they came from - I seem, though, to recognize them as 'remembered'.

THIRD DESCRIPTION: KNOWN SITUATION

Imagined presence: experiencing my living room. I am sitting in my favorite seat next to the hi-fi-speaker and in front of the cabinet where the tuner/amplifier/recordplayer are kept. I look straight ahead of me and see the fireplace, the living room wall on the opposite side and the picture over the fireplace, which is of a horse on a farm mostly in brown tones. I see the brown chair in the corner and the green sofa to my right and to my left are the piano, the French doors, the rocking chair and the green leather chair. (All these things are not constantly there, but appear as I set my gaze to go around the room. They also disappear as I write). The light, green, sort of shaggy floor carpet also comes into view. Now I see the brown coffee table with magazines on it. The bookcase to my left comes into view and as I try to imagine the one to my rear, an automatic shift of perspective takes place: I am standing up facing it and I see its white side. This is a habitual view of it.

Actual conditions. I'm in my host's 'den' in Rio which is furnished in modern style, with black and white colour schemes dominating and street noises continually come up through the open window.

Reflection on process. Here, what can be visualized seems to be controlled by the knowledge of the actual situation via memory - i.e., nothing appeared that was not in my living room and I described only what appeared, but what appeared surprised me sometimes in the sense that my aim was directed only towards a certain 'sector' or 'quadrant' of the room and then something would appear that belonged even though it surprised me at the moment of appearance in the imagined scene, but then I said 'of course' (e.g. Gold magazine rack with Time in it).

FOURTH DESCRIPTION: KNOWN SITUATION

Imagined presence: experiencing my office. I see myself entering my office in my habitual way and putting down my attache case in the hall, on the dirty orange carpet and I unlock my door and turn on the light and then I see myself putting my stuff down by the red reclining chair and then I shut the door, turn to get my key from its place on the shelf. I then pull back my green rolling desk chair and sit down on it and pull close to my desk. I survey what I see - there are piles of papers to my right; actually, articles and reprints to be read; and to my left there is a much smaller pile of papers. I try to focus on them: but all I can see are white, square sheets with vague print; I cannot read them. I try to see what is on top of my in-box (I become aware of memory trying to recall what is there so that I can visualize it - I remember various things, but I keep discounting them as being on top). I finally envision a letter, but all I can see is the white sheet itself - not what is on it.

I look around my office and I can see the dictionaries in front of me, the calendar from Scotland on the wall in front of me, the History of Psychology schema, and try to see some of the pictures of the schema; individual faces vaguely emerge (Rogers, Skinner), but when they do, the whole schema disappears; (If I hold on to the schema, I cannot get the individual faces - nor do I get them in their proper position - they merely emerge from an undifferentiated ground). I can see the file cabinets to my right, and vague stuff piled upon them, but the particulars get vague again unless guided by memory, in which case certain details do spring up, but not completely.

Actual conditions: I am in an airplane flying from Rio to Porto Alegre, Brazil. The roar of the small plane, occasional bumpiness, the stewards' noises while they serve drinks and a light lunch are all around me.

Reflection on process: I am more aware of memory coming in to direct the images that will appear - at least up until a certain point anyway. It seems that I can imagine the normal perceptual objects of everyday life, but it is harder to imagine task-oriented activities completely, e.g., reading, etc.

DISCUSSION OF RESULTS

A number of dimensions of these findings could be discussed, but I shall concentrate on the following aspects:
- A comparison of the familiar vs. unfamiliar presences;
- A comparison of the descriptions from self vs. others;
- A comparison of the description of the imaginative presences vs. perceptual presences.

Familiar vs. unfamiliar imaginative presences.

The first thing to be noted is the relative impoverishment of the descriptions of the unknown situations. Upon reflection, I am certain that this is due to the fact that I not only tried to create an imaginative scene, but also one which I could prove without a shadow of a doubt was strictly imaginative with no tinge of memory. Another hidden demand was that this image also had to be as realistically accurate as possible. While it remained implicit, the above description is a more precise description of my task for the unknown situations. Thus, while I was initially unaware of it, and perplexedly 'lived through' the difficulties of the concrete descriptions, it was only during the analysis, upon reflection, that I became aware that I had placed some very precise and difficult demands upon myself; I had to produce an image that in no way was due to memory, yet it also had to fit in with my preconceptions concerning Rio or my host's apartment.

In other words, in order to counter the possible objection that the presences given to me during the imaginative process were not drawn from memory (and therefore were 'pure' imaginative processes), I tried to imagine something that I never experienced before, but still have it somehow be faithful to a specific place. This set also made me refuse all help from variational past experiences (e.g., a picture of a friend's apartment in Europe came to mind, but since I recognized it for what it was, I wouldn't allow myself to use it).

Now, the choice of a 'real place' to be imagined also revealed another assumption I implicitly brought to the task. For some reason, I also wanted to be able to check the veracity of the imaginative description. Thus I had to choose something that could be checked against a perceptual description, such as I actually did below. I chose this route, in addition, because I wanted to distinguish between imagination and fantasy, and I knew that the latter could have no rigorous check since anything is allowable.

Thus, I would say that I implicitly placed an impossible demand upon myself. I refused to use 'memorial presences' and I refused 'fantastical presences' and thus actually constrained myself to use some implicit sense of imaginary that was in between those meanings. In any event, the above attitude accounts for the relative impoverishment of the 'unfamiliar' descriptions. Perhaps Sartre (1948/1940) was right when he said that the imagination cannot give us anything new.

By contrast, the familiar imaginings offered no difficulty with respect to fidelity to specificity of place. I knew what my living room and office looked like and when the relevant images came before me, all I had to do was acknowledge them and describe them. Obviously, memory was implied in the familiar imaginings or else the project could not be completed. But its role was restricted to the criterion of fidelity to a known place. My imaginative intention directed my 'imaginative gaze' towards a certain sector of space and then created a certain imaginary space to let specific images appear. It was here that memory acted as a sort of 'censor' for what image could appear since nothing not belonging to the setting as I knew it could (or did) appear. Sometimes the familiar images that appeared surprised me in the sense that I had forgotten about certain objects in my settings, but I always recognized them as apt when they appeared. Where familiarity was lacking, as in Rio or my host's apartment, the specific memorial guidance was also lacking and therefore I fell back upon 'airports in general' or 'apartments in general' as guides. These 'general guides', like most anticipatory experiences, were an amalgam of past experiences plus open-endedness, and in general, accounted for the vague and impoverished images of the unfamiliar settings. It is important to note that neither memory nor anticipation produced the image as such, but rather the motive and criterion for the image. In other words, the difference between the familiar and unfamiliar images *as such* can be accounted for in terms of the respective criteria: 'specifically familiar object' and 'object in general'. This could mean that not the contents, but the goal of an act could account for the differences in conscious structures. However, more research specifically directed to the problem of images in relation to memory and anticipation will be necessary to clarify this problem further.

The distinction between familiar and unfamiliar situations allowed another problem to show itself. Apparently, I implicitly used two criteria to evaluate my presence to 'images': a broad criterion, the presence to something that is not in the immediate perceptual environment, and a severe one, the presence to an image that would owe nothing to other modalities of consciousness such as memory, anticipation, dreams, fantasies, etc., nor to previous experience. Indeed, it may be impossible to obtain a 'pure' imaginary experience, but then one would have to re-think the whole question of research in this area. For example, I am aware that experimental studies (e.g. Bentley, 1889; Ogden, 1913) have not been successful in distinguishing between memorial and imaginative images. The former criterion, of course, is too broad to be the basis of the imagination in any meaningful sense. The latter criterion may be impossible to implement. In any event, the implicit stance adopted made the two situations less than comparable from an experiential point of view and a more acceptable and 'practical' criterion will have to be discovered.

Self-descriptions vs. descriptions from others

In a previous study (Giorgi, in press) on the imaginative process I became aware of the importance of contextual factors for the understanding of the image as such. What was available with descriptions from others was a description of the image itself but only vague indications of the perceptual surroundings and some of the other contextual factors, and no critical reflections. Consequently, the latter factors were emphasized with the self-descriptions and some important revelations on the imaginative process were possible because of them. However, later reflections made me aware that the reasons for the differences between 'self and other' descriptions were due in part to instructions because some of the contextual factors could have been emphasized with descriptions from others as well. Nevertheless, I think that it is worthwhile speaking to the following three points:

1) *The role of control:* it surprised me to realize that there was some control over the possible images that could appear. I became aware of this control as I was struggling for an image after I recognized the Rio scene as being from a photo I saw. I wanted to move on to Rio itself but found that the airport scene emerged because I had precommitted myself to a logically constructed development of my entrance into Rio. (I could not be in Rio without first going through an airport. I think the logical structure took the place of the lack of past experience). Consequently, only 'realistic' possibilities were permitted by some part of me (e.g. I could not envisage myself getting off at a space station and still call it Rio), even if they took on a generic character (e.g. the airport scene was a sort of collage of all airports I have been in). With familiar situations, knowledge based upon past experience was the controlling factor. I knew what my office and living room were presently like and this knowledge played a controlling role over what appeared. Instead of logic, the sequence of images for familiar situations was controlled by habit patterns. I saw myself approaching my office in a typical way and I saw the living room from my favorite chair. Thus, at least in these conditions, the degrees of freedom of what could appear, given the aims of the exercise, were far from random and they were controlled by logic or habit (past experience).

2) *Setting of intention or aim:* we mentioned above that we allowed that it was possible that the memorial presences and the imaginary presences (or images) could be identical except for the aim or intention. If this is true, then a complete understanding of the imaginative process would have to take into account the structure of the imaginative act. We cannot go into all of the details here (see Husserl, 1970/1900), but Husserl's theory of meaning claims that meanings are due to what he calls signifying acts. These are acts that are empty but directed toward referents that have the possibility of fulfilling the meaning intentions. The data presented here

suggest that the differences among conscious modalities (e.g. imagining, remembering, anticipating, attending, etc.) may also be due to the signifying acts. Everywhere such an act is copresent even if implicitly and nonpalpably. For example, the act whereby I set the intention to try to make an image of Rio 'realistically' and yet without appealing to memory; or the act whereby I direct my 'mental gaze' to a certain quadrant of my living room and I find that precisely certain pieces of furniture appear; or the act whereby a certain collage of past experiences appear. All of these examples irrevocably point to the fact that the acts of consciousness are equally important, and without them, presences or contents, whether imaginary or perceptual, could not appear as they do.

One other thing also ought to be mentioned in this context, and that is the presence of concomitant awareness without palpable referent. My descriptions are peppered with such awarenesses. For example, in the data is the expression that "I see an airplane circling around the mountains of Rio" (which I quickly recognize as scenes from photos I have seen). Now, this recognition was not a palpable experience. It simply was an awareness that I saw the same view of Rio before in a photo. Moreover, I had no direct awareness that I was producing such a 'memorial content'. I was only aware of the fact that I set the intention to try to produce some 'image' of Rio and up popped (seemingly spontaneously) that particular scene and once it came to view, I became aware of it as something previously seen. But the same thing happened when I said that "I suddenly became aware that the scene is soundless" or when I wrote that "an automatic shift of perspective takes place" or when I wrote "I became aware of memory trying to recall what is there so I can visualize it", etc.

There are also the awarenesses by which I judge the contents of the experiences as 'new' or 'familiar' or as 'memorial' or 'imaginative'. These, too, refer to no contents, but are concomitant awarenesses of various contents. I am not even sure that such awarenesses belong to the realm of the imagination, but I simply include them because they are descriptive givens.

Again, it seems that more clarity regarding what we mean by imagination is called for. The data provided by these self-descriptions in the form of the reflections on the imaginative process, with their emphasis on acts and nonpalpable awarenesses provide findings that parallel those of the Wurzburg school when the latter claimed to discover both 'determining tendencies' and 'imageless thoughts'. We can not probe this relationship further here, but Humphrey (1951) provides a good summary of the history of and controversies surrounding the Wurzburg school.

3) *Objects vs. tasks:* the descriptions of imaginative experience show that the imagination is better able to present static things or objects than tasks. I'm not completely sure why this is so unless it is because things can be presented globally more readily than activities or perhaps because they have clearer boundaries. For example, when I tried imaginatively to

read what was on the top of my paper pile, I was not able to do so. The actual imaginative presence was blurry and it seemed as though my memory was not detailed enough to provide an accurate account. On the other hand, my attitude was set for accuracy because I wanted to give a true account of my office. Perhaps, too, objects can be imagined more easily because they are confronted more habitually, just as white pages are, but the text on a page varies quite a bit.

Imaginative vs. perceptual scenes

The contrast between these two types of presence could not be greater. The contrasts include simultaneously being in an airplane on the ground perceptually and imaginatively flying and landing in Rio; perceptually sitting in an airport in New York and imaginatively entering a new apartment in Rio; perceptually sitting in a room in Rio and imaginatively being in a room in Pittsburgh; and finally, perceptually being in a plane in flight and imaginatively being in an office in Pittsburgh.

Naturally, I am not able to explain this power of consciousness whereby it can put one in the presence of absent things or scenes. I can only affirm that consciousness can do this and describe some of the characteristics whereby it does. I can ascertain that the different modalities of consciousness present presences that have characteristic differences. Sartre (1962/1936) and Casey (1076) have already given lengthy descriptions of imaginative presences and have characterized it as a form of consciousness that is spontaneous, mobile, quasi-real, indeterminate and relatively self-contained. I can only confirm these characteristics, and of course, they are determined by either implicit or explicit contrast to perceptual descriptions. In order to make the difference explicit, I went back and described the perceptual presence to my desk for about the same length of time and I produced the following:

> I push my 'desk-chair-with-wheels' up to my desk and I begin to write. As I write I am aware of the blue inkblot desk pad with brown corners beneath my paper. As I look to my left I see a type-written letter of yellow carbon paper that needs to be filed. To the left of it is a pile of papers, mostly copies of talks by myself. Above the latter is another pile of papers that are in a brown, wooden 'in-box'. A paperweight sits on them and next to the paperweight is an envelope. I look closer to see if I can read the cancelled stamp and it says 'Pittsburgh, PA'. To my right there is also a pile of papers and the top one is entitled "The Existential Parameters of Psychotherapy". Just to the left of the latter pile is my tan telephone and to the left of it is my desk calendar and I can see that I have a 7:30 appointment written down for tonight.

When we compare the above with the description of "Known situation - Imagined presence" above, we can see the difference in the level of detail even though the descriptions are generically similar. This indicates what others have noted, namely, that the perceptual world is explorable in an inexhaustive way, but the imaginative world has limits in this respect even though it, too, is infinite when one moves from object to object.

Reflections on study

The first major point of this study is a tracking of the modifications introduced and the hidden assumptions uncovered. This study began as a simple contrast to the study of descriptions of imaginative experiences by others. It seemed as though descriptions by oneself would provide more of the contextual factors that are copresent with images per se. After the descriptions of the imaginative presences were obtained, the contrast with the perceptual surroundings was so great that descriptions of the perceptual situation were added so that the reader could also intuit the contrast. In addition, the specific content of the imaginative descriptions indicated to the researcher that only non-experienced scenes were being described by him. Thus, he decided to add imaginative descriptions of familiar scenes as well.

While in the process of reflecting on these descriptions, it was discovered that I was implicitly avoiding memorial and fantastic images, so that the meaning of the imagination in this study was more restricted than previously assumed. It really means imagining experientially real situations that are familiar versus those that are unfamiliar with minimum influence from other conscious modalities. This is the way that the 'researcher-subject' systematically implemented the general intention to provide descriptions of imaginative experiences by oneself. It shows that a host of presuppositions are necessary in order to execute concrete actions. But it also shows that careful analysis can uncover many of these presuppositions. The main methodological implications are that piloting is strongly recommended for qualitative research and that being truly empirical in terms of retrospective analysis is also very important for interpreting the meaning of qualitative data.

With respect to results, much of the data confirmed what has already been discovered from a phenomenological perspective concerning the experience of images. One previously unknown or unemphasized finding is that tasks seem harder to imagine in detail than objects. In addition, at least for this subject, there was severe constraint exercised over the kinds of images that could appear because of an unaware implicit acceptance of a restricted task: to imagine only realistic situations. Just what it means that consciousness can so carefully control the presence of images without the subject realizing it while performing is something that will have to be explained further.

Finally, the importance of signifying acts in Husserl's sense was noted. The reflections of the researcher indicated that the images *per se* were not different with respect to familiarity or unfamiliarity, but that the consistent differences concerning which images appeared in the two conditions could be related to the signifying acts that specified 'known, familiar presence' or 'something in general'. The role of signifying acts in the imaginative process also requires further research in order to obtain a clearer understanding of the entire imaginative process.

REFERENCES

Barlett, F.C. (1916). An experimental study of some problems of perceiving and imagery. *British Journal of Psychology,* 8, 222-267.

Bentley, M.B. (1899). The memory image and its qualitative fidelity. *American Journal of Psychology,* 11, 1-48.

Casey, E. (1976). *Imagining: A phenomenological study.* Bloomington, Indiana: Indiana University Press.

Dearborn, G.V. (1898). A study of imaginations. *American Journal of Psychology,* 9, 183-190.

Giorgi, A. (in press). Phenomenology and the research tradition in the psychology of the imagination. In E. Murray (Ed.), *Imagination and phenomenological psychology.* Pittsburgh, PA: Duquesne University Press.

Humphrey, G. (1951). *Thinking: an introduction to its experimental psychology.* London: Methuen.

Husserl, E. (1970/1900). *Logical investigations.* (Transl. J. Findlay). New York: Humanities Press.

Kuhn, T.S. (1970). *The structure of scientific revolutions.* 2nd ed. Chicago, Illinois: University of Chicago Press.

Lay, W. (1898). Mental imagery. *Psychological Review Monograph Supplements,* 2 (3), 1-59.

Ogden, R.M. (1913). Experimental criteria for differentiating memory and imagination in projected visual images. *Psychological Review,* 8, 183-197.

Sartre, J.P. (1962/1936). *Imagination.* (Transl. F. Williams). Ann Arbor, MI: University of Michigan Press.

Sartre, J.P. (1948/1940). *The psychology of imagination.* New York: The Citadel Press.

Weill, M., & Nellen, M. (1910). Contribution à l'étude des images chez l'enfant. *Revue Psychologique,* 3, 343-348.

REFERENCES

Chapter 4

METHODOLOGY IN EVALUATIVE RESEARCH ON TEACHING AND LEARNING

Mariane Hedegaard

A methodological dilemma faces qualitative psychological research. On the one hand, it is desirable to avoid such a rigidly operationalized sharpness and certainty that the answers and results could be deduced, in advance, from the theoretical point of departure. On the other hand, an atheoretical approach is equally unproductive since without goals empirical research results only in a collection of 'objective' facts.

To approach this dilemma for a solution, the relation between theory and the concrete objects and facts has to be conceptualized. This relationship forms the focus of Davydov's (1977) theory of scientific thinking. In scientific thinking, according to his view, a problem area is looked upon as a whole. In this whole, a single object is always related to other objects. The transition from one object to the next delimits the specific in the object through its contrast with the others. Therefore the inner connections are the real focus of scientific thinking. The connection between the general and the specific is the content of the theoretical concept and thereby reveals the concrete unity in its many-sidedness (Davydov, 1977, p. 254).

Scientific thinking presupposes an image of the undeveloped homogeneous wholeness which reflects the problem areas. Therefore, the scientific process has at least two main phases: the first pertains to the undivided image of the problem area and the second constitutes the analysis of the relations of the specific objects in the wholeness of the problem area.

Davydov's theory about scientific thinking (which is grounded on the philosophical work of Iljenkov, 1972) forms the basis for the hypothetical supposition that there are two phases in the research process. In the first phase, where the research is closely connected with the life situation of the subjects, the researcher's model of how to invent and what to ask about is very vague. The researcher (more or less intuitively) records his impression of the changes and contradictions in the process of which he is part. From this protocol record, some general and vague conceptions about the object of research can be formed. In this first phase, the researcher goes from reality to some very vague and fragile general concepts which will gradually lead to a more integrated system of abstractions about the phenomenon under study. In the second phase, the research moves from these abstractions to the complexity and fulness of real life. The goal of the research is a conceptualization of the concrete which can determine every step of action made in the intervention and the generalization.

The above mentioned first phase can have different variants, depending on the objects of research. I see both Giorgi's phenomenological interview approach (Giorgi, 1976) and my own interaction-based observation in the form of descriptions of pre-school children's play (Hedegaard & Hakkarainen, 1986) as instances of this first phase.

The methodological aspect which differentiates the second phase in the research process from the first phase, is the researcher's intentional transformation of the object researched in order to bring out the object's inner relations. This methodological aspect forms the basis for an explanatory and guiding possibility of the research. It is the transforming or interventive aspect of the second phase in the research process which will be the topic of this paper, illustrated by means of the teaching experiment.

THE TEACHING EXPERIMENT

The teaching experiment as a research method may be characterized as a coherent and systematic intervention in the natural conditions under which learning and teaching take place (Markova, 1982). The intention in the teaching experiment is that the pupil's learning activity forms itself as a coherent whole, which results in the pupil's acquisition of a profound understanding of the material's essential and general fundamental features. The goal of the traditional experiment is to explore and examine the child's skills and capabilities at a particular stage of development. The goal of the teaching experiment is to reveal and to realize the child's hidden potentials via a combination of systematic instructions through the use of tasks throughout the teaching process. A way to record the qualitative progress in the pupils' acquisition of a subject is participant observation. The tradition of participant observation has been changed into activity-based observations for the following reasons.

CHARACTERISTICS OF ACTIVITY-BASED OBSERVATIONS

Participant observation is a well-known method in classroom research (Jackson, 1968; Adams & Bidde, 1970; Good & Brophy, 1973; Delamont, 1976). In traditional participant observation research, the observer behaves neutrally with respect to the research situation. He keeps a distance between himself and the subject researched in the name of 'objectivity'. This neutrality is an illusion. Instead, the research situation has to be conceptualized as a communication situation in which the researcher has a role (Hedegaard, 1984). It is more relevant to understand *how* one participates as a researcher than to try to eliminate one's existence in the research situation, which is an impossible task. Therefore, the researcher's description of the activity in the class also implies his being part of this activity.

The characteristics of activity-based observations are inspired by Giorgi's research (1976) and his conceptualization of meaning as the inevitable focus in research. They can be summarized as follows (the argumentation for these characteristics can be found in Hedegaard, 1984):

1) The observation is focused on the content of the activities in the class situation.

2) The researcher actively interacts with the children in the research situation when she finds it appropriate.

3) The researcher describes what is meaningful to her.

4) The researcher focuses upon themes in the situation.

5) The themes focused upon are related to the aim of the research and the theoretical framework for the research.

6) In relation to these themes, the researcher focuses on the subject's motives and intentions through the subject's activities and actions. It is not only a behavioural description.

7) The researcher delineates the essential aspects of the phenomena through his interaction with the subjects.

8) The protocols tend to reflect the conflicts and the problems of the subjects.

9) The protocol, which is a result of this procedure, tends to be a basis for further interaction with the subjects, described in connection to the themes of the research.

CHARACTERISTICS OF INTERPRETING ACTIVITY-BASED OBSERVATIONS

The results of the intervention in the teaching situation are reflected in the activity-based observations. This registration can take the form of a written research protocol, which contains a description of what was going on in the classroom. The writing of this protocol implies some vague conceptions about the phenomenon studied. The interpretation of the research protocol has to be seen in light of a more connected theoretical framework and as a further development of the concepts used in the description phase. There is a mutual dependence between data gathering and interpretation. Neither can be seen as an all- or none-phenomenon. However, despite this continuity between the writing of the observation protocol and the interpretation of it, there are some essential differences between these two aspects of the research process.

The description is based upon an interaction between researcher and subjects in the classroom. This interaction is a person-to-person relation.

Description focuses upon the specific child's problems and activities. More than the theoretical concepts, concrete themes in the situation determine the writing of the protocol. Furthermore, the describer tries to understand more than to explain what is going on in the research situation.

Interpretation is, on the other hand, not based on interaction but on reflection. The person-to-person relation disappears and the lived world relations, referred to by Giorgi, become a context for interpretation wherein the specific child's problems are only interesting for what these reveal in terms of general knowledge. Furthermore, the focus is changed from the concrete themes to the concepts of a theory in which the relation and explanations are the points of interest.

The interpretation is a dialectical process between the protocol and the theory. A theoretical frame of reference is a necessary precondition of writing the protocol and starting the interpretation of the protocol. Using a theoretical frame of reference in relation to a specific protocol both changes the content of this protocol and develops the theoretical considerations into a framework.

THE PRESENT STUDY: A TEACHING EXPERIMENT[1]

In the following, the methodological aspects of an interventional research strategy will be the focus of interest. Results from the project are presented and discussed more systematically elsewhere (Hedegaard, 1986). However, I have to present a rough outline of the teaching experiment first, to be able to use it for exemplification of the methodological aspects.

This teaching experiment concerns teaching history, biology and geography in elementary school (3rd - 5th grade). The aim of the project was to develop and evaluate a new form of teaching on a scientific basis, with an emphasis on the pupil's employment of models, whereby an integration of both motivation and cognition, knowledge and skill is achieved.

THE THEORETICAL FRAME OF REFERENCE

Thinking and knowledge

Davydov gives a theoretical framework for describing the difference between the empirical classification of the environment on the basis of the immediately perceivable (empirical thinking) and the theoretical understanding of the environment (theoretical thinking).[2] The difference between the two forms of thinking and knowledge can be exemplified by the difference between Linné's classification system for plants and Darwin's general theory of the origin of species.

The fundamental, characteristic features of theoretical understanding are the following: things and phenomena must be understood in a connected conceptual system and not as divorced, separate entities. Things and phenomena must be understood on the basis of their origins and inner relations and not only on the basis of the immediately perceivable features. And they must be understood in a process of development and not as being static.

Teaching based on empirical knowledge leads only to classification of things and phenomena on the basis of their characteristics. Teaching based on theoretical knowledge, on the other hand, attempts to promote a mediation by the general laws and development of the phenomena.

The 'germcell' model

Teaching which leads to pupils' learning activity and the development of theoretical thinking must be based on the teacher having, in this teaching, a scientifically based conceptual foundation which he utilizes in order to turn his teaching activity into learning activity in the pupils. The teacher's knowledge must be theoretically anchored so that he and the pupils do not drown in 'facts' or, at the other extreme, end up in pure and simple social interaction without any content in the teaching.

Scientifically based teaching aims to develop the pupils' general conceptual system, through their learning activity, in the form of a model of the subject. What is required of such a model is that it aids the systematization of the subject and is applicable to the socially and historically determined reality in which the pupils live. The pupils' model system is developed on the basis of those models the teacher and researcher use in their planning of the teaching activity. This model has been called a 'germcell' model because it reflects the historically developed, fundamental concept-relations within a subject area. That is to say, the concept-relations which enter into a teaching model must be the historically developed and, contemporarily, functionally applicable concepts in relation to natural and societal problems. The application of the germcell model as a teaching model implicates another important condition. The model itself is in a state of constant development and change through its application to problems in a subject area. The teacher uses the germcell model in preparing the curriculum, as a basis for working out the pupils' tasks and the logic which guides the teaching process. Through the task sequence, the teacher must try to get the children to develop their own general model system. Therefore, he does not present the general concepts or the germcell model directly.

Towards a psychological theory of learning activity

The development of the pupil's theoretical understanding brought about through teaching in school, requires a particular type of pupil activity. Learning is here seen as a form of activity that is based on particular types of tasks and on the development of particular motives and learning structures (Leontiev, 1978; 1981).

The basic psychological principles in this approach are the following:
1) Concepts cannot be passed on in pre-packaged form. The pupils must acquire concepts through their own activity.
2) General principles and generalized knowledge must precede concrete knowledge in the course of instruction.
3) The purpose served by concrete tasks and actions within a subject area is that the pupil, through them, acquires insight into the fundamental principles of the subject.

This form of learning must take its point of departure in the pupils' experiencing of a problem or a conflict relation which, for example, can consist of different explanations of the same phenomena.

THE EXPERIMENTAL INTERVENTION IN THE TEACHING SITUATION

The curriculum plans for teaching biology, history, and geography in elementary schools in Denmark suggest that these three subjects are to be integrated into one subject called 'orientation'. We decided to follow this suggestion by planning a teaching sequence which would proceed through the following three thematic areas which develop logically from each other: the development of species, the origin of man, and the historical changes of societies. These three themes were chosen in order to underline the developmental aspects of nature and society as well as to show that natural and societal development are related and influence each other. By working with concepts and models that, in addition to being a description of nature and the various steps in the history of society, contain the development of nature and society, one makes it possible for the children to become oriented towards the development and the changes that continually take place in nature and society.

The experimental intervention in the teaching included the following steps:
1) Together the teacher and the researcher planned each period of class teaching (a period was three hours). This planning reflected the didactic considerations put forward in the theory and the logic of the basic concepts of the subjects biology, geography and history. Each teaching period of three hours was therefore planned by specifying the goal of teaching, the concept to be taught, and the teaching materials to be used.
2) The performance of the teaching was registered by the researcher in the form of a written protocol of what was going on in the classroom.
3) Together the researcher and the teacher evaluated the actual teaching and the children's activity.
4) Together the researcher and the teacher planned the next teaching period and so on.

COLLECTION OF DATA IN THE TEACHING EXPERIMENT

We collected the pupils' written task solutions throughout the year along with the teaching plans from each lesson. The teaching plans are necessary for the analysis of the effects of instruction and the change in the pupils' learning activity. Furthermore, observing each teaching period makes an analysis of the teaching and learning process possible, both as a general process in the class, in the form of teacher/pupil interaction, and as a focused description of some of the pupils.

INTERPRETATION RELATED TO THE PROJECT DESCRIBED

In order to be able to follow the planned intervention, we have to analyse the relations between the planned teaching activity, the development of the real teaching activity in the classroom and the development of the pupils' learning activity. In the pupil's learning activity, we want to discern three aspects: the pupil's development of motives, changes in the pupil's way of thinking about and conceptualizing the topic, and changes in the way the pupils work together and with the teacher.

A conceptual framework was gradually developed through the research which has its origin in the author's earlier conceptions of knowledge (see Stenild, 1977; 1978; Hedegaard, 1984b) and methods for describing development in real life situations (Hedegaard, 1984a). This framework was only a starting point for the interpretation of the protocols. When the protocols had been interpreted, the conceptual framework was made into a categorial list. The categories in this list are changeable through application because the data give content to the concept and also provide new aspects of the concepts used, aspects which have not been thought of before. Consequently, the checklist now presented is not immediately apparent in the concrete interpretation.

CONCEPTUAL CATEGORIES

Teaching activity
a) How is the instruction process between teacher and pupil formed, and what does it concern?
b) Does the teacher teach in accordance with the plan? Are the digressions due to:
 - the teacher's flexibility in relation to the instruction process?
 - pressure from the children that makes it difficult to carry out the plan?

Learning activity
a) Development of motivation.
 What are the children's interests and wishes?

How does the teacher create interest on the part of the children?
Which conflicts does he work with?
Can the teacher carry through the intentions sketched in the plan?
b) *Development of concepts*
How does the pupil's own learning activity progress in the lessons and
how is it structured?
- Are the children's comments relevant to the instruction?
- Do the children anticipate the course of the instruction?
- Do the children keep the teacher to the topic?
- Do 'why' questions arise?
- Do the children seek coherence rather than categorial solutions?
- Can the children work with the modeling of their knowledge?
- Do the children direct questions at the model?
- Can the children accept that the model develops/changes? Do they
  themselves contribute to this?
- Does an increase of the children's ideational and imagery production
  take place?
- Do the children set themselves tasks?
c) *Social coexistence*
What is the nature of the interaction between children and teacher? In
what way does he help and discipline them?
What is the interaction among the children like?
In what way do they help each other, compete with each other, quarrel
with each other?

PROTOCOLS AND INTERPRETATIONS

The experimental teaching has run for one year and consists of 36 periods
of instruction plans and protocols of class observation.

The material chosen to exemplify the intervention strategy and the
interpretation of the protocols are the first period of instruction and the
18th period of instruction. The first period of instruction is the period
just after the summer holiday, the period in which the children were
introduced to the subject 'orientation'. The 18th period is the last period
before the Christmas holiday. Between these two periods, there was a
whole semester of teaching/learning the subject of orientation. Each
teaching period lasted three hours. Between the two observation protocols,
there were 16 teaching periods, amounting to 48 hours of teaching. To
illustrate the planning of instruction, the plan for the 1st period of
instruction is presented in Appendix A.

We have chosen to present the interpretation of the first period and the
18th period of instruction (the observation protocols are presented in
Appendix B and C) in order to show the contrast between the pupils not yet
having any knowledge in the 1st period and their being capable of making
models in the 18th period.

We will not make any conclusive statements about the results from the interpretations of these two protocols because such conclusions require an analysis of the change as a process developing through all 18 periods of instruction.

The interpretations were made by two researchers, one who planned the instruction observed the class (M. Hedegaard) and a second who had a neutral relation to this research but who has knowledge about the general theory of activity, thinking, and knowledge which guided the planning of the experimental teaching (J.W. McLaughlin). Disagreement in interpretation was solved through discussion of the point in relation to the context of the observation protocol as a whole.

INTERPRETATION OF PROTOCOL I - 8/15/84

Teaching activity
a) How is the instruction between teacher and pupil formed and what does it concern?
The lessons begin with a discussion of what the children learn in those subjects with which they are familiar and what they must learn in the 'orientation' lessons. The teacher asks questions and the pupils answer. The children focus on the content of the subject 'orientation'. The teacher reformulates their answers, attempting to bring forth change in the children's knowledge about the content of the instruction (observations 10, 13, 25). Also, the teacher reformulates the children's answers so that they become more general (23) and concern development (25) and the concept of historical time (26).

The next phase in the instruction contains a drawing task, in which the children must illustrate what the subject 'orientation' is concerned with. In relation to this, the teacher expands the concept of development and historical time (50, 70, 78). However, even though the teacher repeats the theme for possible content (34), it is not these themes that the children choose to draw (36, 38, 39, 40). This is perhaps because the children conceive of the themes in 'orientation' very broadly and loosely and do not relate them to time and development because it is the first lesson they have had in this subject.

In the second lesson, the concepts 'animals' (44) and 'change in the earth' (50), were introduced. Two children formulate different answers to the last problem. The teacher follows up one of the answers, in which a child says that the earth was covered with lava (51). The other answer, one about war, is rejected without explanation (59). In the same way, the teacher follows up an explanation that the earth was covered with water (60). Thus, the teacher directs and expands the children's train of thought and answers by expanding on those answers about the origin of the earth. Thereby, the children's answers are indirectly stressed as important or unimportant.

The teacher's indirect commentary is continued in the dialogue about the Greenlanders' creation myth. After reading the saga out loud for the class, the teacher draws yet another theme into the instruction via the question of whether there have always been humans (70). The children tackle the problem seriously but the teacher follows their answers up with questions that are very concrete and can easily lead in the wrong way (74, 78, 81, 86). That is exactly what happens to some of the children (79, 87, 88), even though they try for a long time to keep to the original theme (75, 77, 80, 82, 85). As soon as the teacher brings the original problem back into the class dialogue, the children begin again to contribute serious answers.

The teacher's questions are, however, more an introduction to the next point in the curriculum than a concentration on the children's conceptions (45). Also, the teacher does not give the children much opportunity to comment on some older children's conceptions of the development of animal species which he reads aloud, but uses it to point out that there exist other conceptions as well (101) and that adults can have different conceptions, which are to be found in books. In groups, the children look at books and talk together about what they see. Then they are given a drawing task which has to do with differences between the appearance of animals nowadays and that of prehistoric animals.

b) Does the teacher teach in accordance with the plan?
The teacher teaches in very close accordance with the set plan, which is understandable since this is the first period in a teaching experiment. Unfortunately, however, this probably limits the children's participation in such a way that their conception of the implicit conflicts between the various emerging conceptions (i.e. the development of the world, of animals and of man) is not ensured. It is quite clear, though, that the children are able to formulate their ideas in relation to these themes, even in the first instruction period.

Learning activity
a) Development of Motivation
What are the children's interests and wishes?
How does the teacher create interest on the part of the children?
What conflict does he work with and what demands does he make?

The children are open, interested and take part in the class dialogue, even though it is quite clearly dominated by a few, very interested children, for example Bent. The children try, throughout, to answer the teacher's questions and to take part in the tasks he sets. The few cases in which the children bring non-central themes into the dialogue (79, 87-88) can be attributed to the teacher's way of asking questions. The children's intentions are centered around the subject content of the themes introduced by the teacher, i.e. the development of the earth, animals and man. The teacher's intention is to work with different explanations of these and, thereby, to form conflicts among the children. It is rather uncertain whether he manages to do so or whether the children, instead, see the various explanations as non-conflicting ways of working with the chosen themes.

It is very clear, though, that the children's own explanations create conflicts among some of them. For example, Lonni's descriptions of the earth's creation as a blending of natural-scientific and religious explanation, "God created dry spots" (57) awakens resistance in Bent, who explains it in a natural-scientific way, i.e., "The water evaporated because of the sun" (61). Bent reacts in the same way against 'the Greenlanders' creation myth' (65), whereas Henrik's comments constitute an attempt to defend it. Thus, the teacher's questions do not create conflict for the individual child but, rather, among the children. The question is, then, how can these conflicts among the children be used creatively, in the further development of their interests and cognition. In this teaching period, they are not directly used to that end.

The teacher also attempts to work with conflicts by asking provocative questions (74, 78, 81, 83, 86), which build on double-meanings in the children's answers. The children have difficulty in understanding the teacher's provocations and answer the questions directly. Doing so leads them away from the themes once or twice.

b) Development of concepts

How does the pupils' own learning activity progress in the lessons and how is it structured?

The children's comments are closely connected to the instruction. They have to do with themes that the teacher has introduced. None of the children can say in this first lesson what the difference is between animals nowadays and prehistoric animals. But many have ideas about what the earth looked like in early times.

The following different conceptions are apparent in the class:

John: Believes that the earth has been different because there have been wars (54).

He attributes the difference to personal relations (58).

He believes that there has always been life on earth (72).

His conception about the development of man is rather vague.

Lonni: Believes that the earth has, at one time, been covered with water, but that God caused the transformation (57).

She refers to personal experience when apes are mentioned (79).

Bent: Believes that the earth was covered with lava and can explain the origin of the lava (51, 53, 55). He can also accept Lonni's description of what the earth looked like earlier, but not her explanation (61).

Also, he still tries to reject 'the Greenlanders' creation myth' (65). And accordingly, to reformulate some of it to a natural-scientific explanation (69).

He has a clear conception of the development of man and of time (73, 80, 82, 85).

c) Social coexistence
What is the nature of the interaction between the teacher and the pupils and among the pupils?
The teacher completely controls the progress and the course of events in the class activity, but the children respond openly and happily to his questions and tasks. Only once does the teacher set an openly disciplinary requirement (47), but controls, or attempts to control indirectly a couple of times (40, 59, 89). In all cases, it is in response to the children's unstructured interest in the themes that the teacher has introduced material into the instruction.

The children listen to each other and do not repeat each other's answers. They also react to each other's answers in some cases (61, 66, 88).

INTERPRETATION OF PROTOCOL OF II 12/19/84

Teaching   activity
a) How is the instruction between teacher and pupils formed and what does it concern?
The lesson begins with class dialogue aiming at making a resumé of what the children can describe of the problem area "the evolution of animals". The teacher follows the research schema (which contains a resumé) in his first questions. He asks: What are we investigating? (2) What do we know about it? (2, 5).

Bjarne answers concretely with the names of animals, and the teacher generalizes this to a new question. He introduces the sub-theme 'survival and what is important for survival' (11, 12).

The teacher requires specific formulations, because this is a resumé (15, 18, 22).

The theme 'parental care' captures the children's interest and the teacher and the children go more deeply into this for some time (23, 46). Lonni, who wants to continue with the original problem, only manages to put forward her view (28, 47) some time later. The teacher subsequently stresses that 'survival' is the problem that must be completed (54). Then he relates this theme to the model (61) and asks for a child to, first of all, draw the model on the board and then to relate the various features in the 'survival' category to the model. The children are then given the task of formulating, by themselves, a generalized model for 'survival'.
b) Does the teacher teach in accordance with the plan? (The teaching plan for this period is not presented in an appendix because it requires too much space).

The teacher is still teaching in accordance with the plan, but concentrates now, along with the children, on a relevant   subordinate point, 'parental care'. It is, however, still the teacher who directs   the course, even though the children now also actively hold the discussion to the themes.

Learning activity
a) Development of Motivation
What are the children's interests and wishes?
How does the teacher create interest on the part of the children?
What conflicts does he work with and what demands does he make?

The children are still absorbed in the content of the themes. This time, the teacher tries to make a resumé and does not build the instruction around conflicting conceptions of the themes. However, he does create a conflict by formulating a mistake, i.e., that the cod gives birth to its young (30), and by contrasting the cod's and the chimpanzee's parental care (38). The children react directly to this provocation and become absorbed with the theme 'parental care'.

A conflict arises spontaneously, thereby, between Bent, who wants to continue concentrating on the theme 'parental care', and those children who want to go on with the problem of animals' development and survival (49, 51). The teacher supports the general problem formulation and the class continues with that. In the middle of the conflict, Henrik tries to distract the class' attention from the subject content (52). The manœuvre might be due to the conflict, but, in any case, it is rejected by the teacher (53). This illustrates for the children that he demands concentration on the subject content.

b) Development of Concepts
How does the pupils' own learning activity progress in the lessons and how is it structured?

It is quite clear that the children are absorbed in the relations among survival, parental and coexistence. It is only at the beginning of the lesson that there is an enumeration of animal names (7). Otherwise, it is the relations that the children concern themselves with. One or two of the children also anticipate the course of the teacher's instruction. Gunnar does so by drawing the general model for the survival of the animal species before the teacher has set the task. Similarly, Lonni tries to anticipate (28), by reading aloud the problem: 'Why do some animals die out'. The teacher tries for a time to hinder her in doing so, but it is still an anticipation when she does it (47).

The contributions (by Lonni, Tina and another child (47, 49, 51) are attempts to keep the teacher to the original theme (27). Bent also takes over the teacher's role by exemplifying the teacher's concept of parental care (25) and by asking questions of him (43), as does Dennis by praising the observer's writing (46).

The children are absorbed in the model and are interested in drawing it on the board. This is particularly apparent when Bjarne helps Rasmus and when Rasmus changes the teacher's suggestion (65, 66).

c) Social coexistence
What is the nature of the interaction between children and teacher and among the children?

The teacher still directs the course, but Bent is so absorbed with the problem 'parental care' that he assumes control for a moment. Also, a child corrects the teacher's mistake in the 'parental care' theme (30), as does Rasmus with the teacher's drawing (66).

The children listen to each other and perhaps compete a little in answering (47-51). However, Bjarne wants very much to help Rasmus when he is up at the blackboard.

The teacher disciplines by saying, "Wait" (29, 53).

TENTATIVE EVALUATION OF THE INTERPRETATIONS

Teaching activity
The teacher is a little more flexible to the children's introduction of topics in the 18th instruction period than in the first which can be seen in the children's focusing for some time on parental care. There is little digression by the pupils from the themes introduced by the teacher, in both the first and the 18th period of instruction.

The teacher adheres very much to the plan in both instruction periods.

Learning activity
The lack of digressions by the pupils can be taken as an indication of their interest in the teaching.

In the 18th instruction period, in contrast to the first period, the children spontaneously focus on relations and development and they directly contribute ideas to the teaching and also want to control   the focus of teaching. The children listen to each other's answers in both lectures. It cannot be seen from these two teaching periods how the social coexistence has developed among the children.

CONCLUSION

Each protocol has been used as an evaluation of each period of instruction. The common sense comments are related to this evaluation.

The overall evaluation of the results of the teaching experiment is based on the interpretation of the observation protocols from each instruction period. These interpretations will be fit together to form conclusive general interpretations by explicitly using the conceptual category system. The aspects of teaching and learning differentiated by using the category system will be used to evaluate the general character of the progression of the teaching and learning process.

It has to be stressed once more that the items in the categories are not only determined by the theory but are also changed and developed from the interpretation of the specific observation protocols, because aspects not previously conceived will hopefully arise through the analysis of the protocol. Further evaluation of the results of the teaching experiment will be based on the pupils' solutions of tasks given throughout the year which will be related to the interpretation of the observations so that the progress of their development of skills and knowledge throughout the year can be seen. Finally, interviews will be used to evaluate a possible change in the children's conceptions of the development of animal forms and the origin of man and to evaluate the extent to which the pupils' conceptions are related to the concepts of the teaching material.

The value of this methodological approach will depend on its ability to develop theoretical conceptions which can guide teaching and learning activity in the future according to specified objectives.

NOTES

[1] The project is carried out in cooperation with Esben Hansen, Uffe Juul Jensen and Yrjö Engeström. The research project is supported by The Danish Research Council.

[2] This differentiation between these two forms of thinking was already undertaken by Vygotsky in the beginning of the 1930's (Vygotsky, 1962) and has since then been developed and extended by Davydov and his co-workers (Davydov, 1977; Davydov, Lompscher & Markova, 1982).

REFERENCES

Adams, S., & Biddle, B.J. (1970). *Realities of teaching. Explorations with video tape.* New York: Holt, Rinehart and Winston Inc.

Davydov, V.V. (1977). *Die Arten der Verallgemeinerungen im Unterricht.* Berlin: Volk und Wissen.

Davydov, V.V., Lompscher, J., & Markova, A.K. (1982). *Ausbildung der Lerntätigkeit bei Schülern.* Berlin: Volk und Wissen.

Delamont, S. (1976). *Interaction in the classroom.* London: Methuen.

Giorgi, A. (1975). An application of phenomenological method in psychology. In A. Giorgi, C. Fischer & E. Murray (Eds.), *Duquesne Studies in Phenomenological Psychology,* Vol. II, 82-103. Pittsburgh: Duquesne University Press.

Good, T.L., & Brophy, J.E. (1973). *Looking in classrooms.* New York: Harper & Row.

Hedegaard, M. (1984a). Three essays about how the child becomes conceptually related to the world. *Psykologisk Skrift-serie Aarhus,* 9, 5.

Hedegaard, M. (1984b). Interaktionsbaseret beskrivelse af småbørn og børnehaveklassebørn i deres dagligdag. *Psykologisk Skriftserie Aarhus,* 9, 4.

Hedegaard, M. (1986). *Instruction of evolution as a school subject - and the development of pupils' theoretical thinking.* To be published in Proceedings from the "1. Internationaler Kongresz zur Tätigkeits- theorie", Berlin, October 3-5.

Hedegaard, M., & Hakkarainen, P. (1986). Qualitative research as instructional intervention. In P.D. Ashworth, A. Giorgi, and A.J.J. De Koning (Eds.), *Qualitative Research in Psychology.* Pittsburgh: Duquesne University Press.

Iljenkov, E.V. (1972). Die Dialektik des Abstrakten und Konkreten im "Kapital" von Marx. In Schmidt (Ed.), *Beiträge zur marxistischen Erkenntnistheorie.* Nordlingen: Suhrkamp Verlag.

Jackson, P.W. (1968). *Life in classrooms.* New York: Holt, Rinehart and Winston,Inc.

Leontiev, A.N. (1978). *Activity, consciousness and personality.* New Jersey: Prentice Hall.

Leontiev, A.N. (1981). *Problems of the development of the mind.* Moscow: Progress.

Markova, A.K. (1982). Das ausbildende Experiment in der psychologischen Erforschung der Lerntätigkeit. In: Davydov, Lompscher & Markova: *Ausbildung der Lerntätigkeit bei Schülern.* Berlin: Volk und Wissen.

Stenild, M.H. (1977). *Begrebsindlæring en procesanalyse.* Copenhagen: Dansk Psykologisk Forlag.

Stenild, M.H. (1978). *Spæadbarnet og førskolebarnet.* Copenhagen: Dansk Psykologisk Forlag.

Vigotsky, L.S. (1962). *Thought and Language.* M.I.T. Press.

Appendix A

Plan for the 1st period of instruction

The goal of the instruction

To introduce the children to the subject 'orientation' as a single subject (i.e. an integration of biology, history and geography).

To initiate the building of a basis for the teaching/learning of the subject and its fundamental questions: the origins of man and how the animal species evolved. We wish to acquire insight into the children's conceptions of these and at the same time to evoke in the children an interest in these questions.

We attempt to strengthen this interest by working with the contrasting explanations of man's origin, how animals have developed and how life arose.

Concepts of instruction

Conceptually, orientation includes the development of the earth, plants, animals, and man.

The organization of the instruction

The teacher's activity	The pupil's tasks
1) Distribute work folders and note books - explain how they are to be used We must make our own book in the teaching experiment.	Write name on the notebook
2) Focus our attention on the subject in relation to other subjects.	What must one learn in Danish, Mathematics and art? What must one learn to be good at in 'orientation'?
Conclusion: Learn to be good at finding out how the earth, animals, plants and people have developed. How the earth, animals, plants and people have developed is something that people have always wondered about and there have been many different conclusions.	
3) Tell/read: the Eskimo creation myth.	
4) The children's conceptions of evolution on the basis of questions.	You all know that there are many different kinds of animals on the earth nowadays, from whales to aquarium fish and from people to mice. You also know that there are animals all over the world; from the rain forests to Greenland and from the oceans to high up in the mountains - But tell me, where do they all come from? Have all of these different kinds of animals always lived on earth? What do you think? Do you think that the animals that lived on earth in earlier times look the same as animals do today?

Do you think that there have always been people on earth?
How did people begin to be people?
Where does man come from?

5) Other children's conceptions - read aloud from an interview protocol.

6) Present adults' conceptions and ideas of the first animals and man from books with illustrations.

Look at the books.
Find the animal that you believe is most different to animals nowadays.
Write and draw in the note book on the basis of the question: Which animal is the most different animal from those we know today?

Mariane and I go around in the class and make the children show, draw and write down why they think the animal pointed out is the most different.

7) Distribute copied material
   - for the next lesson you must read these pages.
   - include, possibly, fossils in the next lesson.

Appendix B

Description of "class activity", August 15th, 1984
- 2 first hours
Describer: Mariane Hedegaard

Observations   Common sense interpretation

1. The teacher is learning the names of the children.
2. Then she askes the name of the subject.
3. They say:
4. Biology - geography - history.
5. The teacher asks for what they call these   Introduce the subjects by asking for their
   subjects when they are put together.   common name.
6. Gunnar says 'orientation'.
7. The teacher writes it on the blackboard. Then he writes 'Danish'.
8. Asks: what are you supposed to learn in the Danish lessons?
9. To read and write, Lonni says.
10. The teacher adds: To be good at reading   Teacher reformulates the answer so it
    and writing.   becomes adequate in relation to his
11. The teacher asks for more.   expectation.
12. Child: To write stories, to spell.
13. Teacher: Yes, to be good at using one's   Teacher extends the child's description.
    imagination.

14. The teacher asks about mathematics.
15. Afterwards he asks about creative art.
16. Gunnar: To learn how to draw.

Gunnar has caught the teacher's point that they should learn to become good at something.

17. Mette: You must learn how to use your hands.

Mette and other children have also caught the teacher's point.

18. Child: Learn how to shape things.
19. Teacher: Then why do we have 'orientation' as a subject?
20. Gunnar: We must learn about animals.
21. Child: About plants.
22. Child: About nature.
23. Teacher: Yes, that's right. Plants and animals are parts of nature.

The teacher links up the children's formulation to a larger whole.

24. Rasmus: We must learn about old days.
25. Teacher: Yeah, that's right you must learn about how things develop.

The teacher reformulates Rasmus' answer about the old days so that it also includes development, although it was not intended in his answer.

26. Teacher: Were things different in earlier times?

Teacher focuses on time concept.

27. Rasmus says something about the time of the Vikings, but is not, however, able to explain himself.
28. The teacher writes the formulation of the problem on the blackboard.

Teacher formulates this first theme in writing.

29. I believe the children are anxious to see the books they are to receive.
30. Teacher explains that they are to make their own books.

The teacher changes the subject to a practical one.

31. The children seem contented.
32. The children receive a plastic folder for their loose-leaf book and a green exercise book; they are told that they may draw in it.
33. They are told that they may draw something on the first page: What is 'orientation'?

The children are invited to a drawing task.

34. They may draw animals, plants, human beings or something from earlier times. The children's summary - the teacher repeats twice.

The teacher uses the children's formulation of the problem area.

35. John: May we draw a dog?
36. John: How do you draw old cars (asks me)

Understands that it should be something from earlier times.

37. Henriette says: I have never been able to draw a Viking ship.

Addresses the observer, focus on the time aspect.

38. Mette draws herself. Mikkel and John are fetching picture cards from Rasmus - cards with pictures of cars - in order to draw old-fashioned cars.

Mette and Henrik have not got the point that it should be something from the old days they should draw.

39. Henrik goes to the teacher and asks whether he may draw an aquarium with

fish in it.

40. The teacher asks Mikkel whether it would not be too difficult to draw from a card, because then one would expect it to be the same, and whether it wouldn't be better to draw a model which is in one's imagination only.

41. The children are quiet while they draw.

42. The bell rings.

----

43. The children are told that they have to finish their drawings at home.

44. The teacher tells them that there are a million different animals. He mentions some names, and the children add to the list.

Teacher and children delimit the focus of their future activity to the concept "animal".

45. Do prehistoric animals look like the animals we know today?

Teacher intends to lay the foundation for the concept of adaptation and introduces the problem area by asking a question about appearance.

46. The children: No.

47. Put up your hands when you want to say something.

Direct disciplining.

48. Gunnar: No.

49. None of them can tell the difference.

50. Teacher: The earth - has it always looked the same?

Teacher expands the concept of development and time.

51. Bent: No, it has been filled with lava.

52. Teacher: What is lava?

53. Bent: Melted rock coming from the middle, where it's hot.

Teacher asking the pupil to elucidate his answer which the child is able to.

54. John: There have been wars.

Child introduces another aspect.

55. Bent: It may also come from volcanos.

56. Teacher: Yes, volcanos eject lava.

Teacher follows Bent's themes because it can be related to the creation of earth and animals. Teacher neglects John's comments.

57. Lonni: Before any human beings were born there was water all over. Then God created dry spots.

58. John: My grandfather took part in the 2nd world war.

John sticks to history.

59. Teacher: I would like to hear about it some other time.

Teacher wants to postpone John's theme.

60. The teacher returns to the subject of God and the dry spots.

Teacher takes Lonni's comment because it can be related to the creation of the earth. Pupil supplies the conflicting views involved.

61. Bent: No, the water evaporated because of the sun.

62. Teacher: Does everyone believe that it happened that way?

63. Children: No.

64. The teacher reads from the Greenlanders' creation myth.

The teacher demonstrates another conception.

65. Bent rather promptly says that it is wrong.

66. Henrik replies that one could eat dogs.

A comment which is close to the myth read.

67. Teacher: I don't think they did. He keeps on reading from the myth.

Teacher avoids the diversion, follows the plan.

68. Bent: I know all that about the rocks.

Bent comments very much because he is interested and perhaps also because he wants attention.

69. Bent refers to a passage in the myth about the rocks falling down from space - they probably come from the stars - (he immediately fits the creation myth into his naturalistic conception).

70. Teacher: Do you think that human beings have always existed? For how long? Well. Have there always been animals?

A new theme is introduced, possibly too early. Focuses class effort on further development of the concept of time via description of past and present time.

71. John: Yes.
72. John: Flies and things like that.

Probably John does not have any conception about animal evolution, but Bent has.

73. Bent: I know how human beings were created - from apes.
74. Teacher: Did the apes create the human beings?

Teacher provokes but the question may lead the children the wrong way.

75. Henriette: No, the apes turned into people.

Corrects the teacher.

76. John: Because they ate bananas.

John is probably making fun.

77. Mikkel: No, because they turned into apes.
78. Teacher: Do the apes in Zoo turn into people, and then they can be let out?

Teacher focuses class effort on further development of the concept of development and time.

79. Lonni tells about the Zoo.
80. Bent: Our ancestors were apes.

Though the teacher asks concretely, Bent demonstrates knowledge of evolution.

81. Teacher: Your grandparents?

The teacher follows Bent's answer up with a very concrete question about time relation.

82. Bent: No, it's a long time ago.

83. Teacher: Did human beings once exist who turned into apes?

The teacher asks a question with a wrong content.

84. Teacher: I can also ask you whether human beings once looked like they do today?

The teacher asks about appearance.

85. Bent: No, once they were hairy all over.

The question is seriously tackled.

86. Teacher: Could it happen that you would lose your hair in two years time?

The teacher makes a provocation to get the pupil to clarify further.

87. John tells about Dracula - where there is a man who turns into an ape.

But it results in digression.

88. Bent: I remember that from the ghost train - there is a monster.

89. Teacher: Human beings didn't always look like they do today.

The teacher brings aspects from the original problem back to the instruction.

90. Teacher: What about the animals, did they look like they do today?

Observations	Common sense interpretation
91. Gunnar: No, many other animals have existed.	Gunnar also demonstrates knowledge of the evolution of animals.
92. Gunnar: They have died out.	
93. Teacher: But how did it happen?	Teacher leads the development of the problem in directions of adaptation.
94. Bent would like to tell about the Eskimos. The barkmen dig up some kind of fruit.	Bent uses the just told myth of the Eskimos to answer.
95. The teacher reads from an interview research a girl's description of how species of animal evolved.	The teacher follows the teaching instruction instead of the child's answer because his question was meant to lead to this.
96. About how she has thought it over.	
97. Reads another girl's description about prehistoric animals.	
98. Each time John asks whether the children attend this school.	John is very concretely oriented to the topics introduced.
99. Teacher: What do you think of this?	
100. Child: Yes, it's true.	
101. Now you have told me what you think, and I have read to you what other children think, now I have some books showing what adults think.	Formulation of a new step in the instruction period.
102. Groups are arranged.	A new task is introduced.
103. After a while the children are to point out which animal is most different from the animal they know today - because afterwards they are to draw it in their exercise books.	
104. The children are very busy looking in the books.	
105. 10 Minutes before the bell rings the children are told to draw.	

Appendix C
Description of class activity, December 19th, 1984,
2 first hours
Describer: Mariane Hedegaard

Observations	Common sense interpretation
1. The teacher says that we are going to talk about what we have been doing since the summer holidays. Summarizes from the model for scientific work which has been written on the blackboard once and for all.	

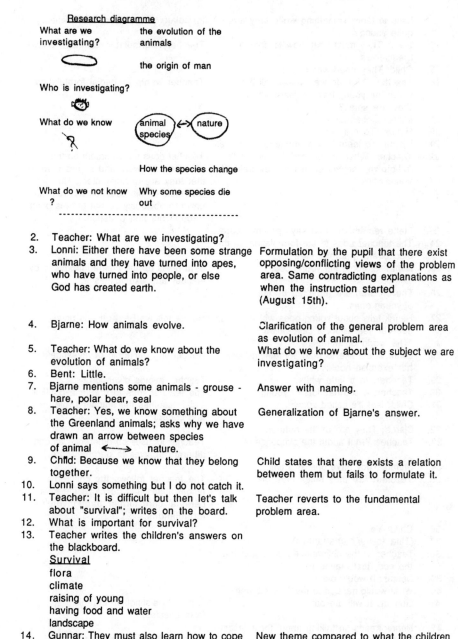

Research diagramme

What are we investigating? the evolution of the animals

the origin of man

Who is investigating?

What do we know   animal species ←→ nature

How the species change

What do we not know ?   Why some species die out

2.	Teacher: What are we investigating?	
3.	Lonni: Either there have been some strange animals and they have turned into apes, who have turned into people, or else God has created earth.	Formulation by the pupil that there exist opposing/conflicting views of the problem area. Same contradicting explanations as when the instruction started (August 15th).
4.	Bjarne: How animals evolve.	Clarification of the general problem area as evolution of animal.
5.	Teacher: What do we know about the evolution of animals?	What do we know about the subject we are investigating?
6.	Bent: Little.	
7.	Bjarne mentions some animals - grouse - hare, polar bear, seal	Answer with naming.
8.	Teacher: Yes, we know something about the Greenland animals; asks why we have drawn an arrow between species of animal ←→ nature.	Generalization of Bjarne's answer.
9.	Chîld: Because we know that they belong together.	Child states that there exists a relation between them but fails to formulate it.
10.	Lonni says something but I do not catch it.	
11.	Teacher: It is difficult but then let's talk about "survival"; writes on the board.	Teacher reverts to the fundamental problem area.
12.	What is important for survival?	
13.	Teacher writes the children's answers on the blackboard. Survival flora climate raising of young having food and water landscape	
14.	Gunnar: They must also learn how to cope with other animals.	New theme compared to what the children have told.
15.	Teacher: What do we call that - that they	Teacher attempts at getting the pupil to

	have to learn something while they are quite young?	formulate the name of the relation.
16.	Lonni: They must learn how to defend themselves.	Teacher reformulates Gunnar's answer.
17.	Child: They need water.	
18.	Teacher: What do we usually call that which the young have to learn when they are small?	Teacher wants a special formulation.
19.	Mette: Cohabitation.	
20.	Henrik: To practice.	
21.	Bjarne: To learn how to manage in nature.	
22.	Teacher: What do you call that which the full-grown animals do when they train the young ones.	Teacher does not comment on the children's answers and shows thereby that they are unsatisfactory. He then reformulates his question because the children obviously do not get his point through his first question.
23.	Mette remembers and says parental care.	
24.	The teacher adds to the formulation on the blackboard: parental care	
25.	Bent tells about the young cod.	Bent takes up the theme introduced by the teacher and exemplifies it.
26.	The children are attracted by the subject of young ones.	
27.	Henrik tells about young ones which he has seen on television, a cast called "The world of animals".	Henrik follows Bent on this point.
28.	Lonni would like to read something from her exercise book.	Concerning our topic of investigation.
29.	Teacher: In a little while.	Teacher avoids diversion.
30.	Teacher: A cod has lots of young.	The teacher tries to create a conflict.
31.	Child: No! it's called spawn.	Child assumes the teacher's role and control.
32.	Bjarne: They are at the bottom.	
33.	Teacher: What about the cimpanzee?	Teacher focuses on difference among different species in parental care.
34.	Stefan: They have one at a time.	
35.	Teacher: Are they taken care of?	The teacher follows the children's tangilizations and develops the topic of parental care further through their formulations.
36.	Child: Yes.	
37.	(Tina is very unattentive).	
38.	Teacher: If the chimapnzee does just like the cod, just leaves it?	
39.	Dennis: It would die.	
40.	What would happen to the species then?	
41.	Gunnar: It will die out.	Is able to distinguish organism from species.
42.	Henrik keeps on talking about the telecast.	
43.	Bent: Do you know how many eggs a common mussel lays?	Asks the teacher a question.
44.	Teacher: No! - he is supposed to	

make a guess.

45. Bent tells that it lays 25 million eggs.
Side-tracks but close to the theme.

46. Dennis tells me that I have a nice handwriting; probably because I told him that his handwriting is nice.
Praises the observer, but thereby goes away from the teaching themes.

47. Lonni reads from the paragraph she found in her exercise book: Why do some animals die out.
Insists on the teacher's original way of presenting the problem at the beginning of the lesson.

48. (One of the questions we formulated that we wanted to investigate).

49. Child: Gradually, more and more animals go on land.
Also a comment on the first questions from the beginning of the year's teaching.

50. (We have dealt earlier with the subject of how in the past aquatic animals developed into terrestrial animals).

51. Tina: I know how man came to existence. She does not get the chance to tell it because Bent keeps on talking about the cod.
Conflict between the children who want to follow the subjects as introduced by the teacher, and Bent who has been caught by the new problem about young and survival.

52. Henrik: Me and Mikkel have a secret from the class.
Attempt to divert the instruction.

53. Teacher: Yes, I am anxious to know but not right now.
Which is acknowledged but delayed.

54. Teacher: Have we considered all that is important to survive?
The teacher stresses that the subject is survival.

55. Tina: That they have warmth so that they don't freeze to death.

56. Bjarne: Defence against enemies.

57. Teacher: What do we call that?
The teacher asks about something which has already been formulated by Bjarne. Then Tina repeats the answer.

58. Tina: They must learn how to defend themselves.

59. Teacher: Against what?

60. Child: Other animals.

61. Teacher: Now we will see if it fits into a model.
The children have been working with the model for a while.

62. Teacher: Can anyone draw a model? Several put up their hands.
Draws the pupils' activity into the solution of the problem.

63. Rasmus goes to the blackboard, he wants to draw a model for a polar bear.
Believes that he can do it.

64. But when the teacher says that he has to include everything in the model, he hesitates. The teacher assists him by drawing the first part. The teacher draws:
But becomes nervous because teacher formulates the task again.

65. Bjarne shows Rasmus the model   Gets help from another child.
     in his book.

66. Rasmus (after having drawn part of the   And corrects the teacher in his way of
     model): Polar bear is wrong. (It looks   helping with the model.
     different in his book).

67. Rasmus draws correctly, although
     Greenland is differently placed
     in his model.
     Rasmus draws:

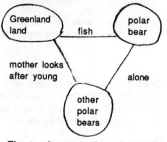

68. The teacher goes through the drawing from   Teacher wants to summarize their
     the items on the blackboard about survival,   knowledge.
     which the children have already suggested,
     by asking them where it belongs on the
     research scheme.

69. Teacher: Where do I write other species?

70. Mette wants him to write it next to food.

71. Teacher explains that it has to be in the   Teacher corrects directly, but does not
     circle for Greenland.   explain.

72. He says that they are going to make a   Teacher gives a new task.
     model for all animals in the next lesson.

73. Gunnar goes to the teacher and shows him   Gunnar solves the task before it is given
     his model, it really is a general model.   and is eager to show his results.

74. Gunnar shows me his ballpoint pen, he has
     also shown me his model - I may keep his
     drawing of the model.

Chapter 5

CREATIVITY AND THE METHODOLOGICAL DEBATE:
A MYTHO-HISTORICAL REFLECTION

Mike Arons

QUALITATIVE RESEARCH: MYTH AND HISTORAL REALITY

In Antoine Saint-Exupery's (1943) story, *le Petit Prince*, a Turkish astronomer, garbed in his native dress, presents a paper at an international conference describing his discovery of a new asteroid. His announcement is met with polite indifference. He returns several decades later to the conference, but now in European garb since Turkey had meanwhile modernized. He presents the same paper about the same asteroid and he is acclaimed for his great discovery.

Something like this is the reason that human science and qualitative research are having such a struggle trying to gain recognition. Those for whom it is suited have not yet recognized their need for it. This is due, largely, to its wrapping which is confounded with philosophy and introspection. The philosophical critique of the old psychology methods and the digging of the groundwork for new qualitative research in the social sciences have been in the process of development for a century, particularly in Europe. In the United States, the Duquesne school, above all, has been Spartan in its labour of translating philosophical foundations into rigorous, fertile and original research methods for the social sciences (e.g., Giorgi, 1970).

I would like to propose and defend a more optimistic view about the future of qualitative research. We may be at the point of beholding the mountain coming to Mohammed. For good reason, which will become evident, I am going to put my focus on American psychology in this paper and suggest that as a delayed reaction, it is about to open up to human science approaches. In the end of his life, Carl Rogers, for instance, was enthused and enthusing others about new qualitative approaches that are so well attuned to the demands for meaning, complexity and wholeness inherent to the humanistic vision of man (Arons, 1985). American psychology had, after all, undergone, during the sixties and seventies, a major shift in faculty and student interest from the academic-research (dominated by natural science models) to the professional-applied end of the field. Rogers had helped lead this displacement of psychology's center of gravity. It is encouraging just to have heard him re-emphasize research in its newly developing qualitative approaches.

But, my basis for optimism is only bolstered by such good signs. What is being expressed has, in my opinion, a much deeper foundation. The dialectical movement in the direction of qualitative approaches to research in American psychology began in the fifties with the emergence of a historical clash between two Titans. One Titan was the quantitative methodology which dominated American psychology. The other was a human subject matter called 'creativity', so dreaded by the former. Yet, the encounter was fated. Since the confrontation has all the qualities of myth, it is best to at least introduce the story by taking full advantage of the power of myth.

Quantitative methodology ruled the entire kingdom of psychology and all its neighbouring social sciences. So consolidated had become the dominance of this approach and so distanced by apparent success from its own family origins, that these origins were never spoken of except in terms flattering to the method. This methodology would tell stories about itself and its ascendancy to dominance. It would read from the scriptures of Auguste Comte about the primitives who inhabit both history and subjectivity, of the slow rise of its ancestors from animism and projection through noble attempts of peoples and the mind to grapple with realities beyond their fears and desires.

Mentioned often is Uncle Physics, who by his boldness and originality conquered the physical world from the aging and waning King Philosophy. He had lithographs of Uncle Physic's conquests which he showed whenever asked or given the opportunity. All knew that Uncle Physics was the model for this methodology's conquests in the land of the psyche (in any event, the land had once been called psyche).

What was never told, or perhaps even remembered, in royal circles where background is a matter of some consequence, were the differences between the ways that this methodology achieved dominance in psychology as compared, really contrasted with the ways Uncle Physics had taken over from old King Philosophy. If the truth be known and honestly stated, this methodology, ruler of psychology and the social sciences, inherited nearly everything of what it has become from Uncle Physics.

Of course, Uncle Physics had earned his success the hard way. The methods of Physics evolved slowly and in relationship to the encounters with the physical world. And at a point it became evident to both winner, Physics, and loser, Philosophy, that the latter had nothing comparable to offer. Philosophy retired from the psychical world with dignity. Being a noble fellow, he helped out Uncle Physics when and wherever he could.

But things were different in psychology and the other social sciences. The philosophers knew that while the method had introduced a new language and a set of impressive formalities, psychology had never left the oldest questions asked during the days when King Philosophy reigned. It simply crowned itself a better manager of these questions than philosophy who had centuries earlier raised them. But this was merely a matter of double theft: questions from Philosophy; method from Uncle Physics.

The story of ancestry is more sordid though. It starts with an incestuous relationship. Uncle Physics was ruling a land of subjects who were natively different from himself. Thus he could more easily respect them as strangers and employ the most effective, if necessarily indirect, means to get to know them and by this understanding of their ways would they come slowly to yield to his rule. But, alas, the relationship between the psychologist and his subject matter was - to put it discreetly - more intimate. Indeed, if in psychology there was to be a relationship at all which could appear honourable, it was necessary that the new reigning methodology forced, by extraordinary double contortion, a distance between the human psychologist and the human subject matter.

The first part of the contortion was not hard to effect because the prying instrument to gain cleavage was borrowed from Uncle Physics. It was called the objective attitude through which the psychologist could distance himself from himself. Kings must always keep this distance. There was a ritual called scientific education which taught how this is done. Or, if one were clever, he could merely recite the incantation, over and over, that I am a scientist, and all the rest of his humanness, especially that nasty pre-scientific stuff, would just vanish. But to assure this, the method as applied had built-in constraints and red light signals just in case some lyrical subjectivity managed to whistle its way through.

The second part of the contortion was hard, for this was something the methodology in psychology never could borrow but had to improvise on its own. Here it was a matter of making human subjects into objects, like those of the physical world. This double contortion had put a strain in the land of psychology. The philosophers have never ceased to talk about this strain because, after all, they are concerned with ultimate truths. They not only sense, but fully understand both the basis and burden in debt to fate which psychology carries.

Some who tell stories, liken the situation of the psychology's natural science methodology to the Hindu symbol of the snake which is eating its own tail, pretending not to know or being dumb to the foreseeable consequences should this incestuous relationship continue unabated. In any event, the method assures that the distinction between pretending and dumb is merely academic. Once the method starts eating away, it never sees more than a nibble in advance and, at that, has established all the skepticism and safeguards to assure no recognition of itself in its mouth.

Others liken the strain to the story of Oedipus, who while escaping his fate becomes, like the method, king, intelligently ruling over subjects whose problems he cannot possibly understand, for lack of understanding of himself. The strain is not reduced until Oedipus encounters pre-scientific subjectivity through a primitive yank at the emotions. I like this version because it offers me the lever to move to the major point of this article. That is, that American psychology in the 1950's met Tiresias in the form of creativity.

HISTORICAL STATUS: SOMEWHERE BETWEEN THE DUMB AND THE BLIND

Nearly anything that was new, democratic sounding and not boring was welcome to America at the time it gave refuge to functionalism in its behaviouristic form. It is as if William James were a bridge between a boring German and an evangelical American attempt at objectivity - a role for which he would certainly not wish to be remembered. But he might have been dismayed, though not surprised, to have seen the day when the latter became as trivial and pedantic as the former. Given its early promise of instant success, one might wonder how the new American psychology could have postponed its day of reckoning until the 1950's.

That question lends itself to interesting thoughts. Survival of the new psychology, once defeated in its introspectionist form, rode on playing safe and dumb. Its safety was a cocoon it built around itself, making it impervious to criticisms from without and even within. As a science it was now in a class progressively beyond philosophy - out of earshot - and, in any event, it spoke a new and esoteric language of jargon and operational definitions intentionally disconnected from natural language. Its taste for elements served to segmentalize its enterprises into micro-specialities and increasingly isolated psychology from the once related, but now distant, fields of social science. But even these seemed not much more distant than any subfield of psychology from another. If the cocoon developed on the outside, the isolating mechanism operated from within. It was a new science which, it seemed fair, could only approach the subject matter incrementally beginning with the simplest indications of 'humanness' first - which often meant animal studies. However, this was the way of forestalling the day when that psychology had to encounter a humanness more than its match. That would turn out to be the Titan Creativity.

It could avoid thinking about such things by substituting for a reality check of its own, *a priori* assumptions borrowed, like its method, from other fields about the depth and scope of the human subject. Hedonism largely provided the energetics and functionalism the telos. This obviated the need for a philosophy of humanness and also provided the inherent justification for predictability and potential control. The Amercian society, stretched by pluralism, needed a psychology of adjustment just to collectively breathe. Its past, like that of its psychology, viewed obsolescent, left nothing but progress to consider. And signs of progress were everywhere in America. Psychology benefitted here. For unlike its unfortunate European cousins who had to communicate with their pre-scientific colleagues, American psychology was granted early and total autonomy from philosophy.

Playing dumb was a game learned from the positivists who called it objectivity. By this, for whatever else it benefits, a split occurs between the man and the scientist. The scientist played dumb to the man, to his feelings, to his personal experience. He was already playing dumb to the pre-sciences. Its was fair for the scientist to peek, on off-hours, in the interest of his creativity - which he was allowed to call a "gut feeling" - but none of this stolen fruit was to be recognizable in the scientific formulation of the product.

By an interesting pact, ratified in the American constitution, to insure the purity of both, a stiff arm distance was also to be kept between the secular and the religious. Max Weber (1958) thinks that Protestantism is that arm. This situation also permitted psychology to play dumb to the claims of an invisible spiritual world proclaimed by those of blind faith. There is no doubt plenty of room for misunderstanding and mischief when a society stands between the authorities of the dumb and the blind. One really does not understand where either of them is at or if they at all have anything in common. The Church-secular split in America took a different form than that tried elsewhere. In America, students received their spiritual training in Sunday School and not, as in France, as historically raised spiritual questions now examined in secular philosophy. Where American education, after formalities were dispensed with, led unabashedly towards the functional, i.e., social adjustment and jobs, French education led towards 'culture générale' and 'l'année philosophique'.

Where the disturbed adolescent in France was likely seen as passing through 'la crise spirituelle', requiring intimacy and self-exploration, his counterpart in America was sent to the counselor for a dose of 'social adjustment'. Those in America who found no comfortable home in the dogmas of the church and yet found adjustment less than a satisfying escatology, and who had abandoned past cultural and ethnic identities in the name of progress, could easily feel like spiritual orphans. It was a state of uneasiness widely enough spread to spawn the sort of social reaction which erupted in the 1960's. This same spiritual void would spawn the creativity and humanistic reaction within American psychology.

But that is the key encounter we are not yet prepared to face. The matter of playing dumb took several forms: e.g., split of scientist from man [himself] and his object [once man]; split of positivist from philosophy and pre-science; split of autonomous psychologist from colleagues and split of thinking man from blind faith. The matter of playing dumb was supported from within by *a priori* motor-telos assumptions of wholeness, and supported from without by a society sharing values of the functional subject and progressive methods. Combined, these all amounted to the obverse side of their promised benefits, to massive suppression.

The combination of a sequestered dumbness, as our educators and psychoanalytic colleagues would remind us, is pregnant with explosive future possibilities, both fortunate and unfortunate. One might say that the form American psychology took amounted to a bet with very high stakes. The bet was that the method with its progressive objective of prediction and control could ultimately devour, at least on its own terms, the subject. The price of failure would be that not dissimilar to the fate of Wundt and Tichener's structuralism, but perhaps much worse, given the magnitude of the suppression of history and subjectivity required by the boldness of this new leap. To the advantage of American psychology, the day of the crucial test could be forestalled for reasons offered above, until something unexpected, outside the method's control capabilities, would occur, i.e., a rebellion from its supportive society and/or from within in a form psychology could not ignore without denying itself and its *raison d'etre* .

CREATIVITY: INTERNAL COMBUSTION

By the 1950's social adjustment and conformity had become less distinguishable, at least in the public mind, and the latter had reached stages of epidemic proportions (e.g., Goodman, 1960). The Sputnik shock bolted its way into the complacent social consciousness prodding an immediate and subsequent realization. The immediate, that America produced few of its native born or educated creative scientists and, subsequent, that science and technology for all their contributions to progress and material gifts were providing little concomitant self-understanding or personal satisfaction. Remedies for the first, i.e., a tight return to the intrinsics of education, especially to mathematics and science, were reversed and finally overwhelmed by attempted remedies for the second. American education offering little to satisfy the hunger for self-exploration and science offering little in this direction or even personal satisfaction from its products, resulted in an extreme loosening and broadening of education. This reaction was coupled with a growing aversion to science, technology and materialism, and also to conformity, making jobs and professions. The social revolution of the 60's was on. But it's parting shot, creativity, preceded it by a decade.

This new hunger for self-exploration made Euopean-based existentialism, and Western and Eastern transcendentalism widely popular reading. The psychedelic movement gave an instant vision of the universe within, paling by contrast social life as lived and, especially, psychology's laboratory version of it (Leary, 1983). The interest in both existentialism and mysticism, though from different tracks, led towards and from the central station of creativity. Creativity was now on the table for psychology, forced by the society. Why had not the functionalistic model in psychology, education and life produced the source inspiration for progress? Why were the "obsolescent" cultures, at home or by immigrant ambassadors, producing the basic creative stuff of science? From the side of the students of psychology came the question: "is that all there is?"

The subject of creativity provided a perfect vehicle to negotiate a break from fixed patterns of thinking and unquestioned assumptions both about giftedness in the scientist and personal growth. Creativity had that horizontal quality of what Merleau-Ponty (1964) called "ultra choses", very apt for an area of recognized human potential historically ensconced in such an aura of respect, awe and mystery. Creativity had other special qualities not easily dismissed, mechanized or reduced away by psychologists trained in such arts. It had tangible and valued utilitarian products, unlike religion and mysticism whose experiential claims could be reduced to illusion, delusion and consolidation. These creative products were often authored by psychologists themselves and placed as originating in their "gut feelings". Science itself was becoming a contemporary expression of the new, the novel - of creativity and, as Bronowski (1958) was to claim, the scientific method was itself the single most creative product invented by Western Culture. Creativity could not be denied legitimate status as a research subject without at the same time denying the self-image of the scientist.

What was to make creativity particularly indomitable in terms of resistence to dismissal, mechanization or reduction was the inherent significance of the term 'originality', which by definition implies the unpredictable. This was the most inherently frightening aspect of this word, to a psychology operating from a model of prediction and control. It posed the distinct possibility of a human process itself unpredictable. Furthermore, 'originality' is a two vectored word. One vector is towards the new, the unique, but the other vector is towards the origins. Here, in the regressive relationship of the new to the origins was the spector of possibility most ominous in its implications for a psychology which had in the name of positive progress expediently suppressed its historical past and personal subjectivity (Krippner & Arons 1973).

Indeed, the studies on creativity were to reveal a great distinction between the creative and non-creative scientist. The latter, like his method, more characterized by repression or suppression of complexity, disdain for ambiguity and equivocal symbols, compulsive rigor and preference for control and order at all stages. The former, characterized by much the opposite plus a non-pathological emotional lability; strong 'primary process' activity; holistic or Gestalt, rather than elementistic life and organization styles; and strong interest in self-discovery and personal development. Above all, the creative scientist, and more so the artist, were hardly recognized by their exemplary social adjustment (MacKinnon 1962; Barron 1963).

Maslow (1962) was to find in the profile of the creative individual, among whose ranks he recognized few of his colleagues, striking correlaries to the traits he was finding in his self-actualizing subjects. For instance, the literature on both groups speaks of 'peak' and 'transcendent' experiences (which would become one of the foundations for transpersonal psychology). Maslow discerned two versions of creativity: one centered on talent, the other characterized by a special spontaneity and originality of life style. Here Maslow both popularized creativity - a spur to the human potentials movement gathering rapid momentum in the United States - and linked creativity to Eastern philosophies. For instance, he drew analogies between creative and Zen perception, and frequency of peak and mystic experiences among creative self-actualizers. The artist John Ferran had come to make this link between the traditionally 'talent centered creative' and the 'mystic' in a more direct manner. He suggested that the artist would be drawn by inspiration towards completion of the work of art. The mystic would reinvest his inspiration towards self-expansion and greater mystical unity. The creative process in the scientist was presumably similar to that in the artist, both having a potentially mystical side. Such links between creativity and mystical experience have a considerable history in the humanities at large (e.g., Laski, 1962).

This creative-mystical nexus represented in positive and psychologically healthy terms that which had been fundamentally rejected in favour of the method (e.g., consciousness, ambiguity, equivocal symbolism, the mythological and even the mystical). Psychology did what it could to turn torrid creativity into a tepid sub-field except in applied areas (e.g., Torrance, 1976) where it has pretty much languished over the years or has been theoretically reduced to a form of information processing. But as the emergence of cognitive psychology itself indicates, along with dozens of new professional divisions, psychology has never been the same since the creative part of the creativity revolution occurred. Both its foundations and *a priori* models of the human have been wounded and remain vulnerable.

CREATIVITY: REACTION WITHIN PSYCHOLOGY

While the more mystical dimensions of Maslow (1971), and certainly much of the popular extensions of the creativity revolution, could be underplayed or dismissed by academic psychology, other more indigenous and traditionally empirical wings of the rebellion opened by creativity research could not, at least not without intolerable family squabbles. Some of this research was quite explicit in confronting itself to both the method and major productions of psychology at that time. In his 1950 Presidential Address before the American Psychological Association, Guilford (1952) explicitly set up such an opposition. Among the four reasons he gave for the relative lack of interest into creativity prior to the fifties (fewer than one hundred publications before and over one thousand by the end of that decade) were: excessive preoccupation with I.Q.-tests; domination of learning theory; and prevalence of excessively rigid methodological standards. The fourth, lack of adequate criteria by which to define creativity, has its own interest for us which we will come to in its time.

But the opposition was more often implicit in the form of focus, questions asked and research variables selected for study. In a nutshell, the criteria developed for defining creativity were fashioned largely in terms of what was now recognized as *not* creativity or even anti-creativity or, put differently, in terms of those characteristics in psychology and society now being recognized as sterile. But this meant that the creativity research itself was largely fashioned by that which it opposed, making this research a significant expression of the local socio-historical context. Some examples of the implicit oppositions characteristic of the creativity research of the period will be discussed.

Historically, interest in creativity had largely focused on art and the artist. The research interest flourishing in the 1950's focused more on science and the scientist. As Hudson (1966) conjectured on this shift, creativity was being updated to the new cultural heros. The scientist was now seen in a new light, previously reserved mainly for the artist. By that widely held view, artistic products such as Shakespeare's character, Hamlet, were unique, irreproduceable, products of the creator's imagination. On the other hand, scientific products such as laws of conservation of energy were mere discoveries of realities that any scientist at some point would potentially find. Now the updated formulation expressed by Bronowski (1958) suggested that great scientific products, like art products, were unique individual construals of reality.

This new formulation - linking science to individual originality - had significant implications as regards the status of scientific method. For, in science viewed as discovery, the role of the (discovering) method becomes dominant. But if the great leaps of progress of science churn around the individual creative scientist more than around the method, then an understanding of that uniqueness is essential. This leads to such questions as to the conditions for creativity, implicating the educational, laboratory and social conditions. Opposing existent to ideal conditions in creativity research, the former were found seriously wanting and even antagonistic to the latter. In a word, turning particularly to psychology, the overemphasis on the importance of method and, as Guilford states, this particular objectivistic method as then applied, proves to be an obstacle not only to the study of creativity but to nurturing creativity itself.

What of the values of personal selection and educational preparation for science? With a stress on the power of method, these are one thing; a stress on the creative power of the individual, these are quite another. Preparation to serve the method more appropriately stresses the systematic, standardized and that which is convergent towards broad and specific ends; that requiring precise and efficient thinking within defined parameters; that affording a great tolerance for deferral of reward; that social in the sense of shared mission, forms and communication and that void of the personal subjective. By contrast, preparation to serve personal creativity more appropriately stresses the pre-systematic or that largely aimed at intuitive development; that which stresses the ideographic, impulsive, divergent towards possibilities, the metaphorical and symbolic; that which is open to the 'chaotic', iconoclastic and rebellious and that which is strongly dependent on access to vital emotion and personal experience (Barron, 1963).

To the question of what are, in fact, the generalized characteristics of those selected (or who self-select) to enter science, Hudson (1966), no uncritical supporter of creativity research, acknowledges that the creativity literature supports a view that physical scientists do evade personal issues and the psychologist "does something even more odd... he tries to make sense of the human experience by reifying it". These observations are relative to the larger point made earlier in this chapter that scientists tend to be deniers or suppressors of the personal.

The area of creativity research which provokes Hudson to these observations is that in which creative potential is differentiated from intellectual potentials as measured by I.Q.-tests. The I.Q.-test, as Guilford suggests, becomes an important symbol and concrete vehicle for creativity research. The creativity research expresses at once that which is inadequate in terms of educational preparation and personal selection for science and that which is inadequate to both the psychological and social view of 'functionalist' man. The consistently high correlations boasted between I.Q.-scores and educational, social and vocational success, prove to be the lever which energizes the new assault on educational, personal and social values. Convergent thinking is centrally valued in both test items and educational curricula, at the nearly complete expense of 'divergent' thinking (Getzels and Jackson, 1962).

Both in I.Q.-tests and in education, pure convergent thinking comes to be recognized as leading to standard conservative goals and values. Both turn out to be vehicles expressing and enforcing functionalistic values, including social, professional and psychological goal-directedness. Both value, first of all, goal directedness itself and both value externally set socially reified goals such as scientist or professional, which require step by step purging of all 'irrelevancies' not pertaining to these socially valued ends. This is where, once again, suppression comes in. For both the answers to tests and vocational goals are measured by reduction to simple form, exclusion or rational instrumentalizing of emotion in the service of goals (called motivation), preference for symmetry and preference for the efficient rather than the complex, ambiguous or paradoxical (Getzels and Jackson, 1962; Torrance, 1976).

The relationship between I.Q. and functionalist psychological and social values had been made decades earlier by Terman himself, whose standardized Stanford-Binet test accounted for much of the popular wide appeal and application of I.Q.-tests in American education. Arguing generally against past conceptions of the frail and emotionally unstable caricature of the creative genius, and specifically a renewed version of this caricature proposed by Lange-Eichbaum (1932), Terman and Oden (1947) concluded that their follow-up of high I.Q.-subjects had shown them to be biologically superior and to be characterized by "all around social adjustment". In a word, Terman's I.Q.-tested geniuses were models of Darwinian survival. Of course this was the correlary of psychology's model of superior psychological health, notably with its stress on adjustment to social reality.

Now contrasted to these values implicit to I.Q. and explicit to psychology generally, the new model for psychological health and success emerged in the name of creativity. Counted among Terman's geniuses "were no individuals who succeeded as Shakespeare, Goethe, Tolstoy, etc." an admission Terman explains away by the role luck plays in achievement of creative renown and by contemporary pressures towards specialization. The creativity literature suggests, quite differently, that lack of creative renown of Terman's high I.Q. geniuses is more associated with the values and forms which underly his testing instrument itself. The creative individual reaches into inner resources: these he has nurtured and to them he has continuous access. He prizes both self-realization and self-actualization, deals with the experienced world intrinsically rather than instrumentally and is prone to take psychological, creative and spiritual risks (Maslow, 1971).

Yet the creative individual measured for originally, or other creative characteristics and those who were already recognized for their creative contributions now serving as subjects, are not lacking in social or psychological reality orientation. Quite the contrary, so strong, characteristically, are the 'egos' of the creative that like the Master at martial arts, these persons could skillfully suspend their 'secondary process' functioning in the interest of exploring the possibility of greater unities of reality (Kris, 1953). This process of "regression in the service of ego", indeed the entire process connected with creative activity, not infrequently opened the individual in the creative process to experiences and realms of reality inaccessible to those centered mostly on the task of survival and adjustment: connections between the archaic and novel; psi and mystical connections between individuals; sense of personal and collective teleology beyond survival; and ability to see the sacred - at least significant - in the 'banal'. Frank Barron, among others, was to draw this relationship between the creative individual and the new vision of the psychologically healthy personality (Barron, 1963).

Enough has been said to indicate how much the creative research was connected with and an expression of a reaction from within and against the standards of the time in American psychology and society. Yet the point seems self-dedeating. For if we are dealing with a local revolution limited to a mid-twentieth century American context, then the implications for the broader question of methodology seem weak or non-existent. I suggest the contrary is the case. It is precisely the relativism of the event which gives it more universal meaning.

BROADER IMPLICATIONS FOR THE FIELD

It is the uniqueness of context and meanings which makes the creativity revolution both a matter of local and international relevance. If one can look at America as the California of the Western World, it can be viewed as an experimental laboratory of that world. These are terms that many American psychologists would likely feel at home with. However, psychologists wrapped in the notions that their approach is 'objective', i.e. not culture-bound, and their knowledge a progressive product of slow methodological accrual, would be less likely to acknowledge or appreciate the experiment, or test, in which they have been key participants. Even more certainly, the psychologists would likely not admit or realize what was at stake in this test: the very foundations of the method itself as applied in the human sciences.

But events cannot be denied. After the fifties, American psychology exploded into literally hundreds of splinters, represented by the proliferation of divisions and specialties in the American Psychological Association. Its gravitational center shifted to cognition, but now within seeing range of the more extraordinary possibilities raised during the creativity revolution and its even more radically suggestive offshoots. The research-academic, once unchallenged king, has been supplanted in popularity and influence by the professional and applied ends of psychology. In brief, American psychology has been altered radically since the 1950's, but has yet to take full stock of the directions and meanings suggested by these changes or to reformulate its subject matter and methods in terms of these.

The conservative temper which currently eclipses the United States, has led to a period for reformulation. The reformulation has begun at the quilted and political end. Lost territories are being reclaimed (at the academic-research level); newly gained money, power and influence consolidated (in the applied areas). The academics are moving towards more standardized curricula and more control over even the applied ends through means of accreditation. The professionals, big political winners of the past twenty years, are attempting to consolidate their gains through control of professional schools, licensure, political lobbying, control over state organizations and other guild serving instruments. The battle passes through the political arena. It has not yet passed through the ideological arena.

Yet, in my opinion, it is the ideological reformulation which is brewing beneath the surface and which strongly favors an opening to human science or qualitative research. The past twenty years have been characterized by a mass migration from the research end of psychology. The period has been characterized more by personal search than collective research. This was, in a sense, a return to the medieval, but also to the Eastern emphasis on personal and direct salvation rather than on the rationalist collective and indirect salvation represented by the model of science (Arons, 1976). Unencumbered by positivistic skepticism and methodological presuppositions, universes of human possibility have been opened during this period of search. The search has carried the searchers to and through vast territories rejected or deferred by scientific psychology but now, by its own routes, reopened ironically in certain areas of quantum physics and neurology (Wilber, 1984). This search in its many forms has been largely centered around consciousness, that term most completely rejected by the behaviourists.

These forms have been psychological, spiritual and social as in expanded or altered states of consciousness and Black, Feminist, Gay or

Ecological consciousness. The paths of consciousness have not led only to, though perhaps through, a new 'individualism' in the form of narcissism but, rather, to two newly realized or newly appreciated planes of intrinsic human connectedness. The first is ecological, the second spiritual. I stress here the intrinsic connectedness. These planes of connectedness are there and call for discovering and preserving rather than to be formed actively in individual and collective self-interest.

With this new awareness, the post-Renaissance rationalistic necessity for mastery and control of self and environment is relativized. The other planes of human connectedness, such as the social, economic and political become less ends in themselves for survical and more instruments in the service of personal and collective fulfilment. People are less to be seen as instruments who sacrifice their awareness of intrinsic planes of connectedness in the interest of deferred rewards from science and society.

These reflective observations are not, I concede, measurable facts which describe current realities. But they are also not merely subjective fantasies in the sense that they now have natural, i.e., scientific factual (e.g., ecological) and experiential (e.g., spiritual) grounding. What is significant about the double sense of connectedness, ecological and spiritual, is that they are now directly and popularly experienced as realities. Intuitively, they have been grasped and by their intrinsic natures, provide, ontologically, an existential ground for humanness. Epistemologically, they make more palatable the Kantian based intuitive mode of knowing rather than the skeptical Humian based philosophies. The need to find external sources of knowledge and causality and even the need for 'motivation', in that extrinsic sense which fueled the past models of the human in the social sciences, is now situated rather than absolute. Seen in this way, epistemology now has regained intrinsic sources, opened and directed by awareness from that of which it is aware. In this same view, axiology is now intrinsically grounded, raising serious questions about the long range prospects of success for a 'value-free' science. Explanation, which implies an inherent pre-rational dumbness to that area which 'connects' a cause and an effect, is supplemented by understanding which speaks to an awareness of the necessity of reflectively thematized connections.

Such a climate, which is largely the legacy of the informal exploration of experience and consciousness of the past two decades, bodes well for human science or qualitative research. There is now a research void to be filled. It is likely that those who have been influenced by the climate of that period, whatever the disciplinary choice, will be more amenable to, even insistent on, a reformulation taking into account dimensions and domains of human experiences no longer hidden by suppression or dogmatic philosophical assumptions of the past. Indeed, the holistic values of these past two decades portend a breaking down of the walls separating past disciplines which were predicated on elementism and certain alineating assumptions which are now relativized. There is evidence at symposia on qualitive research and also within academic settings, of the preference of many young faculty and students for more integrated or multidimensional approaches to the human sciences.

CONVERGENCE OF CREATIVITY LITERATURE AND PHILOSOPHY OF METHOD

The above speculations are based not solely on conjecture from current observation of trends. They have a base in necessity, the necessity revealed within and about the human subject, starting with the creativity revolution, which require new epistemological, ontological and axiological assumptions to ground research into the human. The creativity revolution reveals a different human potential from that assumed by current research philosophies. For example, originality, by definition, is not predictable. Creative science is powered by this apparent potential for unpredictability but its methodological assumptions ignore it. In fact, developing philosophies of method which emphasize understanding and recognition more than explanation and utility, seem more attuned to the human potential revealed by the creativity literature than the tenets of natural science. Let us consider examples of this attunement, or at least the apparent convergence between new methods and creative potential.

The phenomenologist-hermeneutican, Ricoeur (1970), is one of several who have formally observed the relationship between the psychoanalytic 'topographical domain' of the preconscious central to creativity, and meanings of consciousness reached through the process of phenomenological reduction. In creativity, Kris's "regression in the service of ego", though not identical, has some correspondence in terms of process to Husserl's phenomenological reduction, centered on the term 'epoché' which intentionally 'frees' or gives access to preconscious material. This particular form of suspension of judgment, this bracketing, has its approximate correlary in the creative process in terms of putting 'aside' one frame of reference, letting it 'gestate' while dealing with others - all awaiting a 'deeper' sense of meaning or unity - a new essential relationship. Suspension of judgement is hardly a concept alien to the methods in the natural sciences. But where and how it is founded 'topographically' relative to creativity or phenomenology is an issue of theoretical and practical importance.

The creative process follows, again, along the lines of phenomenology in terms of the relationship of the subject-object, in acknowledging the inherent kinship of the 'two'. Nonetheless, this explicit admission allows for differentiation and for appreciation of uniqueness, a basis for unpredictability of the subject-object. This recognition of difference within continuity and inexhaustibility places much of the field of understanding in the domain of immediate diversity and conflicts of lived world meanings. These lived conflicts appear in the creative process as a tolerance for ambiguity and complexity and a resistence to reductionism from consciousness or convenient but distorting tendencies towards the normative.

This same multi-significant and contradictory world has focus both in phenomenology and, particularly, in hermeneutics where the passage from meaning to meaning both differentiates and reveals essential relationships not grasped in the state of "première naivité". The creative potential to subtly attune to isolated but significant indications of essential meaning - e.g., Freud's example of the unstable position of the tablets in Michelangelo's sculpture, Moses - suggests correspondence to the significant experienced-revealed essence relationship recognized in phenomenology.

Little need be said about the new appreciation in many fields, including philosophy and hermeneutical psychology, for the creative value of the symbol. This newly rediscovered appreciation for symbolism coincides with the characterization of creative thinking as 'metaphorical'. For all the justified objections to language, symbol and, particularly metaphore, as subjective obstacles to scientific knowledge, much creative thinking even at the scientific level proves to be metaphorical. This implies that one does not pass to the complexity of creative human thinking, experience, meaning and action without passing through the thickets of language and symbolic thought, and "language is the source of all misunderstanding", wrote Saint-Exupery (1943).

Specific suggested correlaries can be added to and even multiplied. But there is a much broader level at which creativity research and human or qualitative research join. They both push subjectivity to its limits, and although the former path is not made explicit, the latter's is. For both, subjectivity is a form of objectivity in the sense that the object is the guide and the relationship called for is one characterized in the creativity literature as 'detached-engagement'. One could speculate that this relationship to the world experienced has its own correlaries in the philosophies of religion, East and West, a 'Taoist' perception or a Biblical view of the "in but not of the world". Implied is a respect for uniqueness as well as the continuity and extension presented within creative 'space' or 'distancing'.

The 'intelligence' required of both human science research and creativity is recognized as broader and different from that measured by utilitarian tests, particularly standardized tests. Such an expanded sense of 'intelligence' or 'esprit' is not apart from empathy, sensitivity, self-awareness, emotional validity, significance or values and the sense of personal and human destiny. Human destiny is different from but evidently implicated in progress of the scientific variety. The studies on creativity have undermined much of, at least, the common meaning of progress associated with Positivistic assumptions (these implicit as well to I.Q. testing). Maslow (1962) realized this but stopped short of smashing the idol of science as the only form of inquiry which could 'progress'. He asked that science take into account, as heuristics, the contributions from the pre-sciences, i.e., art, poetry, philosophy, theology. However, he fell into a trap of contruing all progress in a single, more linear, manner like that characterized by technology.

Boirel (1961) points out that the pre-sciences also progress but in a qualitatively different way. The relationship in technology between a TX-1 model and an advanced TX-2 model is one of defined improvement. The relationship between Impressionism and Cave Art, on the other hand, is one of expanded views and meanings of reality. In art, unlike technology, the recent progression does not render the earlier product obsolete. Science, according to Boirel, has dimensions and qualities of both technology   and the consciousness expanding presciences. The creativity literature is rather explicit in establishing the essential relationship in the interest of creative contributions to 'progress' as, to use Ricoeur's (1970) terms, one of Arché-Telos. It offers the resources for and the possibility of revitalization of the sedimented symbols and meanings of the past, historically and personally, in the interest of the creative work or creative living. The creativity literature, best illustrated by the work of Barron (1963), insists on the creative individual's access to continuity between early and recent experience, all of which serves as resources in the creative effort. This continuity with 'past' or 'the subjective' - living with all the meanings and complexity - makes for a better understanding of the non-pathological personal and social instability often observed in such creative individuals.

There is a type of validation inherent to the creative process - a discrimination of the true and real - which differs from but both precedes and antedates the validation process valued in science using a positivistic method. It is the validation of the poet, or philosopher, and lies in a sense of necessity, harmony and elegance. It is aesthetic as well as logical and heuristic: aesthetic in the sense that the ideas are congruent; logical in the sense of coherance, or recognition of that which is intellectually discordant, incompatible; and heuristic in the sense of suggesting new, potentially harmonious paths. The creative process has a 'built-in' dimension of criticality which is recognized in the fresh yet plausible quality of the creative product, which in science then makes it a candidate for positivistic validation, e.g., as an hypothesis, theory, model, etc. Of this creative pre-science of the scientific process itself Einstein (1934) wrote:

"Science as something existing and complete is the most objective thing known to Man. But science as an end to be pursued, science in the making, is as subjective and psychologically conditioned as any other branch of human endeavor" (p. 112).

But is there not also a 'creative post-science' which seeks validation of scientific results in the various value and meaning contexts which give significance to the scientific project itself? For, even after the scientific validation process has been applied, its results also must meet the intuitive criteria for coherent reconnection with other validated products of the method. In this relationship of creative validation which is pre- and post-scientific, we find a correlate to phenomenology. The phenomenological process - not totally dissimilar to the creative one - operates along lines of inherent validation: necessity, intuitive coherence, and heuristically suggestive of the next paths to follow. Like the creative process, but as a well thought-out method which has the essential quality of reversibility, phenomenology is both a pre- and post-scientifically validating enterprise.

One of the reasons offered by Guilford to explain the psychology's retarded interest in creativity was the lack of adequate criteria. Although the products are enormously different in quality, both a child's doodle and a Rembrandt painting can legitimately qualify as 'creative' products. Later, Maslow was to extend the word creative to a 'productless' but recognizable style of personal growth which he discerned among his 'self-actualizing' subjects. Harmon and Rheingold (1984) see in the same creative process two distinct possible paths, one towards tangible art (science, etc.) and the other towards mysticism. Little wonder that creativity is so difficult to define.

Yet its recognized presence everywhere, even at the heart of a science which denied it in its subjects, reveals the fuller socio-historical significance of a rediscovered creativity. It is a reminder of the inexhaustibility of the human subject when researched by the human subject. Yet the very limits which forecast an ultimate inexhaustibility, provide the steps of potential coherence from which the phenomenologist moves systematically towards the inexhaustible. Each step provides simultaneously coherence which reveals its limits and new potentially meaningful directions. For as creativity has two sides, one of product and one of personal growth, so also does phenomenology which reciprocally in process reveals the subject studied and the subject inquiring. Neither is the same afterwards.

Nowhere in sight is the 'definite' study which rests as the ideal for the naive-arrogant scientific psychology which had, until its household encounter with creativity, monopolized the twentieth century.

It appears to me that what is required if we are to achieve a larger view of science which incorporates different forms of inquiry and still avoids a 'tolerant' but sterile eclecticism, is a hermeneutic seeking the integrity of different methodological 'missions' - their uniqueness - as well as an understanding of the greater integrity which links their discontinuities. Such a hermeneutic could well begin with an inquiry into the questions of distancing, validation and progress in natural science, human science, personal self-understanding and creativity.

SUMMARY

The present chapter thematizes methodological critiques in psychology in a broader mythological and historical context, proposing that a mid-century surge of interest into creativity has historical implications conducive to new qualitative methods. The historical uniqueness of American psychology is seen as a dialectical "prise de conscience" potentially recentering the broader field.

REFERENCES

Arons, M. (1965). *Le problème de la creativité: questions méthodologiques.* These, Bibliothèque de la Sorbonne, Paris.

Arons, M. (1976). Presidential address. *Newsletter,* Division of Humanistic Psychology, 4 (1), 1-2.

Arons, M. (1985). A quarter century of humanistic psychologies. *The humanistic psychologist,* 13, (2), 55-60.

Asch, S.E. (1952). *Social Psychology.* New York: Prentice-Hall.

Barron, F. (1963). *Creativity and psychological health.* Toronto: Van Nostrand.

Barron, F., & Young, H.B. (1970). Rome and Boston: a tale of two cities. *Journal of cross-cultural psychology,* 1, (2), 91-114.

Boirel, R. (1961). *L'Invention.* Paris: Presses Universitaires de France.

Bronowski, J. (1958). The creative process. *Scientific American,* 199, 59-65.

Burtt, E.A. (1952). *The metaphysical foundations of modern science.* New York: Doubleday.

Einstein, A. (1934). *Essays in science.* New York: The Philosophical Library.

Freud, S. (1968). Moses and monotheism. In J. Strachey (Ed.),*The standard edition of the psychological works of Sigmund Freud.* Vol. 23, 3-140. London: Hogarth Press.

Getzels, J.W., & Jackson, P.W. (1962). *Creativity and intelligence; explorations with gifted students.* London: Wiley.

Giorgi, A. (1970). *Psychology as a human science.* New York: Harper & Row.

Goodman, P. (1960). *Growing up absurd.* New York: Random House.

Guilford, J.P. (1952). Creativity. *The American Psychologist,* 5, 444-454.

Harmon, W., & Rheingold, H. (1984). *Higher creativity: liberating the unconscious for breakthrough insights.* Los Angeles: J. Tarcher Inc.

Hudson, L. (1966). The question of creativity. In P.E. Vernon (Ed.), *Creativity.* Middlesex, England: Penguin Books.

Krippner, S., & Arons, M. (1973). Creativity: Person, product or process? *Gifted Child Quarterly,* 116-129.

Kris, E. (1953). Psychoanalysis and the study of the creative imagination. *Bulletin of the New York Academy of Medicine,* 29, 334-351.

Kubie, L.S. (1958). *Neurotic distortion of the creative process.* Lawrence: University of Kansas Press.

Lange-Eichbaum, W. (1932). *The problem of genius.* (Trans. by E. Paul & C. Paul). New York: MacMillan.

Laski, M. (1962). *Ecstasy: a study of some secular and religious experiences.* Bloomington: Indiana University Press.

Leary: T. (1983). *Flashbacks.* Los Angeles: Houghton Mifflin.

MacKinnon, D. (1962). Personality correlates of creativity: a study of American architects. In P.E. Vernon (Ed.), *Creativity.* Middlesex, England: Penguin Books.

Maslow, A.H. (1962). *Toward a psychology of being.* New York: Van Nostrand.

Maslow, A.H. (1971). *The farther reaches of human nature.* New York: Viking Press.

Merleau-Ponty, M. (1964). Maurice Merleau-Ponty at the Sorbonne. *Bulletin de Psychologie,* 236, 18.

Ricoeur, P. (1970). *Freud and philosophy.* (Trans. by D. Savage). New Haven: Yale University Press.

Saint-Exupery, A. (1943). *Le petit prince.* New York: Harcourt, Brace & World.

Terman, L.M., & Oden, M.H. (1947). The gifted child grows up. In L.M. Terman (Ed.), *Genetic studies of genius.* Vol. 4. Palo Alto: Stanford University Press.

Torrance, E.P. (1962). *Guiding creative talent.* New York: Prentice-Hall.

Torrance, E.P. (1976). Creativity testing in education. *The Creative Child Quarterly,* 1 (3), 136-148.

Weber, M. (1958). *The Protestant ethic and the spirit of capitalism* (Trans. by T. Parsons). New York: Scribner.

Wilber, K. (Ed.) (1984). *Quantum questions.* Boulder: Shambala.

PART TWO

QUALITATIVE RESEARCH STUDIES

Chapter 6

AN EMPIRICAL PHENOMENOLOGICAL APPROACH TO DREAM RESEARCH

Diane L. Reed

The purpose of the present chapter is to introduce an alternative approach to dream research. Specifically, I intend to show that dreams can be studied in a phenomenological, yet still scientific way. My emphasis here will be on explaining the rationale and the need for an empirical phenomenological approach to the study of dreams, and on describing a particular method that was worked out through a dialogue with the phenomenon. The type of findings such an approach can lead to will be illustrated by two preliminary studies. Because of the space constraints of this chapter I will briefly review the results of the first study and show how those results led me to undertake the second project. The second study will be presented in greater detail.

I am interested in the study of dreaming largely because I am interested in better understanding that domain which traditional psychology refers to as the unconscious. Because of the opacity and involuntary character of dreams, they have given rise to countless theories and assumptions about an alien mind located within the dreamer. For a variety of reasons, the unconscious has become a dubious concept within the scope of psychology as a science. Nevertheless, various phenomena, such as the dream, continue to be indisputably present. Hence, I am interested in looking anew at this domain. And, according to many in traditional psychology (e.g. Freudians, Jungians, and numerous others), the dream is a, if not the, primary access to this realm.

Speaking more specifically, the ongoing and still to be met aim of my research is to arrive at a structural description of the essential features that characterize dreaming as such and allow us, therefore, to speak of 'the dream' or 'the world of the dream'. A primary focus of that project will be to characterize the nature of the horizons within which the dream events cohere into a meaningful unity, and how waking consciousness can gain access to those horizons. Such findings will have direct implications for our understanding of the so-called unconscious. The two preliminary studies which are presented in this paper provide a significant step towards attaining the aim mentioned above. They each involved a different perspective on the phenomenon, with however, the same ultimate goal in mind.

In both studies I used the phenomenological psychological research method described by Giorgi (1970, 1985). Clearly, my research interest does not meaningfully lend itself to the natural scientific research methods used by most psychological researchers (i.e. experimentation and quantification). It calls for a qualitative, descriptive approach. The guidelines set forth by Giorgi for phenomenological research in psychology provide a means of dealing empirically with qualitative research interests such as those that I have posed. The method he describes allows one to approach psychological subject matter in a phenomenological and yet scientific manner.

The approach is phenomenological in that it follows the phenomenological invitation to 'return to the things themselves' by setting aside conceptual and theoretical assumptions and proceeding descriptively to see what can be learned from the direct study of the experience of the phenomenon being investigated. Furthermore, the researcher's aim is to systematically determine and explicate the essence, or *eidos*, of the experience being described, that is, the necessary and sufficient constituents of the phenomenon which make it what it is and without which it would no longer be that phenomenon. This is what is sometimes referred to as the structure(s) of the experience. To describe a structure is not simply to describe the various elements which can be found in an experience. Nor is it to extract certain features that correlate positively or add up facts in some pre-established way. Rather, to describe the structure is to describe how the elements of a phenomenon function constitutively, how they interrelate to form the unity of the experience. In Merleau-Ponty's words, the structure describes "...the sense of what is lived through by oneself or by another" (1964, p. 64). In addition, with this phenomenological research approach one departs from concrete lived experience so that the specific steps for arriving at the structure(s) are specified and worked out in dialogue with the phenomenon rather than beforehand.

The research approach described by Giorgi also uses the criteria of science. The vision of science he endorses is, however, broader than that of most natural scientific researchers. The latter employ, almost exclusively, the methods of experimentation and quantification. To be considered scientific according to Giorgi's approach, the following criteria must be met: It must be possible for the activity to be performed by many researchers; the findings should be intersubjectively valid; and there must be a definable method. Furthermore, the researcher must approach the phenomenon being investigated in a methodical, systematic, and rigorous way. The specific approach taken is guided by how the appearance of the phenomenon invites the researcher to be methodical, systematic, and rigorous. For further elaboration of this procedure, one may refer to two recent publications: *Phenomenology and Psychological Research* (1985), edited by Giorgi and *Exploring the Lived World: Readings in Phenomenological Psychology* (1984), edited by Aanstoos.

As stated previously, the goal of my research is to explore the salient experiential parameters that characterize one's immersion in the dream world and thereby arrive at a specific description of the essential features that characterize dreaming. The existential psychiatrist, Medard Boss, provides significant beginnings toward such a project in his celebrated book *The analysis of dreams* (1958). In my opinion, he offers many valuable, original, and interesting insights into the phenomenology of dreaming, but the task is not yet complete. A possible limitation of his work is that he did not have available to him the specific phenomenological research method that I employ. With this systematic method I hope to pursue the phenomenology of dreams even further.

The results of my first study showed that the sequence of dream events emerges as a unity. The dream is not just a hodge podge of disconnected moments. It is not a sheer multiplicity of unrelated events. Rather, the dream events progress and cohere in a meaningful way for the dreamer, at least as long as he is dreaming. For instance, there is nothing astonishing to the dreamer that he can be in one location at one moment and then suddenly, with absolutely no effort and no sense of having actively moved, he can be in a different location the next. The two scenes have some connection, at least in so far as it does not surprise the dreamer that one situation followed the other and they can later be reported in a unified story.

These adumbrations of the total dream, in so far as the dreamer is not surprised by them, would fit together if, like waking experiences of the lifeworld, they were part of one spatial-temporal-social horizon. But they are not. The research revealed that one cannot point to how these events fit together in a spatial, temporal, or social way. During the dream there is an effacement of the natural lifeworld horizons. They are not operative in the same way that they are in waking life and they are not what holds the dream together in a meaningful unity. Dream settings and events appear to operate according to their own internal logic. Differences occur in dreams that are beyond the range of what could be expected in ordinary waking life. For instance, self, others, and objects can assume radically different meanings, properties, and capacities which would be impossible or unthinkable for them to assume in a waking context. During ordinary waking experience, settings and situations do not undergo the same abrupt, effortless changes. Every situation assumes its context within the world such that the connections between situations or settings are typically, specifiable, rememberable, and meaningful. Yet, as has already been pointed out, the dream events are not radically incoherent. They do fit together.

Thus, the questions that arose for me were: What does determine the coherency of the dream? What could be the principle of unity that allows the various aspects of the dream to come together so that it is experienced as a coherent, meaningful whole? What are the horizons which hold together the dream, and by what processes can waking consciousness gain access to them?

APPROACHES TO DREAMS WITHIN THE CONTEXT OF TRADITIONAL PSYCHOLOGY

Turning to the traditional psychological literature, one can find numerous theories and studies pertaining to these questions, and each one has its own particular emphasis or variation. (The position of Freud's psychoanalytic theory, for instance, would be that the horizonal significance of a dream lies in unconscious instinctual wishes and that one can gain access to them through the method of free association. Carl Jung, on the other hand, would point to the archetypal content of the collective unconscious). In my opinion, although these theories and studies are interesting and valuable in many respects, they ultimately fail to provide an adequate answer to the particular questions I am raising. A reflective review of the literature reveals why.

Although the diversity of viewpoints and the immensely varied treatment that has been accorded to dreams is staggering, this vast literature can basically be divided into two broad categories. One category includes approaches to dreams that were developed or carried out within a therapeutic context where dream analysis was done with the specific goal of helping a patient live his or her life more effectively. The other incorporates approaches and theories that were derived independent of therapeutic aims. The first category typically includes Sigmund Freud's psychoanalytic theory of dreams, the existential-phenomenological approaches of Ludwig Binswanger and Medard Boss, Fritz Perls' Gestalt method, and countless others. Although all of the approaches that can be subsumed in this category can be assessed individually in terms of their values and limitations, they can also be looked at collectively in so far as they all use dreams, within the framework of therapeutic praxis, to understand waking life. Patricia Berry, in an article entitled "An Approach to the Dream" (*Spring*, 1974), provides an excellent critique of all forms of dream analysis done within such a context. Although her questions and critiques are directed specifically at the Jungian approach to dream interpretation, they can, in my opinion, be equally applied to all forms of dream interpretation done from within a therapeutic context. The gist of her argument is that we cannot arrive at a comprehensive understanding of dreams as long as we are simply using them to achieve our therapeutic aims. Such a practice may tell us more about the client and his waking situation (which of course is very important if we are doing therapy with him), but it does not clarify our understanding of dreaming per se.

Furthermore, many therapists contend that a dream is truly understood when the interpretation 'clicks' for the person. However, as Berry points out, this pragmatic approach opens itself to countless difficulties. In her words:

> ...it conceals an essential difficulty having to do with what might be called theoretical sensitivity... It opens the way to an aspect of psychotherapy little different from charlatanism, syntonic transference neurosis, hysterical suggestion, doctrinal compliance, religious conversion and political brainwashing. For these too 'click' and in these too the subject feels himself changed for the better on the basis of insights revealed. (1974), p. 60).

Berry goes on to argue that:

> Without a sensitivity among theories, it no longer matters what theory we have; one idea is as good as another providing it 'works'--and everything works equally. If there are better and worse theories about dream interpretation, they cannot be based on what 'clicks'--for when we lose sensitivity here, we lose it in practice as well. (1974, p. 60).

Berry thus makes a plea to researchers to distinguish practical therapeutic ability from a theory of dreams and points to the need for a systematic study of what does positively unfold a dream.

Nevertheless, the problems are not eradicated by simply studying the dream world and its unfolding outside of a therapeutic context and independent of therapeutic goals. The second of the two general categories of dream literature encompasses those theories and studies that were derived and carried out independent of therapy. This category includes, for instance, experimental studies of physiological aspects of dreaming, content analysis of which Hall and Van de Castle (1966) are representative, and James Hillman's approach of archetypal psychology. These theories and studies likewise do not provide an answer to the question of the essential features of the dream and its horizons. Many do not provide an adequate answer because they bias their results by either imposing on to the dream and its unfolding certain biasing presuppositions and/or theoretical frameworks or by guiding the interpretative process toward some preconceived desired end (e.g. Hillman). Other studies only focus on the physiological correlates of sleep and dreams which do not speak to what is experienced by the dreamer or to the meaning of that experience. Others emphasize normative data, i.e. group comparisons, rather than in-depth exploration of a single dream (e.g. content analysis).

In an effort to avoid the aforementioned pitfalls, and throw light on the perplexing issue of the dream's horizons and how one can gain access to them, I undertook a second empirical phenomenological investigation, to be described here. As a possible point of access to the horizons which hold the various aspects of the dream together so that it is experienced as a coherent, meaningful whole, I studied the moves that subjects spontaneously make that both do and do not lead to the successful unfolding of their dream images. It yielded some intriguing, although still preliminary results.

METHOD

SUBJECTS

There were two subjects, both adult males. One of the subjects was a graduate student in philosophy and the other was a special education teacher.

PROCEDURE

First the subjects described a dream they had in the form of written protocols. The instructions that were given to each subject were: "Describe a dream that you had in enough detail so that someone reading or hearing the report would know just what the experience was like for you and would know everything that happened in the dream". I then typed verbatim the descriptions from each of the subjects.

Next, I interviewed the subjects with a procedure I called "walking through the dream". This involved reading the dream back to the subject in stages and allowing him to associate to it in whatever way he chose. The following instructions were given for this procedure:

> We're going to walk through the dream together just the way you wrote it. I'll read a short bit of it, then stop, and I would like for you to describe for me anything that comes to your mind about the scene, incident, or image I just read. You may provide further details about it, describe any thoughts or feelings you have, relate any puns or metaphors that come to your mind; in short, just let yourself go and associate to it in whatever way you choose until you feel ready to stop. We'll then move on to the next scene.

The subjects' responses to this procedure were also typed verbatim. Each subject made moves that both did and did not lead to successful unfolding of the dream images. However, as a result of the process of 'walking through the dream', one subject experienced a radical regestalting of the meaning of the dream for him. He connected previously enigmatic and seemingly unconnected scenes, unfolded the dream's horizonal significance, and was emotionally moved by the experience. The other subject experienced no such essential unfolding of his dream's horizons and coherence, although new qualities, characteristics, and meanings in several discrete images did emerge during the interview.

DATA ANALYSIS

The method for data analysis was the previously discussed phenomenological psychological method described by Giorgi (1970, 1985). I modified the basic procedure he describes in response to the demands of the data and my particular research interest at this point (i.e. understanding the coherence and horizonal significance of the dream). The data (the dream and the interview) were broken down into natural meaning units (i.e. spontaneously perceived discriminations within the subject's descriptions which I, as researcher, delineated while assuming a phenomenological-psychological attitude). The meaning units of the interview were incorporated into corresponding meaning units of the dream description so the two could be analysed concordantly. Each meaning unit was then looked at in terms of two poles.

(1) The noetic pole which describes the subject's perspective and the moves he makes in regard to the dream images (e.g. S. views the dream from within the context of waking life external to the dream itself, and provides an interpretation of what in his waking life the dream image points to or illustrates).

(2) The noematic pole which describes the dream images and any unfolding that takes place. It was possible to discriminate when an image was actually unfolded by seeing where in the data some new quality, characteristic, or meaning emerged in the image during the interview that was not previously present for the subject. In other words, I was able to see if the image itself took on a new meaning as opposed to the image in an unchanged state simply being brought into relation with another image or with some event in waking life. For example, if a subject described a waking experience or a waking correlate of a dream image and did not relate these experiences back to the dream, then one only got descriptions of waking objects and events and hence, no new meaning or quality of the image itself emerged.

From these meaning units, a structural description was arrived at for both the unsuccessful moves (i.e. moves that did not lead to the unfolding of the dream images) and the successful moves (i.e. moves that did lead to an unfolding). These structures were expressed in as high a level of generality as possible, given the limited amount of data.

RESULTS

UNSUCCESSFUL MOVES

The data revealed that there was no unfolding of the dream images when the subject considered the dream from an external perspective - from outside the context of the actual experiences he lived through while dreaming. This occurred in essentially two ways: (1) An external perspective was maintained in so far as the subject described experiences outside of the dream itself and did *not* return back to the dream. For example, a common move the subjects made was to describe the literal waking referents of the dream images rather than the experiences they had while dreaming. One subject, for instance, dreamed of being in a shopping centre parking lot. He states:

> The dream begins in my old home town where I grew up. The time is present-day and the place is a shopping centre parking lot. A great number of tables have been set up, along with a platform stage, and a large, formal banquet is beginning to start.

Rather than further elucidating how he experienced this setting during the dream, the subject described the literal parking lot of his waking life. His associations to this section of the dream were:

> I used to hang out at the parking lot every once in a while. It was on the main drag in my old home town and hanging out there was one of the big things we used to do. Part of it belonged to a shopping centre and part of it belonged to a gas station repair shop.

Thus, the subject told me something about the parking lot in his waking life (which was quite different from the way it appeared in his dream), but he did not return back to the dream. It is left unclear how the two are related or what meaning the one has for the other. (2) Second, an external perspective was maintained in so far as the subject sought an explanatory basis for the dream from something outside of the actual dream experience. For instance, there was no unfolding of one subject's dream in so far as he only considered it as pointing, in a uni-directional manner, to some waking life experience. This waking experience was treated as an explanation or as a reason for why he dreamed what he did. These explanations and interpretations remained external to the dream in so far as the dream itself is not dealt with, but only the dream's possible causal connection to waking life. This move frequently involved guessing or supposing with no move back to the actual dream experiences.

One subject, for instance, dreamed of being chased by a crowd of people who were throwing small tennis-ball-like objects at him that exploded on impact. In an attempt to explain why he dreamed that, he immediately looked for instances in his waking life where he actually had been chased or had felt chased in a metaphorical sense. The subject then thought that perhaps he felt chased at his job because of all the paperwork he had to do. He described the pressure he felt from his supervisors during his waking life, but it was evident that he was merely guessing that the two might be related. Hence, the dream image of being chased remained the same at the end of the dream as it was in the beginning and there was no unfolding of meaning. The subject said:

> ...There haven't been many times in my life that I've been chased. Recently, if there's anything that I might have felt people were chasing me about it's the fact that there's no much paperwork at the job that I have that I always felt that I was being somewhat pressured or chased by my supervisors to get this in, get that in. But that's really not the case anymore.

Another characteristically explanatory move was the use of a psychological concept to account for the dream experience. This is illustrated by one subject who attempted to explain his lack of fear in the face of a threatening crowd in terms of a defense mechanism. He states:

Again, I wonder if that's not just a defense mechanism that I set up in the dream because it seems to happen a lot in the dream that I just know nothing's going to happen or that I'm going to be okay in the end.

Thus, the data shows that there was no unfolding of the dream images in so far as the subject considered the dream externally, either by describing experiences outside of the dream without returning back to it, or by seeking an explanatory basis for the dream from something outside of the actual dream experiences.

SUCCESSFUL MOVES

The data showed that unsuccessful unfolding of a dream's coherence and horizonal significance involved three essential constituents: (1) the subject considered the dream images and experiences within the context of the dream itself and maintained an affective attunement to what he experienced while dreaming, (2) qualities emerged from certain dream images which functioned metaphorically as images (second level images), and (3) the subject considered these second level images in relation to one another.

When I say that the images were considered from within the context of the dream, I mean that the images as they were experienced while dreaming were explored in their own right, i.e. the subject did not attempt to explain or account for them by going outside the dream. This move was manifested in the Protocols in several ways:

(1) The subject described and amplified the dreaming experience and did not immediately look for what it might be pointing to in his waking life. He plumbed deeper and deeper into the experience itself rather than going outside it.

(2) One subject imaginatively re-entered into the landscape of the dream via the concrete medium of a waking referent and from that perspective further described the sense of the dream image. In describing an abstract painting that appeared in the dream, he turned to a real abstract painting in the room in which the interview was being conducted. He then used the immediacy and concrete presence of that painting to help evoke the lived-through experience of the dream.

(3) When images from waking life were brought in, they were not used as a cause or as an explanation for the dream, but rather as an allusion to help elaborate the sense of the dream itself. Thus, the subject always returned back to the dream. For instance, in discussing the frightening chaos and confusion of a classroom setting in one dream, the subject alluded to biblical images and images from biblical movies of the

'Israelites' wild abandon at the foot of Mount Sinai. This was a way of further elaborating the sense of evil and lack of control in that scene.

(4) Through a repeated restatement of the theme of the original dream report, one subject remained connected to the dream experience and to what was important about it. He repeatedly restated the theme 'no one listened' and this kept him close to the dream experience:

> Yea, *no one listened*. I was alone... that's just the image that strikes up when I think of it - *no one listened*. They were just all out there going crazy and I was trying to get some semblance of reason established and trying to act and do things. But *no one listened*, which is very helpless and very lonely, very fatal. It seemed fated that I was to fail. *No one listened...*

(5) Images of the dream were interrelated with each other. Consequently, an enlightening of one image was seen to hold implications for others. For example, one subject related the end of the dream to the beginning and viewed the entire dream as a unity from the end backwards. In doing this, the dream took on a new significance for him. The other subject recontextualized the specific image of seeing his father and sister in the dream in terms of the overall dream setting, i.e. being in his old home with his wife. In doing this, a new aspect of the image emerged - the subject realized that his sister and father were unhappy and were there only out of obligation.

The second constituent of the process of unfolding dream images is that a second level image emerged from the primary dream image which had a metaphorical power of its own. For example, one subject reported that during his dream he experienced himself as being in a classroom at college, then suddenly, with no sense of having moved from one place to another, he found himself in the house where he grew up. In the process of plumbing deeper and deeper into the dream experience, he unfolded the dream settings in terms of their being tombs. The image of the tomb, as a second level image, was unfolded from the primary images of the classroom and home in the following way: First, the subject further described the classroom as he experienced it while dreaming and got increasingly in touch with the affect or mood of the scene. He said, for instance, that it was underground, that there were no windows in the room, that it felt dank, stuffy, etc. He then juxtaposed these qualities and it suddenly struck him that the room was like a tomb. As he continued through the dream, he described the house as it was present for him. Again, similar tomb-like qualities emerged. This is the subject's description evoked by his associations:

> ...Somehow I want to say that the home is just another tomb. The only thing that leads me to think that, the only thing that strikes me, when that thought occurs to me is that there weren't any windows in the house either... *it had the same feel like the other building...* They were very stuffy places and my house had the kind of darkness and dankness of a tomb... It's funny! ... the house! The house seems more like a tomb as I try to think back through the dream again, than the classroom. In real life I can't think of any connection between the two

settings, but it's like it got worse in the dream. It got danker and stuffier, the environment or situation.

Hence, it became evident that this tomb-like quality was a constituent of both of the dream settings (classroom and home). It was this image that tied together the seemingly unconnected scenes. Thus, the tomb image was established as the horizonal significance of the settings of the dream. Both of the settings were seen as a representative or embodiment of this second level image of the tomb which could be described as embedded within the primary image as its depth or horizonal significance.

In another instance during the same interview, the subject unfolded an image of abstract paintings in terms of their being a 'cutting or wounding of the real'. The image of 'wounding the real', as a second level image, was unfolded from the primary image of the abstractions in the following way: In describing the dream experience, the subject alluded to the waking referent of abstractions. Through his description of their artistic character there emerged a quality (i.e. the paintings' imaginative freedom in relation to the real which he described as a wounding or cutting of reality) that has a metaphorical power of its own. This image was then seen as the horizonal significance of the image of the abstractions.

Finally, these second level images (which are themselves metaphors) were brought into relation with one another and there was a radical regestalting of the meaning of the dream for the subject. The image of wounding the real and the image of the tomb were brought into relation with one another in such a way that the subject saw that the specific reality which was being wounded was that of the tomb. Once he realized that the reality which was being wounded was tomb-like, it became evident to him that what was acting against this reality and wounding it was positive and life-like. Previously, the subject viewed the dream as simply a portrayal of him running away from evil and chaos. Suddenly a new meaning unfolded such that he came to experience the dream as reflecting the deadness of his life, the fact that he had not yet truly lived. The chaos he was running from was actually positive (although threatening) because it represented the possibilities of being something totally different, something with life. It meant a breaking away from the dull, highly rational way in which he was living and experiencing his life. The subject makes this evident in the following passages:

".... the classroom itself and the world was a tomb. Going nowhere. But the evil paintings... Maybe the whole point of the dream was that the evil was my salvation.... that classroom where the evil was, that was life.... It's like those painting were luring me beyond what was.... The abstract paintings were the threatening chaos that was breaking through my tomb-like life.... I've only thought about the dream up till now as like a story where I'm running away from all this evil in my life, which makes sense, but then I find out I'm dead... and all the settings I've been in are tomb-like. My life is dead. Which makes me think that the abstract paintings that I was so terrified of and that I never thought of as seductive til right now, were the forces of life, if you want to think of it that way. The possibilities of being something utterly different, maybe chaotic, but.... something with life...."

CONCLUSION

The research indicates that it is at the level of interplay between the subject's affective attunement to the dream experience and the secondary images that emerge, that the horizons which hold the dream together can be revealed such that the dream can be seen to cohere in a meaningful way.

Consequently, the depth of the dream is not to be found simply at the level of an image as an image of a literal thing (e.g. the dream classroom as an image of a literal classroom). This precludes the consideration of the dream as simply pointing in a uni-directional manner to some literal experience outside the dream and taking that experience as an explanatory ground or cause of the dream. These findings also throw into question all attempts to truly understand the dream by applying a predefined theoretical framework onto it (e.g. Freud's theory of symbols, Jung's archetypes, etc.) and by interpreting it from a specifically therapeutic context (i.e. viewing the dream only in terms of what it is pointing to in waking life).

Nevertheless, as the data clearly shows, when the dream itself is taken as an end and its horizons are unfolded, there is still an enhanced understanding of waking life. Thus, there is obviously a relationship between the horizons of the subject's waking world and those of the dream. But, as the research indicates, it is a mistake to equate the one with the other. The subject who came to an insight into his lifeworld did so only as a consequence of exploring the dream on its own terms. Thus, it seems that whatever is said in the dream concerning the subject's waking life can only be comprehended by entering into the dream's own specific language. And, when seen through the reflective gaze of waking consciousness, this language is revealed to be radically metaphorical and radically tied in to the affective significances of the dreamer's life.

These preliminary results only scratch the surface of these difficult issues and I am still far from answering the questions which originally motivated this project. Nevertheless, I hope that I was able to give, at least an initial sense, of how a phenomenological psychological research method can be used to investigate questions that do not meaningfully lend themselves to experimentation and quantification. I also hope that I was able to show that it is possible to reach the unconscious world of dreams through this depth phenomenological approach. Approaching a phenomenon such as dreams in this manner may well set one on a course toward conclusions quite different from those who begin less openly. An empirical phenomenological approach may also help us to better understand the partial truths, limitations, and distortions of many abstract theoretical constructs. In my opinion, more research, with an enlarged data base, is called for to arrive at a greater understanding of the dream and the realm of the so-called unconscious.

REFERENCES

Aanstoos, C. (Ed.) (1984). *Exploring the lived world: readings in phenomenological psychology*. Atlanta, GA: Darby Printing Co.

Berry, P. (1974). An approach to the dream. *Spring*, 58-79. Zürich: Spring Publications.

Binswanger, L. (1978). *Being-in-the-world*. New York: Harper Torch Books.

Boss, M. (1958). *The analysis of dreams*. New York: Philosophical Library.

Fossage, J., & Loew, C. (1978). *Dream interpretation: a comparative study*. New York: SP Medical and Scientific Books.

Freud, S. (1953). *The interpretation of dreams*. New York: Basic Books.

Giorgi, A. (1970). *Psychology as a human science*. New York: Harper & Row.

Giorgi, A. (Ed.) (1985). *Phenomenology and psychological research*. Pittsburgh: Duquesne University Press.

Hall, C., & Van de Castle, R. (1966). *The content analysis of dreams*. New York: Appleton Century Crofts.

Merleau-Ponty, M. (1964). *Primacy of perception*. Evanston: Northwestern University Press.

Van de Castle, R. (1971). *The psychology of dreaming*. New Jersey: General Learning Press.

Chapter 7

DREAMING, REALITY AND ALLUSION:
AN EXISTENTIAL-PHENOMENOLOGICAL INQUIRY

P. Erik Craig

In the following I will explore two basic problems in dream psychology. The first is the problem of the reality of dreams. The second is how this dreaming reality may be related to the reality of waking, and to the individual's existence as a whole.

THE REALITY OF DREAMS

The reality of dreams may be taken here to mean the quality of being real or having an actual existence for a person while dreaming. It may also be understood to mean the historical legitimacy of dreaming, that is, that dreams may be considered legitimate episodes of a person's autobiography, trustworthy manifestations of truth and meaning as lived by the person.

In this chapter I will approach the problems of the reality of dreaming and its relation to waking phenomenologically, beginning with descriptions of that which appears with the life-world of dreaming itself and then returning to these manifestly dreamt things themselves as the final arbiters of meaning. My investigation will draw significantly from the works of Medard Boss (1958, 1963, 1977, 1979), the Swiss psychiatrist and psychoanalyst, who collaborated with the German philosopher, Martin Heidegger, in applying Heidegger's analysis of dasein to problems in psychology and psychotherapy and, in particular, to the analysis of dreams. The purpose of this chapter, therefore, is not only to take up the above problems but also to illustrate aspects of an existential-phenomenological approach to understanding dreams in human science and psychotherapy.[1]

THE BETRAYAL OF DREAMT REALITY

Dreaming has long been one of the most intriguing and mysterious modes of human existence. Yet it is this apparent mysteriousness, the exotic enigmatic nature of dreams, that ensnares us in a profound duplicity. On the one hand, we are drawn to the tantalizing secrets we imagine our dreams contain and, on the other hand, we are all too ready to disown and dismiss them as frothy illusions, as nonsense, unreal, as "*only* a dream". What deft sleights of hand we perform with our own experience, capriciously separating out the real from the unreal to suit our private convenience!

Commonplace Criteria for Reality

But what is it, exactly, that we mean when we say dreams are unreal? Let us consider a concrete example, the dream of a successful, thirty-four year old family physician, whom I shall call Dr. M., who was on the staff of a family practice clinic in a respected university hospital and who had sought out psychotherapy for depression and difficulties in intimate relationships. One night, three months into his twice-weekly therapy, *Dr. M. dreamt that a czarina had taken him captive and was going to have him shot on the pistol range. She had been watching over him as he stood hand-cuffed outside a small building beneath the midday sun, when he slipped out of the cuffs, and, with a single leap, flew over some woods to a field and then further to a nearby street. The scene switched and the dreamer found himself, some time later, at the house where he lived at the time of his dream. Suddenly he realized that the czarina and her henchmen were in that area, too, and that she was still prepared to kill him, this time with a bazooka.*

When Dr. M. woke up from this dream, he thought it nonsensical and dismissed it as "unreal", as "only a dream", especially since it seemed to him to be completely unrelated to anything which was happening in his waking life. But what is it that Dr. M. might have meant when he declared his dream unreal? One possibility is that Dr. M. meant simply that his dream was *weird, bizarre, unlike anything in his ordinary waking reality.* He might have pointed out, for example, that his dream was incompatible with his own personal experience (he had never met a czarina), with common sense (the idea of a totalitarian regime within a democracy was ludicrous), and with the lawfulness of nature (which does not permit unassisted human flight). Another possibility is that Dr. M. meant his dream was *fragmentary or discontinuous.* He might then have noted how the time and space of his dreaming, in contrast to waking, had radically changed when "the scene switched" from one moment on an unnamed street, to a "later" moment at his current home. Perhaps Dr. M. considered his dreaming unreal because it was entirely *private and subjective:* no one in his social world of waking could objectively observe and confirm the presence of this czarina. Finally, Dr. M. might have meant that his dream was unreal because much of it was *contingent* on this instance of his dreaming. The czarina's palpable existence, for example, had completely collapsed as soon as he had woken up and he could not now challenge her over the phone nor force her to appear in court as he might a person who had treated him in a similar fashion while awake.

The difficulty with the above criteria is that they all rely on the norms of waking life to determine what is real in dreaming. But do we have any logical basis for doing such a thing, for judging the reality of one pheno-menon according to the standards and structures of another. In fact, when we carefully consider these criteria we see that not one of them truly distinguishes reality per se, but only what we think of as *ordinarily* real about our waking lives. Is there any reason, then, other than private convenience, for holding Dr. M.'s sense of dreaming reality accountable to his waking reality? What would Dr. M. conclude about the reality of his dreaming if he considered only *his actual experience while dreaming?* Following such a strategy might he not confess that that which encount-ered him while dreaming appeared just as real, just as vital as that which encountered him in waking? How is it then that he so quickly whisked away his dream as unreal, as *only* a dream?

If there is a single feature that distinguishes the existential approach to dreams (Boss, 1958, 1963, 1977; Stern, 1972) from all others it is the proposition that *dreaming is reality.* For example, if we take Dr. M.'s dreamt encounter with the czarina for real, precisely as he experienced it while dreaming, then the handcuffs which bound his wrists were as real as this book you now hold in your hands; the czarina herself as real as the last person you saw today; Dr. M.'s persistence in eluding the czarina as real as your attitude in relation to this text as you sit here reading about dreams.

Theoretical Solutions to the Problem of Reality

Most modern dream theories only partially affirm this view: they accept the dream's symbolic or metaphorical reality but, like many dreamers, reject the fact and significance of its lived reality. Some theories view the symbolism of the dream on what is called the 'object level'. Such theories declare that the dreamt phenomena represent objects of the dreamer's desires, that the czarina, for example, represents the dreamer's mother or some other so-called 'love object'. This view is closely allied with that which was developed by Freud (1900, 1901, 1933). Other dream theories, however, emphasize 'subject level' interpretation, that is, inter-pretation with reference to the dreamer's personality. These theories suggest that the czarina is a composite symbol for unrecognized aggres-sive, controlling and feminine characteristics of the dreamer. This view is akin to that which was taken by Freud's one-time colleague Carl Jung (1954, 1960).

Whichever the premise, most dream theories acknowledge that dreams are real psychological events and that they have real psychological significance. However, while embracing the dream's *psychological reality,* these theories tend to diminish or even reject dreaming's legitimacy and significance as *lived reality.* Such theories suggest that we not get distracted by the czarina for it is what she represents and symbolizes that is real, not she herself. As Medard Boss (1977) has pointed out, "in this view, the dream is said to retain its reality ... but it is a representation of reality, not reality itself" (p. 178).

But what evidence is there that this czarina is a mere symbol, that she did not concretely exist for the dreamer while dreaming? As Dr. M. recounted his dreaming he spontaneously described this czarina's actual bodily appearance there in front of him; how her "icy, arrogant stare" sent "shivers" up his spine; and how the sharp, cold edge of the handcuffs "gnawed at his wrists" as he worked to free his hands from behind his back. Where is the evidence that this encounter did not actually occur, that the czarina was a symbolic facade?

So, while we recognize the psychological reality of Dr. M.'s dreaming, this affirmation alone does not go far enough in accounting for its lived reality. In fact, we wonder if the outcome of the prejudice against the lived reality of dreaming has not been to counter the open physical violence of Dr. M.'s dreaming with a surreptitious, theoretical violence in waking. For just as the dreaming world czarina attempted to execute Dr. M., have not some waking world theories attempted to annihilate the czarina, by erasing her reality in his life? An existential- phenomenological approach to dreaming questions this kind of intellectual violence to our dreamt existence. It boldly affirms the lived reality of dreaming and seeks, first of all, to grasp the salient meanings of the dream as such and, only then, their relation to waking existence.

THE SHEPHERDING OF DREAMT REALITY

But now you may be wondering if it is possible to make sense of Dr. M.'s dreamt encounter with the czarina without resorting to symbolic solutions or falling back on theoretical crutches. Again, let us return to the life-world of Dr. M.'s dream itself and hear more from *him* regarding the particulars of *his* experience while dreaming.

Explicating the Life-World of the Dream

The phenomenological analysis of dreams always begins with explicit descriptions of the concrete life-world of dreaming. "Such 'explicitation'", as it is called by Boss (1977), "requires that the awakened dreamer give an increasingly refined account of the dream.... by letting [him] supplement his first sketchy remarks with more detailed statements. The goal is to put together as clear as possible a waking vision of what actually has been perceived in dreaming" (p. 32). One therefore invites the dreamer to begin with the opening moment of the dream and to wander back through the dream by describing the particulars of his experience while dreaming.[2] In a classical dream analysis, such an explication would include a description of each of the various fundamental characteristics of human existence, or 'existentialia',[3] which always appear with one's dreaming. The following discussion presents aspects of these fundamental characteristics as they appeared in Dr. M.'s dreamt encounter with the czarina and illustrates some of the kinds of questions which may be asked of a dreamer in this phase of the analysis of dreams.[4]

Dream Space. When Dr. M.'s therapist inquired where Dr. M. happened to have been when he found himself handcuffed by the czarina, what this setting was like, and how it changed as the dream unfolded, Dr. M. responded with sudden astonishment. He had completely overlooked the fact that the dream had begun in front of the home where he had grown up in Wisconsin. The czarina had been standing on the lawn between the dreamer and the front door of the house. The dreamer also had been standing on the lawn, with his wrists handcuffed behind his back. As soon as he had slipped out of the cuffs he had flown over some woods to the backyard of a neighbour who happened to have been the only doctor in the dreamer's home town. He had paused only briefly in this yard before having flown on further to Main Street. Dr. M. didn't remember having seen anyone else in town; Main Street had been deserted. He then said that when the scene had switched he had felt relieved to be back at the old farm house where he lived just outside Boston. He had felt safer there in the inviting ambiance of early evening. The air had seemed clean and clear, the shadows were vivid. Again, no one else appeared except the czarina and her henchmen.

Immediately we see that while dreaming Dr. M. was open to appearing in familiar settings which explicitly joined his past and his present and were filled with a variety of meaningful phenomena, most notably with the appearance of a particular kind of womanliness which threatened to annihilate Dr. M.'s very existence. Clearly, this spatiality was not limited to measurable distances and dimensions nor to materially present objects or parameters, for these characteristics are mere mechanical derivatives of the "original spatiality" (Boss, 1963, p. 42f) of dreaming. What actually happened while dreaming was that Dr. M. "gave space" to the appearance of this czarina and, with her, to the sum total of meanings and things to which she refers simply by being the one she is. We will return to this aspect of spatiality again shortly.

Dream Time. Dr. M. has already mentioned certain aspects of his experience of time while dreaming. We have learned, for instance, that this dreaming had unfolded in broad daylight and had come to an end relatively late in the day. We also know that his dream had begun with a historical context and ended with a present context and that the time between these two contexts had vanished.

When Dr. M.'s therapist asked how Dr. M. had felt, while dreaming, about the sudden shift in time, Dr. M. said that he had been initially relieved to have put the incident with the czarina behind him. He was therefore surprised and discouraged to find that she had shown up again after all. In other words, Dr. M. had been surprised to find that this particular form of womanliness, a 'czarinaness', which had inhabited the world of his childhood had actually followed him into his present world. He had been discouraged to find that he still had to deal with this just when he thought he had left it behind.

This taking up of time in a concern with things is the true and original temporality of human existence (Boss, 1963, p. 45f). While various quantities and categories may also be derived from original temporality, our primary interest is with time's 'livedness', with Dr. M.'s unfolding 'use' of time, with his 'concern with' or 'caring for' things in time. With this interest in mind we see that Dr. M.'s entire existence while dreaming had been consumed by his concern with this czarina, either in the manner of being captured and threatened by her or in the manner of escaping and hiding from her. It is not surprising, then, that he had been disappointed by this erosion of his time with defensive attitudes and activities. He had not found a single moment to enjoy his own present or to consider his own future.

Each of these temporal details afford us a more accurate and complete picture of the reality of Dr. M.'s existence while dreaming. We have not once needed to refer to anything which did not appear with the life-world of Dr. M.'s dreaming itself.

Dream Phenomena. As mentioned above, one aspect of the spatiality of dreams is the meaningfulness of the particular phenomena to which an individual gives space while dreaming. A thorough analysis of Dr. M.'s dream would include a detailed description of each of the phenomena, each of the persons, objects and events, which appeared to him while dreaming.

For example, When Dr. M.'s therapist inquired about the czarina by asking, "What is a czarina for you in the first place and, especially, what was this particular czarina like as she stood in front of your childhood home?"[5], Dr. M. responded immediately: "A czarina is a Russian Empress, the female counterpart to a czar; not a pleasant sort; noble, removed from the masses, domineering, autocratic, tyrannical, self-centered. They are constantly meddling in everyone's affairs and expect complete obedience to their rule. This czarina was tall and beautiful, though handsome might be more accurate. She had a hard, angular face and a tight, square jaw. She glared at me with a kind of self-righteous arrogance". Wanting to encourage Dr. M. to remain faithful to the phenomenon itself, his therapist casually asked how this czarina was dressed. Once more, Dr. M. responded immediately: "Oh, she wasn't wearing royal garments, jewels or anything like that, just a long, flowery frock, one of those old peasant's dresses. Oh, that's funny! *The czarina was wearing a peasant's dress!* "[6]

Here Dr. M.'s therapist learned about the particular meaningfulness of that to which Dr. M. gave space while dreaming, the particular kind of womanliness which Dr. M. experienced as opposed to his existence while dreaming. Further inquiry also revealed aspects of Dr. M.'s dreaming which he had not mentioned in his initial report. For example, when Dr. M. described the details of the czarina's second appearance, he recalled that she was being driven ceremoniously past his farmhouse when he realized that she was "giving up her claim" to the territory. Since, however, she was then carrying a bazooka with which to shoot "undesireable subjects", he had hid behind his house and come out again only once she had passed. Dr. M. then recalled, curiously, that he had run up the road after her to the edge of the highway where he had imagined "taunting her with his freedom".

The Dreamer's Presence. In addition to becoming acquainted with dreamt space, time and phenomena, it is also important to learn about the presence of the dreamer himself while dreaming, especially since his own appearance had been the single unifying thread, enduring continuously throughout the dream.

With reference to *bodyhood* we see that Dr. M. became focally aware of his body only when he could not carry out his engagement with the world in a free and spontaneous fashion, as when he was handcuffed for example. Other than this, his body appears healthy, whole and non-problematic. When Dr. M.'s therapist asked Dr. M. what it had meant to him precisely, while dreaming, that he had been constrained in this particular way of having his hands bound behind his back, Dr. M. said he had felt unable to fight back, "to strike out" at the czarina or "grab her by the throat". We immediately see here that Dr. M. was impaired specifically in carrying out his own possibilities for an aggressive response even to that which threatened his life. When Dr. M.'s therapist inquired just how Dr. M. happened to get into such a predicament in the first place. Dr. M. responded that he couldn't remember actually being caught or handcuffed; it seemed that *he had been that way from the very beginning.*[7]

The therapist then asked how Dr. M. had been feeling in this situation and how his *mood* had changed as his dreaming went on. Dr. M. said that he had felt extremely anxious while being held prisoner, particularly with the thought of his impending execution. Though he loathed the czarina, he had been intimidated by her power, so he had remained outwardly docile while privately planning his escape. When he had finally escaped and flown away, he had felt relieved but still anxious that he might "lose altitude" and again fall into her hands. He then recalled having felt lonely when he found Main Street empty. This had been followed by a brief moment of cheerful well-being when he appeared at his farmhouse in the country. However, he had felt immediately depressed again with the czarina's reappearance though this time, at least, he was more confident of himself and of his ability to elude her. At last, as he had run after the czarina and imagined taunting her, he felt both "hatred" and "triumph".

We have already learned a good deal about Dr. M.'s *responses* to that which appeared to him while dreaming. Here two details are worth underscoring: first, that Dr. M.'s initial course of action had been one of withdrawal and flight and not, for example, of retaliation, debate, or seduction; and second, that Dr. M. had awakened at the precise moment which had included the czarina's departure as well as his hatred and triumph but at the same time had excluded any opportunity for being without her in his life.

Clearly, this procedure of simply describing the dream in full is an arduous, systematic process. Although such a method may at first seem quite simple or even naive, one soon learns that the gentle rigour it demands is no easy achievement. In this approach, the most effective dream investigator is one who serves the dream as a shepherd serves his flock, vigilant and protecting of the life within, ensuring nothing is lost, nothing taken for granted.

Understanding the Manifest Dream: Thematic Readings of Dreamt Reality

In renouncing symbolic solutions to understanding dreams we are invited, with a phenomenological approach, back to the life-world of the dream itself. Whereas the prevalent attitude is *"to see through* the dream", our conviction is that we must learn *"to see* the dream" as it is given and *to read* it precisely as it appears in the experience of the dreamer. As Paul Stern (1972) noted, what we need "more than anything else.... is an almost childlike incorruptible simplicity which is not taken in by contrived complexities and is able to see, in the midst of them - the obvious" (p. 43). What is it, then that we *see* when we look at the life-world of Dr. M.'s dream? *What might we say about what was real for him while dreaming?*

The impairment of freedom and the imminence of death. First of all we see that Dr. M.'s existence while dreaming was entirely taken up in a struggle to gain his freedom from a human bondage which began before his earliest memory. Even while dreaming he realized the urgency of his task, that his oppression was no trivial condition for in its shadow he was not only denied the opportunity to move freely in his world, but he was also in danger of being denied the opportunity to exist at all. He saw his loss of freedom and imminent death as coming with one another. While dreaming he never questioned this, he knew only that he *must* be free. Already, we can appreciate how Dr. M. may have preferred to relegate his dream to the realm of unreality. It seems that Dr. M. was simply not open to facing, while awake, these profound matters with which he was inextricably concerned while dreaming. Surely one's very own freedom, life and death are not topics for reverie and pleasant conversation.

Anxiety and the voracity of heterosexual relations. In addition to seeing Dr. M.'s concern with the loss of freedom and the possibility of death, we also see that this concern unfolded specifically in his relations with a woman and with a particular kind of womanliness. It is a striking fact in itself that, while dreaming on this particular evening, womanliness had appeared to Dr. M. only as beautiful but cold, domineering and despotic; while manliness had appeared only as mindless, macho servitude (with the henchmen) or as anxious, submissive enmity (with Dr. M. himself). In addition, Dr. M.'s anxiety about his relations with this woman was so voracious that there was barely a moment in his dreaming for anything else. Relating with this kind of womanliness (appearing as beautiful but domineering, old-fashioned but arrogant, simple but self-righteous) consumed his entire existence. The totality of Dr. M.'s anxious absorption in his dreamt relations with the czarina is conclusively seen in the fact that Dr. M. woke up from his dream before he had barely a moment to himself.

The disavowal of power. In addition to seeing the extent (absorbing his entire existence) and seriousness (coming with the possibility of death) of Dr. M.'s loss of freedom while dreaming, we also see his particular mode of existential impairment. While dreaming he was open to the appearance of human power, but only as 'belonging to' others. In fact, the only assertive act to which he was personally open was running up the road 'to tease' the already leaving czarina. At least then he imagined his own possibilities for feeling "hatred" and "triumph". This, then, is the crux of one of Dr. M.'s unspoken conundrums while dreaming: That he was not open to his own appearance in the world as a person with strength and stamina, who would not withdraw from confrontation and might even welcome the opportunity to engage others on such vital matters as human freedom and the right to live and die as one chooses. How did it happen that while dreaming Dr. M. was not open to appearing as a more powerful, aggressive or even revolutionary presence in the world?

The splitting of power and procreative possibility. Our answer to this question may be that while dreaming Dr. M. was open to human power only as destructive and not as also potentially edifying or creative. For example, while dreaming, the power of possession appeared to Dr. M. only as an imprisoning and life-threatening possibility even though we know that possession in a relationship with a woman may also appear with the tender solicitude of motherly care or with the captivating passion of sexual frolic and dance. Could it be that this kind of perceptual splitting impaired Dr. M.'s recognition of the range and complexity of his own possibilities for being-in-the-world while dreaming? If so, then, though he may have avoided the anxiety of contending with ambiguity and self-contradiction, he paid a heavy price in the currency of his own existential freedom.

Constriction and collusion. Paradoxically, it was Dr. M.'s own existential constriction, his lack of freedom to appear as a powerful and assertive presence in the life-world of his dreaming, that lead to the appearance of the czarina in the first place. For as D.W. Winnicott was fond of pointing out, there is no such thing as a mother alone, a mother can only appear where there is a child. Likewise, there is no such thing as a czarina alone, a czarina can only appear where there is a subject. Dr. M.'s impaired demeanor, his own subjection, thus actually helped to constitute the very arrogance and destructiveness he loathed. His existential constriction colluded in the appearance of the kind of womanliness which he found so threatening and intolerable.

Privacy, solitude and flight: a silent revolution. In light of the extent and seriousness of Dr. M.'s existential impairment while dreaming, it is commendable that he still managed to maintain his own margins of vitality and freedom. Even when faced with overwhelming odds, he was open to his own appearance as an individual of hope and persistence, who claimed a private domain of freedom within which he could think and feel and plan in silence and who steadily struggled to escape that which he found oppressive and life-threatening. Though his victory was not com- plete, and though he was free only in the manner of hiding and fleeing, at least he did not submit entirely to the whims of the czarina, accepting his fate and aligning his own thoughts and values with hers. While Dr. M. may have betrayed himself to the world, he did not betray himself to himself and this "private freedom" is surely the soil from which authentic "public freedom" may grow. His openness to defiantly "taunting" the czarina at the very end of his dream is a positive indication in this regard.

The absence of love and friendship. This leads finally to the significance of that which does not appear in Dr. M.'s dream in any form. In addition to the absence of "procreative power" mentioned above, we see that throughout Dr. M.'s entire dreaming, he appeared utterly alone, bereft of friends or allies. Even in the vicinities of his own homes, both childhood and present, not a single familiar face appeared. There was not a single moment of human love and kindness. Main Street itself was completely empty! Thus in Dr. M.'s struggle for freedom and survival he was without companionship, without tenderness.

Understanding the Dream as a Whole: A Synthetic Reading of Dreamt Reality

In summary we see that, while dreaming, Dr. M.'s entire existence was consumed in his struggle to free himself from a human bondage which began before his earliest memory and which was associated with the possibility of imminent death. Though he escaped this original captivity, which first appeared within the most intimate environment of his youth, he was disheartened to find himself threatened once more in the most personal domains of his adulthood. Although he felt more hopeful in his adult world, the danger was also greater.

In addition, the freedom which Dr. M. sought throughout his dreaming appeared specifically in his relations with a particular kind of womanliness: beautiful but domineering, earthy but self-righteous. Though Dr. M. maintained his freedom of feeling and thought and exercised his capacities for escape and elusion, he was still too anxious and constricted to engage this kind of womanliness directly with confidence and strength. It is, in fact, in this abnegation of his own possibilities for revolutionary being that Dr. M. tacitly contributes to the kind of domination and destructive- ness he feared and loathed. Nevertheless, in the end, Dr. M. at least imagined an assertive act which would have brought him closer to his adversary and would have affirmed both his presence and the value of his freedom.

Finally we see that throughout his search for freedom and safety in his relations with this particular kind of womanliness, Dr. M. appeared entire- ly alone, without allies or any form of human support or affection. How- ever, we also see that at the end of his dreaming Dr. M. was freer and safer, more lively and confident than when it began. Indeed, it was near the end of his dreamt day of danger and captivity; the atmosphere was propitious, the air clean and clear. At last, promise of liberty has replaced the threat of annihilation.

Reflections on the Reality of Dreaming

Reviewing the problem of the reality of Dr. M.'s dreaming existence, we see no indication that his dreamt encounter with the czarina was in any way unreal. Dr. M. himself soon recognized that he could not deny that, in Boss' (1977) words, the czarina's "immediate sensual visibility [had] come impressively, and at times, uncomfortably, close to [him]" (p. 199). Indeed, the very fact of her palpable manifestation with him while dreaming indicates that he was more open to the appearance of these particular human possibilities while dreaming than he had been when he was awake and dismissed their reality and significance in his life. We also see no reason in Dr. M.'s dreaming as such, that this dreamt episode of his existence should be excluded from his autobiography. Even if he persisted in denying his dream's historical legitimacy (which he did not) he would still have to carry it forward 'as denied'. Thus he inevitably carries the reality of his dreaming into his future either as "embraced" and "accepted", or as "ignored" or "denied". Finally, there is no evidence here that Dr. M.'s dreaming was in any way ingenuine, that his experience was not an honest expression of just how things stood for him during the time of his dream. Is there any reason, then, why it should not be regarded as a trustworthy manifestation of the meaning and truth of Dr. M.'s existence while dreaming?

But why, on that particular night, did Dr. M. concern himself with those specific aspects of his existence? Was the reality of his dreaming in any way related to the reality of his waking life?

THE RELATION OF DREAMING AND WAKING REALITY

Although our intent is to examine the general relationship between dreaming and waking, we should acknowledge that the actual practical relationship which exists between the two domains is mightily influenced by the attitude of the awakened dreamer. Surely, those who think dreaming is imbecilic are less likely to discover a relationship with waking than those who consider dreaming to be a meaningful, valuable dimension of their lives. In addition, we must acknowledge that the very problem of this general relationship usually appears to us only when we are awake: the question itself, is primarily a phenomenon of waking and not of dreaming. Having mentioned these general considerations, our challenge is to approach this problem with an open mind, suspending assumptions and prejudices which may cloud our perception and thinking, and to ask ourselves the question "How does the reality of our existence while dreaming relate to the reality of our existence while awake?"

DREAMING AS ALLUSIVE POSSIBILITY

Clearly Freud's assumption of an unconscious mind, whose purpose it was to relate to consciousness by way of delusion, influenced his understanding of the relation of dreaming to waking.[8] If, however, we do not infer an unconscious mind to exist 'behind' our dreaming and if we take our dreaming precisely as it is given in awareness as a spontaneous, remarkably impromptu mode of existence, then our understanding of its relation to waking must rely on what we can observe directly. Cradled in such a phenomenological reverence for dreaming itself, we are led to a perspective quite different from the one suggested by Freud: not that dreaming is delusive but rather that it is *allusive*, that is, that *a dream refers us to itself simply by appearing as itself.* But this is not in any way essentially different from waking existence.

Specifying Conceptual Foundations

Perhaps a brief conceptual excursion will help clarify what we mean. A tree in waking life, for example, simply appears to us as such in the life-world of waking. It does not, apart from our awareness of it, intend to refer to anything. A dreamt tree is just the same: it, too, simply appears to us out of the primordial darkness of the universe and shines forth to us as the very tree it is. Like the appearance-of-the-tree-in-waking there is no evidence that this appearance-of-the-tree-in-dreaming *intends* to refer to anything. It simply appears to us as the tree it is. Thus there is, with both waking and dreaming awareness, this pristine shining forth of the tree as such. There is also, however, with both waking and dreaming awareness, the meaningfulness of the tree which appears to us simply by virtue of this tree's appearing as the tree it is. The appearance-of-meaningfulness is what endows the appearance-of-the- tree-as-such with its *allusive possibility:* that is, *the possibility that once it has shown forth with us and we have become concerned with it, we may then permit it to refer us to its meaningfulness as the particular tree it is.* In this view, dreaming and waking trees only become allusions once we become concerned with them and consider their meaningfulness as the trees they appear to be.

Notice here, even with the dreamt tree, there is no assumption of any unconscious thought or intention. The first and foremost fact about the dreamt tree, like the tree of wakefulness, is simply the fact of its appearance as such. Neither the dream nor the sleeping dreamer intends to allude to anything with this appearance of the tree as such. However, coalescent with the tree's-appearance-as-such is the tree's-appearance-as-meaning, that is, its referring for us to its *immanent* meaningfulness by virtue of our encounter with it as the particular thing it is. I call this the *primary allusion* of dreamt phenomena: *our perception of the reference of the dreamt things to their particular, immanent meaningfulness simply by virtue of their appearance as precisely and only the things they are.*

Thus, the reality of dreaming embodies these two fundamental characteristics: the appearance of the dreaming as such and the meaningfulness of this appearance in and for itself. Our study of Dr. M.'s dream has so far been concerned entirely with these two characteristics of his dreaming: first, with the appearance, for example, of the czarina as such and, second, with the primary allusiveness of the czarina, that is, with her appearance as a meaning bearing presence, a particular kind of womanliness, in Dr. M.'s dreamt cosmos.

Now, I would like to consider the *secondary allusion* of dreaming, that is, just how Dr. M.'s cosmos of dreaming may be related to and therefore refer us to his cosmos of waking. Again, let us turn to Dr. M.'s dream and see, through *his* eyes, how *his* experience with the czarina while dreaming may relate to *his* experience of being-in-the-world while awake.

Explicating the Life-World of Waking
The reader may recall that when Dr. M.'s therapist asked him to describe the czarina, Dr. M. ended with an exclamation, "Oh, that's funny! the czarina was wearing a peasant's dress!" (p.120). Sensing the clarity and energy of this incongruity for Dr. M., his therapist paraphrased his description: "Yes, that is interesting - a woman who appears in humble clothes but who is in control of your entire world, a woman who may be attractive and down to earth but also intrusive and self-righteous..." Dr. M. responded that he was suddenly reminded of a colleague, a staff gynaecologist at his hospital clinic, whom he actually liked very much but who lately had become "awfully opinionated" and "pushy". He said they had often disagreed about their way of dealing with patients. She felt that the doctor "always knew best", while he was much more inclined to consider carefully the patient's perceptions and feelings and to include the patient in developing treatment plans.

In recent months, Dr. M. had noticed that his colleague had stopped referring new patients to him and had grown increasingly dogmatic and self-righteous about her views. Her arbitrariness had become particularly annoying in his work with families with whom they were both involved. Recently he had learned, only after the fact, of various decisions she had made without consulting him. She had even begun treating some of his patients for problems to which he had been attending. Dr. M. recalled that he had, in fact, learned of another such instance on the evening before his dream. Furthermore, over the previous several months Dr. M.'s colleague had begun treating both a former lover and a close female friend, with whom he was occasionally intimate, for various gynaecological complaints. Her involvement with these intimate acquaintances left him feeling like "she was invading [his] entire life". Everywhere he turned, he found her "meddling in [his] world".

Dr. M. said that he was terribly hurt by what he perceived as her personal and professional disregard and, at the same time, he was furious about these intrusions in his life. For some reason, however, he felt crippled in his ability to express these feelings openly and directly with his colleague. Each time he tried he felt anxious, inept and embarrassed, which only made things worse; so he chose instead to remain silent. He was bewildered by the fact that, on the one hand, he could easily captivate a room full of medical colleagues at grand rounds but, on the other hand, be so ineffectual with this one individual. He added that he felt saddened by this whole situation since his colleague and he had once enjoyed an excellent working relationship. He had always felt that she was a "damn good doctor" and a lovely, caring woman. In fact, when they had first met he had fallen in love with her and had even thought about the possibility of marriage. Eventually she had married another man whom she had been dating for some time. At this point in the conversation Dr. M. paused and reflected that there was something unusually irrational about his attachment to this woman and he felt, in retrospect, relieved to have escaped that fate.

Solidifying Connections between Dreaming and Waking.
At this point the therapist was sufficiently impressed by the *similarity between the features of Dr. M.'s dreaming relations with the czarina and his waking relations with his colleague* to offer a more precise connection. He therefore mused, "So she shot you down and gave up her claim to your home and now you feel relieved to have escaped." Dr. M. immediately burst out in guffaw and exclamation, recognizing the essential structure of his dream in this simple, pithy recapitulation of his relationship with this colleague.

Here we see that Dr. M. tacitly acknowledged the correspondence between his dreaming and his waking when he was reminded of his colleague and began to speak of his difficulties with her. When the therapist underscored this correspondence by pointing to additional structural similarities he was clearing the way for a more disciplined inquiry into ways in which the forms and features of Dr. M.'s dreaming may have corresponded with and illuminated those of his waking.

DREAMING AND WAKING: HOMOLOGOUS MODES OF A SINGLE EXISTENCE

Recalling our discussion of Freud's theory of dreams, you might now be asking, if there is no unconscious purpose on the part of the dreamer, how is it that the allusive power of Dr. M.'s dream seems so great, that his dreaming reality seems to have such an extraordinary fit with his waking reality? The existential-phenomenological solution to this problem is relatively uncomplicated: the forms, structures and meanings of dreaming fit neatly with those of waking because a person's waking and dreaming

'belong' to the same individual, are both modes of a singular human existence. Since Dr. M. exists as a single individual who carries out his existence in both dreaming and waking, his dreams must, in some way, relate to
this singularity of being-in-the-world. In this instance, we found that the
realities of his dreaming and waking were manifestly *homologous* with
one another, that is, *they appeared as constituted by corresponding
structures, forms and meanings and as lived-out in corresponding
relationships and proportions*.

Phenomenologically seen, Dr. M. had been concerned with his relations to
a 'czarinaness' in both his dreaming and waking existence. We now see that
he was open to the appearance of this czarina-as-such while dreaming but
that he had been unable, at least prior to his dream, to perceive this same
czarinaness as such in waking, where the clutter of other feelings and
impressions kept him from seeing his colleague for the czarina she was in
those concrete aspects of her being with him. Thus, it was only while
dreaming that he finally and freshly perceived the particular assemblage
of human possibilities which had evoked his anger and anxiety. In the
privacy and safety of dreaming in his own bed, Dr. M. entertained as real
not only the presence of this czarinaness in his world but also his
particular responses to her manifest reality.

Dreaming the Disenfranchised: An Anticipatory Mode of Being.
In this example, we see that what unites and relates the two domains of
dreaming and waking is not the fluidity of appearances as such but rather
the viscosity of meanings which are manifest with those appearances. The
homologous relation between dreaming and waking consists in the carrying
out of the meanings, forms and structures which constitute the particular
"meaning-fullness" of a single human existence in both of its modes of
being. Within the sanctuary of our dreaming mode of existence, however,
we are often open to meaningful possibilities of our lives which we barely
perceive, blithely ignore, or outrightly dismiss while awake. While
dreaming, these disenfranchised possibilities of waking appear to us with
striking clarity as the real and meaningful features of our existence which
they are. In this sense dreaming actually anticipates the possibilities and
tasks of waking. However, almost as soon as we open our eyes in the
morning, we once again invoke the supposedly superior credentials of
waking consciousness and dismiss the realness of that to which we were
momentarily receptive while dreaming. Phenomenologically understood,
then, it is the denied or unrecognized meanings, forms and structures of
waking which, when liberated from the cacophony and reason of everyday
life, may appear starkly sequestered in the light of human dreaming.
Dreaming reality seems bizarre and inconsistent with waking reality only
because we fail, while we are awake, to perceive the meaningfulness of
that which appears as such both in dreaming and waking.

Contemporaneous Homologies and Allusions[9]

With his dream of the czarina, then, Dr. M. had begun to recognize the homologous meanings and structures which constituted his dreaming and waking realities. Following these initial recognitions he began to take up the demanding project of exploring those meaningful possibilities of his dreaming which lay still beyond the edge of his immediate waking recognition. Dr. M.'s therapist continued to assist him in exposing the meaningfulness of his dream and sharpening his awareness of its correspondence with waking. On one occasion, for example, the therapist noted that the czarina had not actually 'shot down' Dr. M. in the dream, that he had escaped before she had managed his execution. Dr. M. responded that that was exactly what had happened in waking. *This woman had kept him 'on the string'* for some time while she was going back and forth about the man she eventually married. When it seemed to Dr. M. that she was not prepared to pursue a serious relationship with him he tried to spare himself a public rejection by *precipitously withdrawing* from the competition while *remaining a 'hostage' to his more private feelings* .

On another occasion, Dr. M.'s therapist had mused that, while dreaming, Dr. M. had seen the czarina as a powerful presence in this dreamt relationship while *his* only strength was in concealment and escape. "How is it", his therapist then asked, "that this particular way of perceiving yourself in this dreamt relationship might also colour your waking relations to your colleague or to women in general?" This question led to a lengthy discussion of Dr. M.'s sense of *basic anxiety and powerlessness in intimate or potentially intimate interpersonal situations.* Generally, he concealed this vulnerability from others and even, to a large extent, from himself. He acknowledged that in this respect he was actually more honest while dreaming than while fully awake, for at least he "had the guts" while dreaming to let his vulnerability be.

Paradoxically, this waking recognition of "having the guts" to be "power-*less*" while dreaming was followed by a series of dreams in which Dr. M. became increasingly "power-*full*'" in response to his colleague's intrusive and domineering behaviour. In one dream he firmly told her to get out of a restaurant's men's room when she walked in and interrupted him in the middle of a bowel movement. In another he simply told her to "keep quiet" when she started lecturing him about the superiority of her approach with patients. In spite of Dr. M.'s increasing confidence and strength while dreaming, it was still several weeks before he permitted himself the luxury of expressing himself more assertively with his colleague directly in waking. These 'follow-up' dreams clearly illustrate the anticipatory relation of dreaming to waking.

While the above inquiries with respect to Dr. M.'s contemporaneous waking life disclose psychologically evocative homologous relations between his dreaming and waking modes of existence, they also lead us to further questions. In particular, we wonder how it is that a man of obvious intelligence and professional success could have come to have had so much difficulty with being himself in personal relationships? Again, perhaps more secrets were contained in the correspondence of his initial dream to his waking life.

Historical Homologies and Allusions.

Since we know that human existence itself is quintessentially historical, could it be that Dr. M.'s lack of freedom in relating with this particular kind of womanliness began even before he had met his colleague? If so, how might Dr. M.'s dreaming refer us to his autobiography and, therefore, to homologous waking realities which might shed light on the origins of Dr. M.'s interpersonal difficulties?[10] As we review Dr. M.'s original explication of his dream, certain remarks suggest that this historical domain of meaning and possibility is centrally implicated in his existence while dreaming. First, in responding to his therapist's inquiry about the setting of his dream, Dr. M. suddenly realized that the dream had begun *on the lawn... in front of his childhood home* (p.119). Second, when his therapist asked how Dr. M. had been caught and handcuffed in the first place, he responded that he *"couldn't remember" when it had happened* and that it seemed as if he *"had been that way from the very beginning"* (p.121) these remarks refer us directly to Dr. M.'s own history and remind us that he was entirely concerned, while dreaming, with that which pursued him out of the past, with that which he had hoped he had escaped but, in fact, had not. Again attending to Dr. M.'s own experience, let us see how he came to understand specific correspondences between his dreaming and his own life history.[11]

The week following Dr. M.'s initial report of his dream, Dr. M.'s therapist casually asked him about the childhood home with which his dream had begun. Though Dr. M. initially responded with equal insouciance, describing its humble appearance, its setting in the woods, its tiny rooms, and its creaky steps. He soon began to choke with emotion as he spoke of how he missed this home and its simple natural surroundings. He said he suddenly realized that in spite of its apparent modesty, he had never loved a home as he had that one. Dr. M. added how disappointed he had felt when he had learned that his mother, who had been widowed since he was six, had sold their home soon after he had left for college. His voice faded as he commented that she had *never even asked him how he felt and had mentioned it only after she had moved* to another house. "I've never been back", he said, "nor felt at home in her home since".

Immediately we see here the homologous structure of meaning which constitutes, first, this historical event in Dr. M.'s relation to his mother; second, the contemporaneous events in his relations with his colleague; and, third, the dreamt events in his relations with the czarina. In each of these instances he had been significantly engaged with a woman who appeared to him in the manner of making decisions and taking actions having import for his life without considering his perceptions and feelings. Each of these women also appeared to Dr. M. as in some way standing between himself and a home. In addition to these already im- pressive homologies, when Dr. M.'s therapist recalled his patient's first descriptions of his mother as a woman of humble origin and appearance who ruled the house with an indomitable will, he was certain Dr. M. had suddenly opened himself to exploring a poignant domain of historical allusions.

When Dr. M. finished speaking of his sense of loss about this home, his therapist simply said: "So, there you were, while dreaming, kidnapped and about to die in your very own yard!" Dr. M. responded that he found that odd but, stranger still, was the fact that this was exactly how he had felt as a child: *trapped by his relationship with his mother.* As he had been an only child, his mother had increasingly turned to him for companionship and support in the wake of his father's death. He remembered having been enamoured with this role and with his mother's affection for him as a young boy, but, with the onset of adolescence, he had also begun to feel suffocated and afraid. Increasingly his mother had seemed to him to be fragile, irrational and arbitrary and her austerity had been oppressive. Looking back on those years, as an adult in therapy, Dr. M. began to see the sources of his ambivalence and confusion, particularly when he realized that in spite of their apparent affection for one another, *he could not recall having received a single motherly embrace* and his mother had sternly refused to kiss him (or anyone) on the lips.[12] Furthermore, when arguments had arisen between his mother and her mother (Dr. M.'s "silent, enigmatic, German grandmother" had lived with them since he was an infant) or between his mother and himself, they had usually ended either with his mother flying into a rage and throwing food or kitchenware around the room, or with her bursting into tears and locking herself in the bathroom while refusing to talk. Each of these alternatives had seemed intolerable to Dr. M., and he had come to feel too afraid and/or guilty to ever express his frustration and anger. Instead he had *"kept [his] feelings inside"* , carrying them alone and in silence. Toward the end of his high-school years he had begun to have a "strange, ghost-like premonition" that *getting away from home was, for him, "a matter of life or death"* . Honour-ing this 'ghost-like' reality, however, he had applied to Harvard College so his mother couldn't dispute his moving East and, the following fall, he left for New England where he has lived ever since.

Dr. M. had spoken without a pause for nearly the entire session, and though his therapist had noticed numerous poignant homologies he once more picked up right where Dr. M. left off, again just like linking the reality of dreaming to the reality of waking: "So you responded then, just as you did in your dream, when you secretly slipped out of your handcuffs and flew off on your own". Dr. M. nodded his recognition and it was clear that he had made an important start with exploring those ways in which *his mother, like the czarina of his dreaming, was "still with him",* as well as those ways in which his existence was *still impaired by his continuing sense of anxiety and powerlessness* in intimate relationships with this kind of woman.

THE CO-ILLUMINATION OF DREAMING AND WAKING

What is evident again in this interplay between Dr. M.'s dreaming and waking is the homologous structure of meaning which constitutes both. It is almost as if one can take an outline of the meaning-structures of the life-world of dreaming and look directly through them, like a transparent template, to highlight precisely corresponding forms and features in the life-world of waking. This remarkably homologous relation is due, again, to the simple fact that a person's dreaming and waking are both carried out by the same individual, are both structured by the meanings of a single human existence.

Our intent here has not been to conduct a classical dream analysis nor to present a complete clinical case study, though certainly we have incorporated elements of each. Instead we have used this single dream to inquire into the problems we had originally set before us and, in the process, to illustrate aspects of an existential-phenomenological approach to investigating and understanding dreams in human science and in psychotherapy. Our concern in these last few pages has been to understand the relation between the reality of dreaming and the reality of waking. This was accomplished, first of all, by inviting a particular dreamer, Dr. M., to describe precisely how his world appeared to him while dreaming. Then later, as Dr. M. began to recognize features of his waking which corresponded with features of his dreaming, he was invited to describe these waking realities, again remaining as faithful as possible to his experience as such. As these two kinds of life-worlds, dreaming-life- worlds and waking-life-worlds, began to illuminate one another. Dr. M. began to see that his dreaming experience was hardly as nonsensical and unrelated to waking as he first thought. On the contrary, he found a striking similarity between the meanings, structures and forms of his dreaming and those of his waking, in both its contemporaneous and historical dimensions. Thus Dr. M. came to see the autobiographical validity of his dreaming, the truthfulness of his dreaming with respect to his existence as a whole. As he continued to explore the significance of his dream he realized that, while dreaming, he had dared to take his first undiminished view of some of the fundamental truths of his existence, truths which he continually had eluded or overlooked prior to his dreaming and which he had spurned once again upon waking from this dream. Fortunately, however, with the encouragement of his therapist, he was emboldened to reconsider this pungent cosmos of dreaming in which his quest for freedom in his relations to this particular kind of womanliness appeared as a matter of life and death.

One striking lesson in this exercise has been that almost everything we have learned about these truths of Dr. M.'s existence had appeared entirely within the life-world of the manifest dream. Although making connections to waking was necessary for Dr. M. to understand his dream's *specific* significance for his life, these waking life realities merely confirmed what we already knew from the manifest reality of dreaming alone. This suggests that the prevelant prejudices against the manifest dream may be misguided indeed and that the manifest reality of dreaming per se may be a sufficient foundation for seeing the truth of an individual's existence, at least with respect to those possibilities and concerns which are encountered while dreaming. In other words, if we have done our work well and if we are able and willing to see what stands before our eyes, then waking life associations and connections merely emphasize and apply what we already know from the manifest dream.

SUMMARY

In this inquiry I hope to have shown that our existence while dreaming is a mode of being-in-the-world which is as real, vital and meaningful as our existence while awake, and that our dreams may be taken as legitimate episodes of our own life histories, as trustworthy manifestations of personal truth. In addition, I hope to have shown how our dreaming may allude, simply by being the particular life-world it is, first to the meaningfulness of that which appears in the dream as such and, second, to homologous structures, forms and meanings of waking existence. Thus, when we are willing to be concerned with them, our dreams may refer us, while awake, to aspects of our lives which we have seen and openly acknowledged on a daily basis. They may also refer us to aspects of our existence which we have seen but chosen to ignore. And, finally, they may refer us to authentic possibilities in our lives which, because of our own existential imprisonment, our own blurred and constricted vision, we have failed to see at all. Thus, in considering our dreams we may be referred not only to what is but also to what has been and to what might yet be. In this sense our dreams may be seen as a refuge for Truth and Possibility in our lives as awakened individuals.

NOTES

[1] As a professional psychologist, one is ultimately concerned with both of these worlds of science and therapy. Hopefully this dual focus will provide a clarity and richness that would not be possible with either focus alone.

[2] Diane Reed has developed a similar technique which she calls "walking through the dream" (chapter 6).

[3] See Boss (1963, 1979) and Heidegger (1962) for a full discussion of these fundamental characteristics of dasein.

[4] Remember, one can rarely, if ever, do a complete analysis of a dream in psychotherapy, where the vicissitudes of the situation determine which aspects of a dream receive attention. The analysis presented here lies between therapy and science. While the therapist was not free to pursue his own scientific curiosity, his therapeutic task was still profoundly sustained by his discipline as a phenomenological investigator.

[5] This technique of describing a phenomenon generically, (see C.G. Jung, 1954, 97-98; and Delaney, 1979, 52-53), unobtrusively evokes the horizons of the dreamer's experience while dreaming. However, because it also introduces waking thoughts that may not be aspects of the dreamt phenomenon per se, it is important to include the question of the particularity of the dreamt phenomenon in order to determine which generic features were actually presented with the dreamt phenomenon itself.

[6] The author's emphasis here underscores the kind of remarkable detail which may be evoked by straightforward questions about the dreamt phenomena themselves. Later, it will be seen how this particular detail was critical in relating this dream to Dr. M.'s waking life.

[7] See footnote 6.

[8] Perhaps Freud's greatest contributions to the scientific understanding of dreams were his inexorable commitment to the essential meaningfulness of dreams, and his insistence that the source of this meaningfulness was the life of the dreamer. However, having declared dreams to be meaningfully related to an individual's waking existence, Freud then had to account for their apparent obscurity and disparateness from waking. He hypothesized that the so-called "unconscious mind" is aware of an array of impulses, desires and memories which, if known to consciousness, would threaten to destroy any semblance of order in the individual's waking life. Dreaming experience is the theater for enacting these tendencies through symbols and images which disguise their true identity and intent from the dreamer. Thus, for Freud, only the hidden, inferred meaning of the dream, its latent content, is real. The manifest dream is merely a shrewd and artful symbolic delusion. The interpretation contains the truth, the dream itself does not.

[9] As it is impossible to discuss all of the homologies and allusions which follow, italics will be used to highlight those which came to have significance for the dreamer.

[10] Whereas most psychological theories emphasize the *casuality* of historicity, existential-phenomenological thinkers, emphasize its *meaningfulness*. They see historicity as that unique convergence of human possibilities as which the individual has existed in the past and with which he continues to exist in the present. The problem of historicity is not how the past *causes* one to be in the present, but rather, how one unwittingly *continues* old patterns and ways of being in the here-and-now.

We are impaired not by the events of the past but by our blindness to the meanings of the present.

[11] See footnote 9.

[12] As soon as Dr. M. mentioned his mother's reluctance to kiss him he spontaneously remembered having been surprised by his colleague's sexual restraint while they were dating. He *"couldn't believe that she was as Victorian as she seemed"* . Clearly the czarinaness of his dreaming was dense with both historical and contemporary meaning. Freud even called this phenomenon con*dens*ation !

REFERENCES

Boss, M. (1958). *The analysis of dreams.* New York: Philosophical Library.

Boss. M. (1963). *Psychoanalysis and daseinsanalysis.* New York: Basic Books.

Boss, M. (1977). *I dreamt last night....* New York: Gardner Press.

Boss, M. (1979). *Existential foundations of medicine and psychology.* New York: Jason Aronson.

Delaney, G. (1979). *Living your dreams.* New York: Harper and Row.

Freud, S. (1957). The interpretation of dreams (1900). *Standard Edition,* 4 & 5. London: Hogarth Press.

Freud, S. (1957). On dreams (1901). *Standard Edition,* 5: 629-686. London: Hogarth Press.

Freud,. S. (1957). Revision of the theory of dreams. In: New Introductory lectures on psychoanalysis (1933). *Standard Edition,* 22: 7-30. London: Hogarth Press.

Heidegger, M. (1962). *Being and time.* New York: Harper and Row.

Jung, C.G. (1954). The practical use of dream analysis. In: The practice of psychotherapy. *Collected Works, Second Edition,* 16: 139-161.Princeton: Bollingen Foundation.

Jung, C.G. (1960). On the nature of dreams. In: The structure and dynamics of the psyche. *Collected Works, Second Edition,* 8: 281-297. Princeton: Bollingen Foundation.

Reed, D. (1987). This publication, chapter 6.

Stern, P.J. (1972). Dreams:The radiant children of the night. In: *In praise of madness.* New York: W.W. Norton and Company Inc., 39-60.

Chapter 8

A DESCRIPTIVE PHENOMENOLOGY OF THE EXPERIENCE OF BEING LEFT OUT

Christopher M. Aanstoos

THE EXISTENTIAL SIGNIFICANCE OF THE PHENOMENON

> To be a consciousness or rather to be an experience is to hold inner communication with the world, the body and other people, to be with them instead of being beside them. (Merleau-Ponty, 1945/1962, p. 96).

According to Merleau-Ponty we are as unable to experience the presence of another person to himself as we are to encompass the moment of our own death. Nevertheless, he argues, just as the feeling of my contingency carries with it the horizon of death, so too do others exist for me within a horizon of co-existence. Thus, Merleau-Ponty concludes, "my life has a social atmosphere just as it has a flavor of mortality" (1945/1962, p. 364).

Yet it is also true that we flee inauthentically from our finitude (Heidegger, 1927/1962). So also can this fundamental sphere of sociality be likewise forgotten. The experience of being with others can then give way to the experience of being beside them. Ontological structures, such as sociality, are not, after all, things in themselves, but are always and necessarily concretely realized in mundane experience. Indeed, our lived experience even discloses its ontological truths through moments in which their typical manifestations are disrupted. When a lover leaves, the consequent anxiety reverberates a greater truth than this particular loss. Its echoes bespeak the contingency of all relationships, that we are not bonded by cement even to our most intimate others, that our security is never guaranteed (Grant, 1986).

The experience of feeling left out provides us with one such exemplar case. In feeling left out, we experience ourselves *beside* the others, no longer *with* them. The social world, as an ontical-ontological horizon of my existence, ceases to summon me. At such moments, what has been taken for granted can no longer be assumed. Strangeness now resides in the house of intimacy.

THE PSYCHOLOGICAL SIGNIFICANCE OF THE PHENOMENON

From the critical viewpoint, the existence of alter egos is the fundamental problem facing a phenomenological psychology. It is difficult to see how a philosophy grounded totally in experience could avoid eventuating in a position of solipsism or pure subjectivism. (Lapointe, 1976, p. 209).

Phenomenologists have been able to advance beyond the solipsistic pitfall precisely by comprehending sociality as an existential horizon of personal experience. Ever since Heidegger (1927/1962), being-in-the-world has been understood to include being-with-others as an essential constituent. As these philosophical foundations are now informing the development of an authentically phenomenological psychology, introductory texts in phenomenological psychology also are beginning to emphasize the importance of sociality (e.g., Keen, 1975; Kruger, 1979; Romanyshyn, 1982; Van den Berg, 1972). Yet, given sociality's peculiar taken for grantedness, it is much easier to indicate its importance than to articulate its concrete manifestations. One study (Wertz, 1983) that was able to illuminate sociality's prethematic significance did so by examining its rupture in the moment of being criminally victimized. In that sense, sociality is like the proverbial well whose water runs dry: its significance is never noticed directly until it becomes problematic.

Mainstream contemporary psychology also affirms the significance of other people as a horizon of psychological life. Typical of this natural scientifically based psychology, however, it does so obliquely and ambivalently, without a coherent understanding of concretely lived experience. Thus, the presence or absence of others (including the experimenter) is usually regarded as a source of 'error variance'. At best, social psychology views the presence of others as independent variables, causally deterministic of the subject's response or lack thereof. Furthermore, the others are typically strangers to the subjects in the experiment, with whom they have no past and no future. Even the place within which they interact is completely outside their familiar world. The proverbial 'room with strangers' setting may be best exemplified by Asch's (1955) work on conformity, though Latane and Darley's (1970) more recent work, still generally regarded as 'ingenious', uncritically continues the same tradition. In their experiments, subjects are confronted with apparent emergencies, such as smoke filling the room in which they are completing questionnaires. The experiment was designed to determine whether the presence of others influenced the likelihood of the subject's acknowledging the situation as an emergency, as measured by their taking the responsibility of acting to report the emergency. Latane and Darley found that the presence of strangers (actually confederates of the experimenter) significantly decreased the number of subjects who intervene by reporting the emergency. In comparison to control group subjects who were each alone when confronted with the experimental situation, those in a room with strangers (who had been instructed not to react to the emergency), tended to ignore the problem.

In contrast to these experiments, it would be simple enough to imagine an alternative one, in which three friends are put in the room together. Undoubtedly, they would more readily react to the emergency. Indeed, feeling free to acknowledge to a friend that one is experiencing the situation as an emergency may well be a key indication of the depth of the friendship. Only with strangers is it even conceivable that subjects would be so under the sway of the anonymous other as to ignore the sorts of emergencies presented in these experiments. With family or friends, the mutuality of 'being-with' the other stands in striking contrast to these cases of being 'beside' but in no sense 'with' the other. Here, again, however, research access to this lived sense of sociality occurs via deflection: by the way it is disclosed in its disruption.

Thus, both phenomenological and experimental psychology affirm the importance of sociality, and both have sought to overcome its peculiar taken for grantedness by investigations of those moments when typical, unproblematic sociality is disrupted. Taking such access, the present study examined sociality through an investigation of the experience of feeling left out. Being left out, therefore, constitutes an odd sort of psychological phenomenon, one whose presence is given as the absence of something else. As will be elaborated in the section on 'Findings', feeling left out is manifested as the felt lack of recognition of one's own perspective by another. There is a peculiar doubling here: the absence of a presence and the presence of an absence. The phenomenon itself is the gestalt, the unity of presence and absence. To comprehend this phenomenal presence through its appearance as an absence, we must of course recognize that an absence is not merely nothing, but another form of presence. Hence the value of an analysis of that which is not there.

THE PRESENT STUDY

METHOD

This research employed descriptive/qualitative procedures in both the data collection and the data analysis phases, along the lines that have been developed by the Duquesne group of phenomenological psychologists (Giorgi, 1985; Wertz, 1984).

Participants

Students in three courses were asked to participate in this study, and all agreed to do so. Two were graduate courses, comprised altogether of seventeen students; the third was an undergraduate course of eight students. A total, then, of twenty-five participated in the research. They ranged in age from twenty-one to thirty-nine, included fifteen women and ten men, and represented a wide geographic cross-section.

One meta-methodological note must be appended here. The circumscription of my research interest was enacted by the way I selected participants from whom to solicit descriptions. I asked for help from students, rather than specifically from those frequently subjected to exclusion, such as racial minorities, handicapped persons, psychotics, criminals, or vagabonds. As I'll suggest in the Findings, I would have become attuned to a different experience had I asked this latter group, yet one with some essential similarity as well. There are those whose apparent differentness results in their being excluded by the social mainstream. Such exclusion of these outcasts operates at an impersonal, sometimes even institutional level. From the perspective of the insiders, the outcasts don't 'fit' or 'belong'. Those so excluded may very well experience a poignant feeling of being left out, and in that sense would be similar in some essential way to my own findings. However, the felt sense of a sedimented socio-cultural isolation is also different than the immediate and personal experience that I am interested in explicitating here. (More precise convergences and divergences will be clarified in the Findings).

Procedures
The participants were each asked to provide written descriptions in response to the following question: "Please describe a particular situation in which you felt left out. Please be as thorough as you can, including how the event began and ended". A sample of sine of these descriptions, with the names changed, are provided in the Appendix to this paper. (The examples referred to in the Results section are for the most part drawn from these descriptions). These descriptions, once collected, were read carefully by the researcher, who subsequently interviewed each participant. These interviews involved only nondirected requests for clarification of details already mentioned, such as "can you tell me more about that?" Interviewees did recall additional helpful specifics through this verbal recounting that had not been included in their original written text.

Data analysis
These elaborated descriptions were then analysed by means of phenomenological procedures, whose aim was to discern the essential meanings of the situation for the person who lived it. Given this interest, theoretical hypotheses concerning causal explanations and questions about the 'objective reality' of the person's perspective were bracketed, or set aside. For example, in Michael's description, he feels that everyone else in the group had actually 'hung out' at the Burger Chef the previous night. Had all these others in fact been there? Had they all ever been there? Perhaps not, but that possibility is not the one lived by Michael. It is possible to

imagine someone else in Michael's position taking that perspective (of doubting they'd been there). And to entertain this imagined variation helps to see more clearly what Michael's perspective was. But it is the person's own perspective that the researcher empathizes with and seeks to explicitate in the analysis.

Implicit meanings were comprehended on the basis of their place in the experience as a structural whole. The findings from each protocol were then compared in order to clarify the general structural coherence of the experience of being left out. This empirical 'cross checking' - completed by imagining additional possible variations - allows the researcher to notice that something essential is shared in each of them. But what is essential to all of them is not any one common 'element'. For instance, some subjects felt left out of peer groups, but others felt left out by their boyfriend, or their family. What is common is not the particular person involved. Rather, it is the emergent *meaning* of being left out that is the shared essence of the experience. And it is this essential meaning that is understood and elaborated as the findings of the research.

FINDINGS

Overview
Experiencing ourselves as left out evokes an intensely disquieting and painful emotional storm. Previously taken for granted meanings of who we are for others, and who they are for us, are sundered from their past familiar anchors, and now become highly questionable. The smooth reciprocity of self-other relations gives way, and we are confronted by a disturbing negativity. This negativity expresses itself as a tear in the unfolding tapestry of mutual recognition between ourselves and the others. This gap may be a fissure or an abyss, but it discloses an essential break in our connectedness with others.

We become attuned to such a rupture specifically in those situations in which we experience a heightened vulnerability to isolation as a virtual possibility, and, with it, a need for reassurance that we truly matter to the other. Essentially, these are occasions in which there is some sort of social gathering, formal or informal: a coming together that will thematize the bonds between people who care about each other. But our own place within this interpersonal circle is unclear, ambiguous; it requires a clarifying invitation from another. We look, with trepidation, to the other; but our appeal goes unheeded, even unnoticed. Rather than finding the mutuality we sought, we discover instead and in horror that we are invisible to the others, to those who matter to us, and whose solicitude we had wanted so badly. In this way, the previous gnawing possibility of isolation proves inescapable; its preceding virtuality now becomes an all-consuming reality. We find ourselves left out of the circle of reciprocal recognition and acceptance.

The explicitation of the details of this experience follows.

The ground of mutuality

The experience of feeling left out, as a problematic mode of sociality, bursts into full presence against its prevailing ground of unproblematic sociality; that is, of previously lived mutuality. Furthermore, the ongoing continuity of this mutuality is taken for granted by the participant. With regard to the experience that is about to unfold the most significant aspect of this lived sociality is the person's tacit sense of nonconditional and nonjudgmental acceptance from others, based upon a felt sense of togetherness and reciprocity of perspectives. Indeed, only because we are so much at home with others can we take the continuity of this togetherness so for granted. To be more precise, others are "those from whom, for the most part, one does *not* distinguish oneself - those among whom one is too" (Heidegger, 1927/1962, p. 154). This experience of mutuality is lived on both personal and prepersonal levels, even to the anonymous level of The They. Specific examples of this social harmony include Mark's 'old group' with which, as he says, "bonds were formed between us that I felt were solid". Also exemplary is Fred's participation in the organizational support of the Navajo gathering as Director of Parking and sharing their evening together by the fire, or Michael's old school, in which he felt an "easy, sunny" togetherness with his classmates. These cases exemplify the person's unquestioned sense of being related to others, and that both self and others have the same sense of this relatedness.

The announcement of possible isolation

Against this ground, a situation arises which changes the participant's social world, that is, the network of their involvement with actually present others. This shift in the existential milieu discloses a certain vulnerability to isolation. It can take one of two forms. First, it could arise following the break-up of the prevailing mutually agreed upon meaning of a relationship. Such a change could be precipitated through an actual breakup, as in Jackie's case when her boyfriend decides that in light of his moving away the relationship should end. Or else the significance of the relationship could be essentially disrupted, as in Sarah's case when her sister announces her impending marriage, or when a couple have their first child. Second, this change in interpersonal relatedness may also be given through a change in the person's location with the consequently different relations involved in that new situation. For example, Glenda goes with her boyfriend to spend the Christmas holidays at his ex-in-laws; Fred is alone in a different culture in a new part of the country; Michael has just returned from two years in Greece; Jim is just beginning a new graduate school, as is Marie.

What is essentially common to these variations is that an existential change has taken place within the person's social network, a change which calls into question one's own position within these relationships. This change reveals a new vulnerability to social isolation. With this possibility, the phenomenon of feeling left out manifests itself as an initially prethematic need to be included within the present social matrix. This need itself may first become thematic through the reflection of an other who is him or herself left out of the social fabric. For example, Michael thinks about his friend John who seemed to have no other friends, Glenda notices her daughter who is being ignored by the only other child at her in-law's Christmas gathering, or the petroleum engineer whom Fred noticed had no involvement with anyone else, or the other Anglos who arrived the next night and remained separate from the Navajos at the fire. This reflection discloses one's own vulnerability to being likewise isolated, as a virtual possibility. It speaks to the person, precisely in the terms of his/her current context of being already out of his/her usual interpersonal milieu. As Romanyshyn (1978) noted, the other's behaviour can reflect my experience.

Finding oneself beyond the circle of mutuality
This need is then brought to fully thematic awareness through the reflection of the presence of interpersonal mutuality among nearby others. For example, Michael notices the other students at recess are already grouped together as friends; Al, upon entering the party alone, sees his friends already coupled off; Glenda notices the closeness and sharing between her boyfriend and his ex-wife; Fred notices the bond among the Navajos; Marie notices the other two students talking together at the lecture; as does Linda with her two friends at their meeting. Essentially, these present others are themselves connected in some basic, shared way, such that who they are as a person seems not to be an issue for each other. With that sense of acceptance, their inclusion is not lived as a question by them. The left out person, on the other hand, does not experience this same non-judgmental acceptance from the others, does not feel a part of that circle. This exclusion can either be a sense of simply not being noticed at all by the other (as in most cases), or of being seen only in a critical way, as in Susan's case, when she attended a ball game with her new boyfriend and was stared at by the others, who were friends of the boyfriend's old girlfriend.

In either case, this exclusion is lived as a fundamental separateness. Indeed, as Jackie said, she felt 'a wall' between her and the other. The gap between the person and the others becomes thematic as a distance. A vast gap or chasm yawns between self and other. Even though objectively they are right next to each other, phenomenologically they are very far apart. As Al said, he felt "totally removed" from the others at the party. This distance is experienced as the lived spatiality of the situation. The others are experienced as "remote", as "distant", as "aloof", as "far away". In addition, this distance is embodied as a coldness, that is, the absence of the warm nearness of another. Linda feels explicitly "cold"; Marie, when she desparately struggles to initiate a conversation, can think only to say that she feels "cold". The distance is such that the person does not feel recognized by the other(s). The others are seen as insensitive to the subject's need for inclusion. For example, Glenda says that at this point her boyfriend "made no attempt to make me feel... comfortable".

The person feels invisible to the others, as not really there as far as the others are concerned. For example, Jim received no feedback from anyone in the class exercise designed to tell others how they are perceived. Sarah says "I was invisible to my sister". Glenda felt that she "did not count" and indeed was merely "in the way". The other is not there with the person, they have withdrawn. And in this withdrawal, the person feels the loss of a part of themselves. (Paul Young: "Every time you go away, you take a piece of me with you"). A shriveling-up takes place. The person embodies this loss in relation to others as a shrinking of their own body. Linda wrote "I feel my chest tighten and my body seems to shrink". In other words, now that the person needs the recognition of the other, they embody the other's perspective on them, which is precisely a lack of presence. Their own body, now as a body-for-the-other, embodies this experience of being absent, insignificant, by becoming the proverbial wall flower. The body as lived, then, far from being an object, expresses and carries out the projects of the person, a "bodying forth" of the meaning they are living, to use Boss's (1983) term.

The dynamic of ambivalent claims

The possible meanings of this exclusion by others exhibit a typology which can be arrayed upon a continuum whose poles are: "I want to be included but am not entitled to be" to "I want to be included and am entitled to be". Basically, the feeling of being left out is essentially founded upon wanting to be included, but varies according to the extent to which the person feels entitled to inclusion. While in every case the exclusion is lived as a lack of sensitivity by the other, in those cases where inclusion is considered a right, the person also experiences the other as being unfair. Basically, the other is seen as treating the person unfairly because "you should have known what I was feeling". In many cases, the person's experience is mixed, between these two poles, so that the person is ambivalent about their right to inclusion (as best exemplified in Sarah's case). This sense of entitlement itself has two types: neurotic or intimate. Neurotic claims are of the structure well-described by Horney (1950), wherein the person asserts a right based on an unrealistic expectation, one rooted only in an idealized image of oneself, which is itself based upon the fear of being unloved for who one is. In other words, one fears that he/she does not matter to the others whose love is important to him/her.

In the case of being left out, feeling entitled to inclusion provides a way to save the assumption of interpersonal continuity when it can no longer be taken for granted. For example, Joy's sense of being entitled to inclusion justifies and so provides her with a way to hold on to her assumption of togetherness even after John's exclusion of her calls it into question. Her psycho-logic here is 'thought it isn't so, it should be so'. A subtle variant of this sense of entitlement arises when one feels the right to be included because he/she so desparately *needs* such inclusion. For example, after Marie's friends left her alone, she expected other classmates whom she did not know to include her in their plans.

On the other hand, not all feelings of being entitled to the other's recognition are based on idealizations. A second type of entitlement rests upon the intimate nature of the relationship between self and other. For example, Glenda's anger at her fiancee reveals her sense of feeling entitled to his including her in the Christmas festivities for which they've gone to his family's house. But, in this case, her sense of having a right to expect such inclusion rests not on an idealized image, but on the nature of their relationship. (Of course, it is always possible that a person may experience neurotic claims toward another with whom they are intimately related).

Distance and reconciliation
What now becomes thematic for the person is that he/she does not share the interpersonal world within which the others are dwelling together. He/she is not at home in the world. The distance between self and other is too great. This sense of distance is lived in either of two ways: as bridgeable or as hopelessly unbridgeable. If lived as unbridgeable, as in Fred's case, the person experiences a poignant and melancholy feeling of being lonely, an aching, as Fred says, "in my throat". Indeed, that marks the possible transformation of this experience into the experience of loneliness, which essentially involves a loss of faith in the possibility of deep connections with others (Ingram, 1985).

On the other hand, if lived as bridgeable, efforts are then undertaken to make contact with the others. Conversation is the key mode of togethering, and is engaged in, not for an interest in the topic, but specifically as a means to connect. Recall how Fred, for instance, upon feeling the togethering to be impossible, felt an aching specifically *in his throat*. The unvoiced voice, the unspoken togethering, aches as it remains in one's own throat. On the other hand, those persons who do see the gap as bridgeable speak out in an attempt to achieve a togetherness. For instance, Linda asks about a tape recording the others are talking about, even though, as she says, "I am aware of using my interest to become a part of their sharing because I do not feel interested in the tape". Marie also wants to join a conversation between two others, but does not know any of the gossip they are talking about. She says, "I tried to keep the conversation going but for lack of anything else to say I simply mentioned I felt sort of cold". Other efforts include acting out, performing outrageous acts to gain the attention of the other as Jackie did with her boyfriend.

What is essentially common here is that both the speaking and acting are fundamentally engaged in as modes of expression, that is, self-expression. The person who feels unnoticed by the other announces his or her presence to the other, by expressing him/herself, as a project undertaken in the hope of gaining the other's recognition. Sometimes these are successful to a certain extent, and the feeling of being left out is gradually overcome as the person feels included. Other times, these efforts fail and reveal that the gap between self and the other was in fact unbridgeable, the differences too extreme or inherent to overcome. For example, Michael tries to join in a conversation with classmates, only to discover that they are talking about experiences he has never had.

In these cases, the failure of the attempt to connect hurts. The person may experience this pain explicitly, or they may anesthesize it in different ways. Some attempt to cover it up, as Michael did by continuing to stand with the group and pretend to belong in the conversation. Or they may flee from the other, as Sarah did when she locked herself in her room and then left the house altogether after her sister announced her engagement to be married. Or they may simply not attend to the meanings of the situation, in which the latent meanings prickle from the periphery, leaving the person diffusely irritable.

The who of the other
Thus, being left out involves a collapse of one's taken for granted ongoing relatedness with others, a collapse of the experience of mutual recognition and respect for each other as persons. With this loss, one's self is lost as well, in the sense in which one's self is the nexus of the specific self-world-other relations one had been living. With this loss of self, the other's perspective is accorded a certain priority. That is, if self and other are no longer related within a fundamental mutuality, there then arises the question of who's on top (and who's on the bottom); or, as Sartre put it, the Master-Slave dialectic of who is to be the subject and who the object. Without reciprocity, we are left in an opposition of perspectives. In feeling left out, the other's perspective takes on a certain priority, especially if the only imagined way to re-achieve mutuality is by giving up one's own perspective in order to merge oneself into the other, by seeing oneself through the point of view of the other. Given that being left out involves the loss of one's mundane self, this consequence is quite near at hand. A particularly clear example is the way in which Michael pretends to the others from whom he feels left out that he does not in fact feel left out by them. Basically, he feels that "if it can't be so, it must look like it is so". Such supremacy is given to the others' viewpoint that Michael feels that salvation from his own feelings lies with others not seeing that he feels them. In other words, Michael feels so objectified by the viewpoint of the other that he can only recapture his own subjectivity to the extent that he can successfully portray for the other that he has not lost it. (Such also was the situation in traditional psychological experiments in which the person didn't feel free to admit to another that the situation was an emergency or that two lines were not the same size).

DISCUSSION

These findings shed light on the everyday horizon of being-with-others, and help to explicate its implicit structure. Specifically, the contingency and disruptability of its typical, taken for granted, mutuality is most clearly brought to light here. Furthermore, these results also point toward an explication of just what it is that we are for the most part included into rather than left out of. Essentially, to share a mutuality of inclusion with other means to experience oneself as accepted nonjudgmentally by the others; that is, one's participation with others can be assumed rather than the subject to the judgment of the other.

To press this issue even further begins to verge on the ineffable, yet the emergent next question is: inclusion into what? What is it that a person for the most part feels nonjudgmentally accepted into? By grasping its absence in the experience of feeling left out, we are now in position to suggest that, at the level of our most basic, taken for granted experience, we live a 'bond' of reciprocity with others. That is to say, we live a 'world' with others, a world of mattering constituted by the bonds of reciprocal recognition. As a consequence, when we are left out of 'their' world, we are left out of 'our' world, of 'the' world. And with this loss of this phenomenological world as "the sense which is revealed where the paths of my various experiences... and other people's intersect and engage each other like gears". This bond is rooted in our basic visibility to each other. That is, it is a bond based upon being both seer and seen for each other. Recall how, in the experience of feeling left out, people experience themselves as being 'invisible' to others. Jim, for instance, is not recognized by anyone in his class; Sarah feels unseen by her sister; Jackie makes desperate actions trying to get her boyfriend to notice her. Perceptual life itself, in other words, is already embedded intersubjectively, with the consequence that, within the social matrix, mutual visibility serves as a mirroring, in which each person reflects the other (Romanyshyn, 1982). More specifically, the other's behaviour reflects my experience, and vice versa (Romanyshyn, 1978). This sense of the other as a reflection of the self's involvement in the social matrix is what becomes especially thematic in the nascence of the feeling left out experience.

A related issue concerns the question of how self and other could get so far apart in the first place. The descriptions show that the person who feels left out has been overlooked by the other, specifically in the sense of being taken for granted. But how is it that one can be so taken for granted by another, an other whose solicitude matters so much? The other is pre-occupied - that is, the other is occupied in advance with other concerns (other people, projects, things, television) and so not able to become occupied with relating to the person who feels left out. There is a profound irony at work here, in the sense that being taken for granted by the specific other is what hurts, and yet the person involved had him/herself previously taken for granted the continuity of a reciprocal sociality. Such paradoxical dynamics of awakefulness/asleepfulness seem deeply engrained within human existence in general, and especially within its intersubjective horizons.

The question of the ground
The analysis of being left out disclosed the significance of the ground of mutuality as that which is disrupted by the experience of feeling left out. But what if this preceding grounding were itself absent? In that variation, the experience itself would be essentially different. It would then not be one of feeling left out, but rather of never having been at home with others in the first place. This latter sense appears to be an essential constituent of some serious psychopathology (Van den Berg, 1972), which is an essentially different experience than that explicitated in this study. However, that is not to suggest that these two experiences have nothing in common. Approached dialectically, it may be possible to determine if there is anything that is essential to both. In both cases, the person involved experiences a loss of the specific self-world-other relations that are habitually lived through. This loss shatters the sleepy taken-for-granted immersion in the mundane, and renders it all very strange and unfamiliar. To that extent, it may be said that the experience of feeling left out is similar to a miniature psychotic episode, with all its attendant losses of shared familiarity.

Reflections on method
The preceding analysis was based upon a specifically phenomenological method - that is, one that began with the bracketing of objectivistic presuppositions about reality, in order to turn from objects to meanings, to meanings as they were lived. It is possible to imagine an objectivistic psychology's response to such a study. From an objectivistic point of view, such a phenomenological starting point must seem inappropriate. To take psychoanalysis as an example, the psychoanalyst would expect to find a mismatch between the objective facts and the experience of the person feeling left out. Specifically, the psychoanalyst would suggest that the others have not in fact left out the person; that he/she is mistaken in this belief. Furthermore, this mistake is not random, but rather is the necessary consequence of the unconscious process of projection, whereby the person has projected his/her own self-hate outward onto the other, and is thus erroneously experiencing the other's disregard in place of their own self-contempt. Such projection is furthermore understood to be motivated by a desire to escape from the anxiety one would experience were one to become fully present to one's own self-hatred. Given this motivated error, it is inappropriate to approach the experience phenomenologically. Rather, it must be approached psychoanalytically in order to grasp the essential role of unconscious projection to the structure of the experience.

In response to this argument, we should return to the experience in order to discover whether we can in fact phenomenologically discern how the participant lived the phenomenon to which the concept of projection refers. In doing so, we find that, as a phenomenon, it is not absent from the findings. Rather, it is explicated in terms of the self-other relation. It is rooted in the feeling that one doesn't matter as much to the other as one wants/needs to. It is thus that the viewpoint of the other acquires such supremacy that it disrupts to mutuality of self-other reciprocity. To return to the psychoanalytic example of the projection of one's own self hatred, in that case, one's own salvation lies in others (Horney, 1950) precisely because when one is so hard oneself, one can only be saved by the good opinion of the other. But that means precisely that others' opinions count for so much. The other matters more than the self. That is the case with the phenomenon of projection in general. One's own perspective loses its autochthonous authority precisely when the felt lack of mutuality so disrupts the typical reciprocity of self-other relations that the presumed perspective of the other assumes such paramount significance as to hold sway over our own. But precisely because the lived phenomenon of projection is itself grounded *in* the experience of being left out, it cannot itself be taken as a conceptual explanation *for* the experience of being left out. Such a conceptual reversal forgets, rather than illuminates, its own experiential ground.

Concluding ontological implications

The ontology of self-other relations is a thorny thicket of competing viewpoints, expressed most articulately by Heidegger (1927/1962), Sartre (1943/1953), and Merleau-Ponty (1945/1962). In contradistinction to Heidegger and Merleau-Ponty, Sartre insists that there is an essential problematic at the heart of self-other relations (the Master-Slave dialectic). In contrast, this paper suggests that such a problematic arises specifically when the prevailing mutuality is disrupted. Only then are we faced with the Sartrean dialectic. It is thus a founded rather than founding mode of social existence, a second mapping rather than a first mapping of the terrain of intersubjectivity.

SUMMARY

The experience of being left out emerges when one's standing with others is called into question, and it presents itself as the absence of the hoped for reciprocity of mutual concern. One's taken for granted sense of being *among* others is thereby negated, and in its wake is a void, a gaping separateness between self and other. In the face of this distance, the self is experienced as anonymous before the other, whose nonrecognition casts no reflection of the self's concern for mutuality.

REFERENCES

Asch, S.E. (1955). Opinions and social pressure. *Scientific American,* 193. 31-35.
Boss, M. (1983). *Existential foundations of psychology and medicine.* (Trans. by P. Stern). New York: Jason Aronson. (Originally published in 1971).
Giorgi, A. (Ed.) (1985). *Phenomenology and psychological research.* Pittsburgh: Duquesne University Press.
Grant, R. (1986). Existential themes and psychotherapy. Paper presented to the meeting of the Depth Phenomenology Circle, Carrollton, GA.
Heidegger, M. (1962). *Being and time.* (Trans. by Macquarrie & Robinson). New York: Harper & Row. (Originally published in 1927).
Horney, K. (1950). *Neurosis and human growth.* New York: Norton.
Ingram, D. (1985). *Losing faith: the experience of loneliness.* Unpublished Master's Thesis. West Giorgia College.
Keen, E. (1975). *A primer in phenomenological psychology.* New York: Holt, Rinehart & Winston.
Kruger, D. (1979). *An introduction to phenomenological psychology.* Pittsburgh: Duquesne University Press.
Lapointe, F.H. (1976). The existence of alter egos: Jean-Paul Sartre and Maurice Merleau-Ponty. *Journal of phenomenological psychology,* 6. 209-216.
Latane, B., & Darley, J.M. (1970). *The unresponsive bystander.* New York: Appleton.
Merleau-Ponty, M. (1962). *Phenomenology of perception* (Trans. by C. Smith). New York: Humanities. (Originally published in 1945).
Romanyshyn, R.D. (1978). Psychology and the attitude of science. In R. Valle & M. King (Eds.), *Existential phenomenological alternative for psychology* (pp. 18-47). New York: Oxford University Press.
Romanyshyn, R.D. (1982). *Psychological life: from science to metaphor.* Austin: University of Texas Press.
Sartre, J.P. (1953). *Being and nothingness* (Trans. by H.E. Barnes). New York: Philosophical Library. (Originally published in 1943).
Van den Berg, J.H. (1972). *A different existence.* Pittsburgh: Duquesne University Press.
Wertz, F.J. (1983). From everyday to psychological description: analyzing the moments of a qualitative data analysis. *Journal of Phenomenological Psychology,* 14. 197-241.
Wertz, F.J. (1984). Procedures in phenomenological research and the question of validity. In C.M. Aanstoos (Ed.), *Exploring the Lived World: Readings in Phenomenological Psychology* (p. 29-48). Carrollton: West Georgia College.

APPENDIX : NINE SAMPLE WRITTEN DESCRIPTIONS FROM THE PARTICIPANTS

Fred's description
An experience of feeling left out occurred a couple of weeks after the Canyonlands incident. From Canyonlands, I had hitched south through the Navajo and Hopi Nations, taking my time. I then headed towards Dalton Pass, northeast of Gallup, New Mexico, to a gathering held to protest the uranium mining going on in the area. Dalton Pass is not a town but a desert crossroads on the Continental Divide. It is in the heart of the checkerboard region, so named due to the interspersion of land areas owned by the Navajo Tribe and individual Navajo families. I had arrived a day earlier than the official beginning date and so helped set up tents, dig latrines and such. Working with the gathering organizers (both Anglo and Navajo) and the handful of others who showed up early facilitated making acquaintanceships and gave me a feeling of belonging. I also took responsibility for coordinating parking for the next day's deluge of arrivals, which added to the feeling. That first evening, before the gathering began, we all sat around a blazing fire eating mutton stew and fry-bread, about twenty of us, old Navajo men and women with creased faces who spoke no English and were at home around a fire at night, Navajo youth with long black hair, and young Anglos, mostly listening. Despite our differences, I felt like we shared something fundamental, though nothing of that nature was spoken. It was a magic time; I sensed a kind of earthy, ancient wisdom. The next day people arrived by the hundreds. Tents sprang up, scheduled speakers and workshops got underway, and I was meeting new people and orienting them to the place. That evening, after eating dinner and night had fallen, I sat with a couple of new friends on a hillside at the periphery of the gathering area. Below was scattered movement as people prepared for the night; groups, couples, individuals here and there, involved in their own tasks. However, around the blazing fire where I had been the previous evening was another gathering - the beating of drums and chanting voices drifted across to me as the Navajo people came together. I longed to be a part of that singing; beautiful, measured, and wild, it seemed to rise from the earth itself. But I knew that even if I walked over and stood with them and tried to be a part of it, they were sharing something that did not include me. I sat there feeling kind of lonely and cut off, a poignant ache in my throat. I mentioned it to my companions, who didn't empathize much. I listened awhile, then with melancholy went back to the tent and joined the other sleeping bodies.

Glenda's description
When I first met John he made it clear that although he was dating me he was still very much attached to his former wife, Barbara, and her family. Instead of us developing our own holiday traditions as time went by, he continued to plan holidays around his ex-in-laws, both at Thanksgiving and Christmas. He could not understand why I had a difficult time with this arrangement and sometimes his devotion to them and his insistence on maintaining traditions that he had developed with them made me very unhappy. We met in August 1980 and the most painful incident connected with a holiday happened the Christmas of 1981. As usual, John called Barbara to make arrangements some time before Christmas and we drove to Columbia - her parents' home - on Christmas day. I was already feeling uncomfortable. My daughter Diana was with us. She had her own 'left out' feeling to deal with. There was one younger child in the family, a girl about six years older than Diana. Diana would have enjoyed playing with this child but she pretty much ignored my daughter. Consequently I worried about Diana too. The day before we drove to Columbia, John had flown in from a business trip to California, loaded down with gifts - mostly for his ex-wife and her family and we had spent hours and hours wrapping them. In addition he had given Barbara's mother money to buy an outfit for Barbara. He had also bought one of Barbara's sisters a beautiful white silk kimono. I could not believe he had bought something like that for someone else. It was such a beautiful romantic garment and it had not occurred to him that I would have loved to have it. After all the preparations I was exhausted and by the time we got to Columbia I was feeling a lot less than festive. John's

whole attitude to me while we were there was defensive and offhand. He made no attempt to make me feel special or comfortable. I could not understand how, if these were people he loved so much, that being with them would not make him happy and therefore glad to be with me. When we got to Columbia, Barbara presented John with a Christmas stocking. He went off with her to open it, and he seemed very happy to have it. I already fixed him a stocking at home to which he had not paid a great deal of attention, and I asked Barbara why she had given him a stocking. "Because he asked me to", she replied. It still hurts to remember how I felt then - so left out. As I recall, he had known that I was going to fix him a stocking and he went ahead and asked Barbara for one anyway. That meant to me that what I did for him did not count. If he had told me that he had asked her for one I would have known what was going on, but as far as he was concerned it had nothing to do with me and there was no reason for him to tell me. The rest of the holiday went from bad to worse. John continued to be rude and offhand to me. I was so hurt that I could hardly keep from crying. Diana was having her own problems with the other child, but I was in no shape to give her any support. Barbara's family was embarrassed because it was so obvious that John's behavior was making me so unhappy. I also felt angry and powerless because I had got into this situation and he had taken for granted that I would put up with what was going on. After Christmas, John was going to fly directly from Columbia to Boston to see his mother. No suggestion had been made that we would have part of the holiday alone to spend together. I was supposed to drive him to the airport, bid him a fond farewell, and then drive home to Carrollton. Here was one point at which I could get some control over the situation. I could hardly stand to be around him so I decided that some member of his beloved ex-family could take him to the airport, and I would leave at my own convenience - which is what I did. It didn't make me feel much better because I was so deeply unhappy, but at least I didn't have to hang around while he made it abundantly clear to me and everyone else that I was in the way. Barbara couldn't see anything wrong with what had gone on and it never occurred to her that her days of making Christmas stockings for John ended when she told him she wanted a divorce. The years have passed and we have discussed this incident. John is no longer deeply attached to Barbara, although she and her family are still important to him. We both understand much better what the other was feeling during times like the Christmas of 1981. Eventually, John told me that I was the most important person in his life, not Barbara anymore, but that didn't happen until we were living together.

Linda's description

I am visiting a friend's house for a coven meeting which occurs bi-weekly. There are three of us in the coven, and we are all friends both within the group and outside of the group. I am sitting on the floor with Sharon on my right on the couch and Elaine of my left, also on the floor. I feel slightly shaky upon being with the group again, because I have not seen either of them since the last time we met. I feel eager to feel connected again with both of them. Sharon asks Elaine if she is enjoying the tape she got the other day from her. Elaine lights up and says she has listened to it several times. I feel uneasy suddenly and somewhat afraid or, more so, more distant than when I entered. I have pictures of them walking to each other's houses to exchange interesting information and to visit over tea. I feel jealous that they live within two blocks of each other, and I live several miles. Suddenly, I believe that if I lived closer I would not be left out of such treasures. As I'm thinking this, I feel my chest tighten and my body seems to shrink. The distance between us seems further, for one brief moment almost a gap that seems unbridgeable. Elaine and Sharon appear very close and their closeness seems to leave no room for me. Then, I gather up the courage and break through the barrier to ask the name of the tape. I am aware of using my interest to become a part of their sharing because I do not feel interested in the tape. I am more aware of not being included. Elaine turns to me and tells me the name. I feel warmth toward Elaine and appreciate her for including me. I ask her what the "Goddess tapes" are about, and she begins to tell me. She has turned her body to face me more and is looking me in the eyes. I feel her acknowledging or recognizing me. Although I still feel somewhat contracted, it is as though a thawing is occurring. I feel warmer or more open although still not sure of my grounding. Elaine feels closer to me than Sharon, who appears cold and distant still.

Marie's description

It was only the second or third time our class had met and we were getting out early to listen to G. Gordon Liddy speak at the Phys. Ed. Building. I walked out of class with the two students I had become friends with. We were halfway to the Phys. Ed. Building when they decided they didn't want to listen to Liddy, so we said good-bye and they headed home. I continued to walk towards the Phys. Ed. Building, suddenly very aware of my aloneness: I wanted to see Liddy but I didn't want to go alone. Looking behind me I saw three girls from my class, and feeling slightly relieved, I waited for them. When they reached the door, we greeted each other as I fell in behind them. Although we were all seated together on the bleachers, I didn't feel a part of them because I was sitting on the end and the girl next to me had her back to me. When she did turn around and acknowledge my presence by asking what my name was again, I was thrilled with the prospect of being included. I tried to keep the conversation going but for lack of anything else to say I simple mentioned I felt sort of cold. She gave me her jacket and then turned back around. They continued to laugh and converse until deciding to leave to get a beer. After they got up and left me sitting there I wondered what it was about me that made them not want to include me. A few minutes later the girl who had been sitting with her back to me came back in the auditorium. Oh, I thought, she has come to ask me to go drinking with them; wasn't that nice of her to come back for me. "Hi", she said, "can I have my jacket". "Oh sure" I said, "good-bye". "Good-bye".

Michael's description

Although I can think of other examples of times when I've felt left out, they seem to be milder instances which themselves point back to a more significant situation, which was the first time I really felt left out, so that's the one I'll describe. It was actually a series of occasions that occurred over the course of a year (the year I was in eighth grade). Though I'll try to focus my description on one particular day, it really fits within this longer time span. That was the year my family returned to the U.S. after living in Greece for two years. Though I returned to the same school I'd been attending before we went to Greece, many of the students were different (in the Washington, D.C. suburbs families were always being transferred in and out), and those that I'd known before had since gone on to share a history of which I'd not been a part. (When I think back on it now, it surprises me how few of the students there had actually been there before I'd gone to Greece. I'd estimate only 10%. It hardly seems possible that it could have been that low, but that's what it seemed like to me). Basically, I felt that I was in a situation in which everyone else was already involved with friendships with each other but me. During class time that wasn't really obvious, it was at recess that I'd become particularly self-conscious about it. Let me now describe a particular instance of it. Lunch is over. Heading outside to the parking lot, to stand around for another recess. Looking around for a familiar face, for someone to hang out with. I don't see John. He's the one person I've become friends with. We spend a lot of recesses together. He doesn't seem to have many other friends either. I can see why, he's sort of out of it. Well, not really with me, but when I look at him as others see him he seems inadequate somehow - "a good boy" - he wants to be a priest. But he's not here today. The parking lot seems to be already broken up into little knots of people, each group already hooked up together with themselves. And I'm left out. I feel so self-conscious not being in a group. I can't help but think how ridiculous I must look if anyone were to see me. So embarrassing. Fortunately, they don't seem to notice. But I hate this, I've got to find a group whose conversation I can join in with. Looking around. (Actually looking at only the boy's groups. They're so gender divided, unlike Ursuline School was in Greece. There I'd already had 'girl-friends', kissed, and written 'love letters'. Here I'm a world away from anything like that. There it was always sunny, easy, here it's overcast). Well, there's Frank, talking in a group. At least I know him a little bit, I'll go over and join in with his conversation.

Just walking over right there next to him now, and pretending it's not such an uncomfortable effort, pretending I don't feel as awkward and out of place as I feel. "Hi". About six or eight guys, they're talking about their having hung out at the Burger Chef last night. Sounds great, but also so unimaginably foreign to my own experience. I've never hung out at the Burger Chef at night - with them or anybody else. They seem so worldly, it's hard to believe we're even the same age. I become self-conscious of my naïveté concerning such worldly affairs. I feel strongly left out of this more experienced world that they share. Not that they've purposely left me out of it, but rather that they've all gone on into it, and I'm left behind because I wasn't around when they entered it. There's such a chasm between my world and theirs, between me and them right now, I feel that I'm simply standing next to them, not really with them. It's like the physical proximity is a disguise, covering over the real distance that I'm feeling, a distance that's so painful, too painful to leave uncovered. So I seek at least to have the form of proximity so that I won't look as left out as I feel. But it's still very awkward, uncomfortable, though not quite as bad. When is this recess going to end, anyway?

Sarah's description
On a bright summer afternoon my sister came home from college with her boy-friend. That night she told me they were going to get married that November. I went to my room and did not come out the rest of the night. My sister and I had been very close. She always petted me. She is a year older than I. But she had nothing to say to me the rest of the weekend. She did not talk to me. It was as if I were not there. When she returned to school I felt as if she hadn't really been home - it had been a bad dream. This was the way is was every time she came until the week of the wedding. She returned home Wednesday before the approaching Saturday wedding. It got worse Friday night before the rehearsal. I felt that no one cared if I were there or not, so I left. I came home late but they were having a party. It was after midnight (go to bed). I was very lonely and there was a house full of people. I was invisible to my sister.

Jim's description
Last quarter I took a course under Mike in which we did an exercise on expressing our desires. Each of us was to write down three desires directed at three different people in the class. Being new at this school, I was looking forward to sharing these with my fellow students. We gave all of our papers to Mike, at which point he began handing out everybody's 'mail'. As he called out names I was eagerly anticipating how much mail I would get and from whom. The pile of mail finally dwindled away. Some people got more than one piece of mail while there were a few who did not get any mail at all. I was one of those who received no mail. I was very disappointed. I just knew that I would get at least one piece of mail, but I did not. I most definitely felt left out. We then went around the class and shared what mail we had gotten and how we felt about it. If we had received no mail we were asked to express how we felt about that. It was curious to me that everyone who did not receive any mail except for me said that it made no difference. I told the class that I was very much bothered by the fact that I did not receive any mail from anyone. And not only was I disturbed by this, but several of the others who had gotten something expressed how badly they felt because some of us were left out. Being new on campus, I already felt somewhat lonely. However, this experience took me from 'somewhat to very'. After getting over the initial trauma, I decided that being left out was not something others did to me, but rather something I did to myself. The responsibility of belonging lay squarely on my shoulders.

Mark's description
Last quarter I was in a class with a group of people that grew to be very close. Because of the nature of the subject matter and the personal sharing that took place, bonds were formed between us that I felt were solid. The quarter ended and everyone went his or her own way. Upon my return to campus I registered for my new classes and found none of the 'old group' in any of them. However, when I finally did see one of the 'old group' I was elated. There were

hugs, kisses and the usual convivialities, but something of the old closeness was conspicuously absent. I found the same lack of closeness shortly thereafter upon seeing another of the 'old group'. I wondered whether their actions were justified considering the circumstances prevailing at that time. I nevertheless felt left out when I overheard one from the old group inviting someone to a party. I was anticipating an invitation which did not come. At that moment I felt that I must have done something wrong to deserve such an obvious snub, and I couldn't help wonder what happened to the closeness that had been established a short time ago. As it turned out, though, the party was for females only and no males were invited. I felt a little foolish and somewhat full of myself for being so judgmental. I have subsequently seen that person many times and none of the left out feelings remained, but the closeness has not been regained.

Jackie's description

Although I have experienced numerous episodes of feeling left out of a situation, one instance in my life stands out from among the rest as a time when I felt most lonely. This event began about a year ago when a very close friend of mine decided that after his graduation from West Georgia College he would continue his education at another college. This change would mean for him the end of our friendship. By the word friend I do not mean just the everyday sense of the word but a much deeper meaning. To me a friend is a very special term to bestow on a person and is one that I do not toss around lightly. The two of us had been close for the past five years. It wasn't so much the fact that Scott had decided to change schools; that is part of college life, and although change in any form is often difficult to accept, perhaps I could have accepted his decision if it had not been for his rational approach to the change and toward me; that was what hurt the most. Scott acted as if our friendship was now at a point that it would simply end and that would be that. He even told me that he did not believe in keeping in touch with letters because all you ended up doing was re-hashing old times. Scott didn't even tell me about his decision, I found out about it through another. I was very angry at Scott for this, but he simply replied "no big deal" and a wall went up from him at that moment. His attitude toward me was impossible to deal with. One hour he would be the same caring person that I had always known and later he would act totally indifferent and even hostile toward me. He never seemed to have time to talk any more or even go to eat lunch, although he seemed to have plenty of time to talk and go places with others whom he was not well acquainted with. This hot and cold attitude built a wall between us. I think I felt as lonely during this time as I did later, perhaps more. I did not know how to deal with this constantly changing attitude; it made me crazy. I experienced a variety of emotions during this period: sadness at losing a person I cared so much for, especially the way I was losing him; anger at both Scott at his being such a bastard through the whole situation and at me for being unable to control my emotions; loneliness because Scott would not share his feelings with me; abandoned because Scott had for all practical purposes gone away already; confused about the emotional roller coaster I was riding; but most of all I felt betrayed by the one person I had trusted and admired for so long, and I hated him for that; I think I still do. I began to commit irrational acts, such as slamming doors around him in public places, driving dangerously in my car when I saw him, shouting in the halls when he was near, and picking fights with other friends when he was watching. My goal was to embarrass him; I succeeded in making an absolute ass of myself in front of others and losing other friends as well. However, I couldn't stop myself and began to drink heavily staying drunk most of the time. I felt lonely and guilty that somehow I had done something that caused his initial change in attitude toward me. Something I had done or not done was responsible for his constantly changing attitude. Blaming myself and hating him, I tried to make him hurt as much as I was hurting. The loneliness and emptiness were almost unbearable;   my best friend was going, and I could not cope with the change. It seemed as if no one cared and that I was all alone to face my loss. Abandoned and betrayed were how I felt during this period. Scott and I ended up hating each other. During his last three months here, we hardly spoke and then only in the briefest and politest of terms. I regret that very much.

Chapter 9

HOW PRIESTS EXPERIENCE CELIBACY

Anke Hoenkamp-Bisschops

Priests in the Roman Catholic church are not allowed to get married. This is for religious reasons: thus they are supposed to become closer to God. Many people consider this obligation to remain celibate an anachronism. However, very little is known about what this obligation means to priests, monks or nuns. The discussion here will be limited to priests, but many of the questions raised will also be applicable to the situation of monks and - perhaps less so - of nuns. In the sixties and seventies a great deal was published about priests who left the church, and in the last few years more has become known about priests who choose to have intimate relationships. However, the media do not cover how average priests experience their celibate life.

How do priests experience their state in life? How does celibacy influence their lives? What effect does it have on their contacts? How do they deal with the inevitable sexual tensions? What limitations do they impose upon themselves in their contacts with others? What role does their own religiosity play in experiencing and shaping their celibate life? These are only a few of the topics we still know very little about.

As a psychologist of religion, working at a training college for priests and pastoral workers, I became more and more interested in priests' experiences of being celibate. It puzzled me that we know so little about such a central domain of their life, one that no doubt greatly influences their work.

I particularly wanted to find out more about how priests in Holland conceive of this obligation. Not getting married may imply several different lifestyles. Some priests, for example, may feel obliged to abstain from any sexual experiences including masturbation, whereas others may have a steady intimate relationship with a woman (or man). Some may be perfectly happy living without a partner, whereas others may continuously be tempted to have a close relationship.

Not only did I want to discover how priests experience all this, I also hoped to gain some insight into why they experience it the way they do. How does the 'choice' for their lifestyle come about?

RESULTS OF EARLIER RESEARCH

Earlier social-scientific research on celibacy consisted mainly of large-scale opinion polls and sociological survey research. However, such research has provided little insight into the experience of being celibate. From the few psychological studies of celibacy, five factors have appeared to be important: an extreme mother fixation, the religious meaning of celibacy, the influence of the seminary training, the lack of correction by a partner, and the age at which the choice for celibacy is made. I will briefly review these results[1]. In a number of research projects, the common characteristics of priests have been investigated (Christensen, 1969; Potvin & Suziedelis, 1969; Rey, 1969). In short, the conclusions are that priests often come from families with a dominating mother and a father who was absent in their (sexual) upbringing. Whether this explains their subsequent choice for celibatarian priesthood is nevertheless doubtful, since other men may grow up in a similar situation and not become a priest.

Traditionally, overcoming genital sexuality by repression, sublimation or integration has been looked upon as the main problem of celibacy. Not until the sixties did researchers become aware of undeveloped affectivity as a problem of at least equal importance. Trimbos (1955) was one of the first to point to the more general problem of affective development in celibacy, by which he meant the growing capacity to entertain satisfying interpersonal relationships (see also Bowers, 1962). Likewise, Plé (1969) speaks of an immature affectivity, which can be expressed in different forms, varying from an unhealthy mother fixation to narcissism and homosexuality. Although Trimbos considers celibacy, when viewed from a mere psychobiological point of view, as a foolish and dangerous venture, he thinks that giving a religious meaning to celibacy can save it.

The cause of the fact that, according to many authors, celibacy often seems such a problem, may lie outside as well as inside of celibate life. Independent of the celibate experience itself, the training at the seminary many hamper affective development. Furthermore, it is inherent in celibate life that one does not have the opportunity to be corrected by a partner; something that constantly takes place in a dual existence (Trimbos, 1955).

The general consensus of opinion is that celibacy is not necessarily harmful, provided that certain conditions are met. These conditions concern the nature of training and the moment at which the decision is made to become a priest, i.e. celibate. Calon (1956) considers the protected education and training of priests to lead to their clumsiness in social contacts. Vergote (1967) puts more emphasis on the avoidance of conflicts in their training. He also points out that the usual repression of sexuality at seminaries damages the complete personality and, above all, affective development.

Mitchell (1970), who takes as a starting point the developmental stages of Erikson, thinks that most of the problems with celibate life are caused by the fact that the choice is made at too early an age. The choice to become a priest is an identity choice and traditionally takes place at the end of training, usually before the age of 25. Mitchell claims that a well thought-through choice for celibacy can not be made until Erikson's intimacy phase is reached, which means approximately at the age of 30.

This short overview of earlier research into celibacy shows hardly any solid results. Even in such a relatively well studied area as the consequences of celibacy, the results are meager. Moreover, this research is on the whole quite old. We don't know how the situation of celibate priests in the eighties looks. How about, for example, the new class of priests who nowadays do not undergo seminary training? But above all, the question of what celibacy means to priests and what kind of place it occupies in their lives remains unanswered.

THE RESEARCH PROJECT

COLLECTING THE DATA

When starting our research project on the celibacy of parish priests, one of the first questions was which research methods to use. Usual quantifying methods such as opinion polls and surveys did not seem adequate, because among other things they can not see through stable rationalizing strategies of the person under study. So the choice was made for depth-interviews, using a semi-structured questionnaire.

It was not clear to what extent priests could be expected to talk in an open-minded way about intimate matters concerning their celibacy, especially with a woman interviewer. It was therefore decided that all the interviews would be held by two interviewers together; the female psychologist together with an elderly priest with a long practice in counseling priests and nuns.

This combination of two interviewers indeed led to a great openness on the part of the interviewed persons. This is partly due to the co-interviewer who enjoys great confidence among his colleague priests in Holland. It also appears to be connected to the fact that the two interviewers combine different characteristics, such as old and young, male and female, colleague priest and outsider. Some people for example find it easier to open up to a woman than to a man, or vice versa. This also resulted in more in-depth probing on the part of the interviewers, since both interviewed from different points of view and from different attitudes towards life.

Wanting to find out about the how and the why of priests' experiences of celibacy, we also needed information about such topics as their growth toward celibacy, their sexual and affective development, their religiosity, etc. For this purpose, a detailed semi-structured list of questions was constructed. It contained such topics as family of origin, reasons for becoming a priest, years of training, history of work (including satisfaction in work), religiosity, sexuality, self-image, significant others, attitude towards the church legitimation of celibacy, and personal meaning of celibacy.

This elaborate list of questions was necessary in order to get an overall picture of the person under study. Because celibacy is a rather delicate subject for many people, especially for priests themselves, they might easily tend to defend their choice. In the interview method the only source of information is the celibatarian himself, and we have no direct means of double-checking his information. Not until we have a more complete picture of the interviewed person are we able to fully evaluate and understand his allegations in some topics.

We especially needed to know whether the respondent is capable of seeing himself realistically, that is, whether he can recognize and acknowledge the good as well as the bad sides of himself. In combination with the impression the respondent makes on the interviewers along with the answer to the question about his self-image, it indicates his capability of reality perception and therefore the reliability of his information. Also, in the first part of the interview we dealt with the childhood years of the respondent at great length. This was partly because talking about this kind of personal and usually emotional childhood memories makes respondents become more emotional and confidential; this means that their information becomes more trustworthy.

We interviewed a total of 25 priests. Respondents were selected by the following procedure: Personnel functionaries of seven dioceses were asked to make a list of 15 to 20 priests in their diocese, who in their opinion might be willing to talk about their celibacy. The priests listed were to vary in age and were not to deviate too much from the average priest in the diocese. From these lists, 51 priests were asked for an interview, which 26 refused. The youngest interviewed priest was 30 years of age, the oldest 67. Eleven priests were under 40 years of age, ten were between 40 and 50 and four were older than 50 years of age.

REDUCING THE DATA

The interviews, which took about five to six hours, were taped and then typed integrally. This resulted in an average of hundred pages of text per interview, altogether about 2500 pages. Since such a quantity cannot be handled, each interview was condensed to an average of 20 pages. The procedure by which these summaries came about will be discussed below.

Procedure for making summaries
First, a list was made of the topics that had to be included in the summary. One such a topic is: "All significant experiences and persons in the past

and the present of the respondent". This is a rather rough description applicable to many subjects. It is chosen to avoid the material not being done justice due to a preconceived scheme (see also Giorgi, 1976). The points for attention in such schemes easily tend to act as spotlights which put the rest of the empirical field in the dark.

The procedure by which a summary is effected is divided in a number of steps:

1. Determining that parts of the text which are important to the topic
   under study.
   After the text of the interview has been read through a few times (if necessary the taped version is listened to), relevant text pieces are underlined. These passages have to meet the condition that they pertain to one of the topics of the previously mentioned list. Notes are made of these text pieces in a slightly condensed form.
2. After the whole text has been worked through in the above mentioned way, the essence of each separate note is written down in one or a few key words.
3. Then, all text-units will be arranged according to the topics they pertain to. In this way a list of topics develops (e.g. childhood years, time at the seminary, friendships), accompanied by all the pages where something is said about that particular subject.
4. Drawing up the final text. In this phase, the topics are placed within larger categories. The final text of the summary comes into being, partly by means of the notes that are made in step 1 and partly by going back to the original text. Here also the decision is made as to which literal quotations are going to be incorporated in the summary. For this purpose, two criteria are used: is it the most perspicious quotation? And: is it representative?

It is obvious that these condensing activities form a risky phase in the research project. Risky, because there is a chance that the data will be subjectively and unconsciously distorted by means of selective reading, tendentious reporting, etc. Reliability is at stake here.

In the following, I will go into the problem of the reliability of qualitative research and the way this problem was handled in this research project.

Intermezzo on reliability
One of the most important objections against qualitative research concerns the often poor reliability of its results. An example that raised a lot of dust some years ago was the case of John Hinckly. He committed an attempted murder on president Reagan and was examined by dozens of psychiatrists for his mental health. Roughly half of these psychiatrists came to the conclusion that Hinckly was temporarily insane. The other half however considered him to be in full possession of his faculties. In cultural antropology (see for example Bovenkerk,1977) several instances of qualitative researches into small communities are known where one researcher came to completely opposite results to those of another researcher. This is because the risk of selective perception is greater in qualitative research than in quantitative

research. In qualitative research, no objective instruments (like opinion polls, tests) are being used; in fact, the researcher himself or herself is the "measuring instrument" and because of his or her subjectivity the results of the research may become distorted. That is why it is required that the researcher makes explicit his or her own - unconscious - prejudices, bias, sympathies, dislikes, etc. Furthermore, several controls on his or her subjective distortions have to be build into the research.

In the interview phase in our project the two interviewers functioned as a control on each other. As a more general control, in order to trace possible unconscious prejudices on my part, I wrote down my own experiences on a number of aspects pertaining to the topics of the research, such as: living without a partner, my own norms regarding sexuality, psychological health, religiosity, etc. Since this self-analysis in itself does not offer enough guarantees against unconscious prejudices, I also discussed it thoroughly with a colleague psychologist.

Furthermore, I agree with Bogdan & Taylor (1975) that in the final report my own procedures should be discussed in detail in order to give the reader the opportunity to estimate for him or herself my reliability as a researcher in this project. There also should be presented enough case material to let readers judge for themselves whether the conclusions the researcher draws from the material are valid.

The risk of uncontrolled subjective distortion in my research is highest in the phase of the summaries. Therefore, here some extra controls were built in. First, independently of each other, an assistant and I made a summary of two interviews. The differences between the summaries were discussed and submitted to an advisory committee. This committee consists of a clinical psychologist of religion, a developmental psychologist and the co-interviewer. As a result there appeared no subjective distortions on my side.

The rest of the summaries were made by me or by an assistant whose summaries I checked and revised thoroughly. Any differences here were also submitted to the advisory committee. In addition, all final summaries were viewed critically by the co-interviewer, who for that purpose once more read through the complete text of the interview. Finally, as an extra control, the summaries were sent to the respondents with the request to check these for errors and incompletenesses.

ANALYSING THE DATA

The next question to be answered was how to go about analyzing the material. We did not only want to do a descriptive study but also wanted to develop some theory about how priests come to their different interpretations and experiences of living a celibate life. For this purpose, the grounded theory method of Glaser and Strauss (1967) seemed suited. However, their research procedures are quite vague. Therefore, we decided to first try it on some of our interviews. Here follows a short summary of the most important elements of the grounded theory method.

Grounded theory approach

Glaser and Strauss (1967) object to the general trend within the social sciences to confine themselves to hypothesis testing and the use of quantitative research methods. According to them, quantitative statistical methods are not always suitable. The need for discovering and exploratory research often is far more urgent than that for purely hypothesis testing. On the other hand, they do acknowledge that not much qualitative research is done systematically. Therefore, they suggest an approach to develop theory on qualitative research data by means of a systematic procedure. Here theory means ideas on a higher level of abstraction than the level of the qualitative material.

In brief, their method comes to this: In the process of researching, a continuous development of ideas and concepts takes place by comparing the incoming data - in our case interview data on respondents - with each other. This means that theory is built in direct contact with the empirical field. By continuously stating similarities and differences, elements of the theory, such as concepts, categories, variables, are being developed. After thus tracing the apparently important elements of the developing theory, one continues to look for more data that can verify or correct earlier findings. In this way one tests and builds up the theory to be at the same time. One continues comparing until no further insights are discovered. The concepts will then be defined and formed into a consistent structure, making relations between them visible.

In this approach, one stays very close to empirical reality and at the same time one introduces a systematics. Theories developed in this way have the advantage of being based on research data and not being opportunistically fetched to fit the data (see also Wester, 1984).

Data on two cases[2] that were used for this first application of the "grounded theory" method are given below, followed by a short analysis of both. Paul conceives of celibacy as living without a partner and having no sexual experiences with others, except oneself. In this freely chosen lifestyle, he is happy. John, however, experienced his living without a partner very differently. He gradually became quite unhappy in this lifestyle and eventually ended up by living together with his girl-friend. He nevertheless still considers himself to live a celibate life.

TWO CASES

THE CASE OF JOHN

John is 44 years old. He is the eldest of five children. His father died when he was 8 years old. At the age of 25 he was ordained a priest. Since the age of 32 he has had a girl-friend, with whom he has been living now for five years.

About his mother he says: "She was full of love for me (...). She was also a devout women with whom I had close contact and who cared for us lovingly (...). She also treated us in a normal, physical way... very close to us". He can still remember very well the following childhood experiences: "It was wonderful to be with her, when we had to collect money from a churchwarden on Friday evenings. Then we would walk together, just the two of us. Collecting money was horrible, but being together... That was bodily contact, you as a child having your mother's arm hooked into yours".

Although leaving home was hard for him, he was not homesick at the seminary: "I looked upon it as something of tremendous wealth: a big house, a beautiful house, with food and games and opportunity to study".

After his ordination John worked for a number of years as a chaplain in two parishes which were known to be 'hard'. In one parish in particular he went through a crisis. The parish priest was a very unpleasant man and, according to John, treated the parishioners in an inhuman way. He nevertheless stayed there for three years. On advice of friends, who saw that things were getting more and more beyond him, he applied for a transfer and finally got it. During this period his relationship with a female parishioner grew into a warm friendship, in which he began to learn to give up his aloofness.

After that, John came to work in a parish where colleagues treated each other well: they went to the cinema and even "had a snack afterwards! Well, just all these ordinary things. That year I felt I was living in heaven, because I did not know what was happening to me, that this was possible, that things could be like this." More and more he began to have confidence in himself: "...to believe in yourself. Because I still had the feeling that I was the guy with that poor mother from the village, who was not able to do anything, and so on".

After spending a number of years in this parish, John went to work in an institution. Two years before that he met his present girl-friend. Under the stimulating influence of another parish worker, he finally made the decision to live together with her. After some adaptational problems, he is very happy with his present work and life situation. At the seminary, he sometimes had problems with his sexuality, because for him masturbation was still in the atmosphere of sinfulness. When he confessed to his confessor, "he did not react to it, he just left it there among all your imperfections". Later, once he was ordained, he thought about it a lot and "everything started to fall into place". He began to think of masturbation as normal and he accepted it for himself. For the rest,sexuality has never been such a problem to John.

His affectivity was giving him more problems. Looking back, he realized that at the seminary he was given a concept of a parish worker that estranged him from himself. Afterwards, colleague students told him that in the beginning at the seminary he had been far more open minded and less stringent than in his later years at the seminary. Not until he came out of his shell through the contact with a women in his first parish, did these colleagues say: "Slowly you have again become the person we knew at the seminary in the beginning".

The one who was responsible for this 'thaw' "was a woman with whom I had conversations, very good conversations, not just small talk. At one point, that lady was to leave our parish and I don't know what came over me, but I went to a shop and I bought her a present. I gave it to her to thank her for the parish work she had been doing. Well, this impressed her so much and me as well, although I was not aware of it at the moment - that she embraced me (...). Well, then it hit me. I thought: what is the matter with me? Why don't I do this more often? Deal with people in such a normal way, you know? And I thought: yes, affection evokes affection, you know. You just have to do it for once!". That woman showed him through her own affection how to live in a more normal, warm and human way.

Although this contact caused him some tensions - "dray dreaming about being married to her, and then again not wanting it because I would not be able to do my work anymore" -, little by little he re-established his peace of mind. The friendship with her "was just getting more affectionate, warmer" and contact remained "friendly, and also affectionate, also physically affectionate, you know. Like: a nice hand-shake and a nice kiss". He says: "She just taught me something like: boy, don't be so afraid and don't act so aloof". She also gave him advice on his problem about the contradiction between his celibacy and these experiences: "Boy, do as your heart says, then the Lord can't have meant it differently".

After a time, he "was not afraid of it anymore, that this kind of experiences happened to me". Since then, he dared to have more fellowship, warmth and physical affection in his contacts with women. It made him in general "more unconstrained in relations with people, no longer aloof. And because of that more things started to happen to me".

The greater freedom in his manner of relating to women clearly contributed to the fact that two years later he started the relation with his present friend. On the advice of a pastoral counselor, he started living together with her. Now, he is glad that he has dared to take this step.

John thinks that the relation with his friend changed him very much, especially on the affective side. He thinks that the most important difference lies in the fact that he now "is part of ordinary life". He goes out shopping, etc. Another big difference is that "you have a home, with a living room. And that there is a place where you don't have to be a parish worker (...). That there is somebody in church who knows how hard you have been working on a sermon. That somebody is there, who knows it and who can later on tell you whether you were sucessful or not. Who also says that it was wrong, that I should have done it in a different way. And not somebody who is always applauding like a housekeeper does because it is the priest who says so and he is always right. All these kind of things".

He also finds that, due to his friend, his pastoral contacts with people have become better. He is more available, available in the sense of: "If you have to be there, you are there completely; you are especially supported by her, to fully be there". He is more able to understand people. People also tell him that themselves. He thinks that "you can only fully relate to people when you have really experienced what it means to have committed yourself to somebody".

His concept of celibacy underwent a remarkable change. For him, celibatarian people are people who are "free. They live in such a way that they are fully available when people call upon them". His relationship with his girl-friend has helped him to reach such an availability. He experiences this relationship as celibatarian, because they are not possessive towards each other, nor do they claim each other. He also experiences a kind of celibatarian renunciation in having to be secret about the relationship and in not being able to have children. Generally, he is very negative about his former conception of a celibate life: celibacy has contributed, for almost all the people he knows, "to estranging oneself from oneself and thus leading you away from the way we were meant to be by our Creator, from your own self".

Celibacy did not have an inspiring influence on his religious experiences. Not until he got this steady relationship and hence could be closer to other people, did his contact with God improve. "Nowadays I feel more like: something is happening to me while praying together with people, while looking back upon what I have experienced with people or while we are together at home. It is not that everything is so 'holy', but that I experience things and then think: they are given to me just like that".

At the seminary, religion was above all a matter of observing the religious practices. "As long as it was done, as long as you prayed your breviary (...) you would keep your faith".

Summarizing, we can say about John that, as the eldest son he had a special tie with his mother. There are, however, no indications of an extreme or unhealthy bondage between the two of them. John is a modest and gentle person; for a long time he did not have much self-confidence. In difficult situations, he often needs a leg up in order to stand up for himself.

That John's affective education was adequate, is also evident from the good friendships he has always had. At the seminary, however, he was gradually taught an aloofness and a formality, which did not correspond with his character at all. In the sexual domain his seminary training did not talk him into feelings of guilt.

During his first five years as a chaplain, John was confronted with extremely malfunctioning priests. All this did not make him feel at home in the clerical world and he gradually began to develop a desire to belong to the world of ordinary people. An abrupt change came when at some point he forgot his aloofness and made a simple spontaneous gesture to a parishioner. From that time on, he was able to handle more closeness in his contacts. His later relationship with his friend resulted more or less from this.

He still considers himself to live a celibate life, though not in the definition of the church. For him, celibacy means being available to other people and being able to fully relate to them. For him, this has a religious quality to it.

THE CASE OF PAUL

Paul is 34 years old. When he was 25 years old, he finished his theological studies at the University. Not until 5 years later did he make the choice of priesthood and of celibacy. Paul has grown up in a rather closed, traditional Catholic family of farmers. He was the sixth of eight children.

He has "very good memories of family life. I think, when I look back, it was a quite warm stock. I don't believe we expressed our emotions very much. It was a bit restrained". At one point his father had problems with his health and this ended up, quite often, being taken out on the family. As a result of their father's problems, the children expressed themselves more to each other. Paul says: "It forced us to be more open towards each other at certain times. When it once again had been too much for us, we had to resort to each other. At such moments we talked about feelings and so on".

The relationship with his father has been difficult for a long time. "At one point I discovered that I almost hated that man". "After this discovery, I spent a long time, partly with the help of a pastoral counselor, anyway, trying to work things through. And now I can say: yes, I do accept him now the way he is".

His mother was a stable, warm and patient person but at the same time she was quite reserved and sober.

When he was 11 years old, the chaplain of the village asked Paul whether he wanted to go to the seminary. At that time, he was quite devout, but not extremely. Furthermore, the old priest in their village had made a big impression on him. "I was very impressed by the fact that such a big, tall man in all earnestness dashed a tear during mass".

At the minor seminary, he felt happy. During that time, he always "swallowed everything about celibacy". When as a matter of course he began his study in theology, he initially had, up to the second year (at the age of twenty), the ideal of becoming a really holy priest.

In the period he did his B.D. he once fell heavily in love. They had close contact for a few days before he found out that the love he felt was not mutual. He then went through some difficult weeks. At about the same time, he was confronted with all kinds of injustices in the Roman Catholic church. This made him angry with the Church and furious about the injustices she caused. In the end, regular visits to an abbey played an important role in renewing his faith. There two monks greatly inspired him: "they were people who could make one choose". He thinks that the monk who is still his pastoral counselor is "a very big man".

An important moment in his opting for or against celibacy was the discovery that sexual needs will not fade away. Besides his crisis of faith and his rage at the Church, the living awareness that celibacy was apparently a risky business arose. He knew himself well enough that he was "sexually very passionate", and he fully realized the ramifications of being celibate.

For some years now, he has been living in a community with people that are more or less like-minded. Just one year ago he was ordained a priest. It is characteristic of Paul that he first wanted to determine whether he could and wanted to be celibate. Not until then did he let himself be ordained a priest.

He likes his job as a parish worker very much and is happy with his celibate life: "I feel I have to live like that and it is in a certain way something I really want, yes, my own desire. Okay, you can say, there are different things you want to do, you know. Now and again I would like to be married or have a steady relationship where... well. But that is somehow not possible because of my religious basis; and I am too happy for that, over and over again".

Especially when he is in love, he misses sexuality and physical affection. He feels a slight pain then, but he also realizes that it will pass. When asked how he deals with this deprivation, he says: "I somtimes desire a sexual relationship, that is what I miss. But it is always temporary. My reaction varies, but sometimes it is very hard. Then I would (just want)... a woman in bed, and nothing else, you know". A bit later: "It hardly ever becomes a severe crisis. I do sometimes fall in love. This happens mostly in my pastoral relations and there I feel I have the duty to keep distance. But at such moments, I do feel the desire more strongly. Still (...) it is a dull pain, I don't really experience a heavy feeling because I know the choice has already been made: I will stop myself".

Whenever he is very much in love, he knows that he will masturbate. He does not experience this to be a sin. Yet he becomes more or less disappointed in himself, but this feeling is also fading. Sober and sensible counselors have always helped him to deal with it in a good way. "At the minor seminary they called it a sin, and that is what it was. So I decently confessed, but happily enough I had a very wise confessor. He said: "Well you don't have to tell me that all the time" (laughs).

Later on, he had problems with the issue of masturbation because he thought that as an adult he should by now have outgrown the habit. "My next counselor also reacted very nicely and soberly to it. He said: "You can talk about it now and then if it is bothering you". But at that time I did not feel it was a sin. With me it is not really sinful, I think. It is more like: I disappoint myself because I think I ought not to. But this is also decreasing. For I notice that I don't have that many ideals any more".

During his studies, he usually functioned in a very rational way. Not until his practical work he did develop his emotional life. His attitudes in contacts changed and improved (although before this change he "was not bad in dealing with people either"). In his contacts with others, two things are very important to him: to express himself about his problems (this is particularly important in personal relationships) and to give enough room to the others.

When he is asked how he experiences solitude, he talks about the kind of loneliness he feels "when something is bothering me and I don't want to talk about it. That can be a loneliness in a group as well; when you are not ready yet to talk about it; it is still mine. You would feel ashamed if others would notice it (...). When you eventually do express yourself, then the feeling of community will be restored again". When he is in love he usually pours his heart out to a friend. "My best friend will say: "Okay, so you are getting one of your hard months". He will say that with a laugh (...). And I feel that they really help me. Like calling me for the second time to ask me how I'm feeling. Giving you a bit more attention (chuckles). Yes, I mean, it makes people nicer".

Friendship means a lot to him. He has two very good friends, both celibate priests. Precisely because of their celibate life, they have a very good relationship. Especially with one, he has frequent contacts: "We interchange experiences and we study together. We study theology each Sunday evening for about an hour or so. Or we just read a book, a difficult one, so that you can talk about it. A book that would have been too difficult to read alone. Now and again, we have a drink together. And then I sometimes realize: A friendship can become so... important. I wonder whether married people have that experience, you know, a friendship relation (...). I am very happy with that".

Further on, he talks about two girl-friends: "I don't have real girl-friends, you know, girl-friends with whom you can have a deep contact. There are a number of women of whom I can say "I like her very much" and "I will certainly visit her on her birthday" and "If we are talking together we don't avoid personal things" (...). But these are not the stable and solid relationships like the ones I have with my two friends". About contact with women in general, he says that in the beginning of his studies he adopted the 'priestly' attitude of being aloof in his relations with women. Thanks to the fact that he has several nice sisters, this aloofness has never become too strong. Also his contacts with people in his parish changed him in this respect.

Without the pastoral counseling and his friendships, he would not be able to bear his celibacy. He too feels the need for affection and security. He gets them from his friends, counselors and family. That deeper loneliness - the loneliness he wants for himself - is hard enough. He needs people with whom he can be totally frank and honest about himself.

In these relationships, he wants to be more concerned about the needs of others than about his own needs. The celibate way of life fits in here quite well and helps him in attaining this goal. The most important thing to him is not to follow his own wants and needs but to see to the needs of others and then again leave them to themselves: "That experience, I think, has a lot to do with celibacy, and with... God himself, yes".

Precisely this freedom in his relationships makes his pastoral contacts sometimes more intense: "What happens sometimes, is that you meet people: like two ships that pass in the night, honk honk. Sometimes I am really very grateful, because the encounter was allowed to have, was more intense than what others maybe experience in ages. And at the same time, it has its freedom: it can be that intense, because more is not needed. It is not a tie for life, because in that case you can not experience such an intensity again and again".

A turning point in the process of deciding to be celibate came during a relationship with a girl-friend. He realized: "If I go on with her, then I will try to have her, to take her. Then I am in the atmosphere of ownership instincts, also sexually speaking, eh... Then I am only paying attention to myself... in all those things. And I cannot do that, it must not be like that". His religious experiences would be damaged by an exclusive relationship with another, because it would mean that he would appropriate somebody else's space. He deliberately chooses not to have an exclusive relationship with somebody else: "If I would start such a relationship I could only think of it as a relation in which I had given way to my passion for expansion, like: I want to occupy that space. In that sense, God does not allow this".

His religiosity has a great deal to do with "being there (free of desires) for the other person". In the space he leaves to the other (and vice versa), he finds God. He experiences this in a very religious way. "When you are busy with somebody else, the space in which you are standing is not yours nor does it belong to the other. That space belongs to a Third: that is... to me it is a holy space". Also his celibacy has to do with this. He wants to keep the space between himself and the other open, because there he can find God. Should he have an exclusive relationship with somebody, for him an important place where he can find God would be gone. He also says: "Those ships that meet in the night, that freedom in there, for me that has to do with celibacy as well. That is also a religious experience. There I experience the letting go, the detachment".

Paul can become very enthusiastic about his faith: "I think we have a grand tradition. I mean, valuable things in the shopwindow. I think our faith in fact is a tremendous one. Yes, it... I cannot help it. If you only take it out of the dust, there is beautiful gold beneath it".

Summarizing, we can say about Paul that already at an early age he became aware of his problematic feelings towards his father. By working them through, under the guidance of a pastoral counselor, he has been able to get through this quite well. He admires his pastor/mentor very much; to a certain extent this man is a father to him. With his mother he had a good - although more or less detached - relationship.

At home, Paul was given a rather sober and rational attitude. The working in the field and the accompanying supervision, among other things, have helped him to develop his emotional life. The friendship with a few good friends means a lot to him. His friends, family and mentor give him the affection and sense of security he needs to be able to endure his celibacy.

Paul has hardly been talked into feelings of guilt regarding his sexual feelings and behavior. He does not repress his sexuality. When he is in love, he has a difficult time. But knowing that it will pass, he is able to bear it. Also the conviction that in the end he will always choose for celibacy helps him. He thinks that his religious and priestly life is worth not being able to fully satisfy his physical desires.

In his pastoral contacts, Paul wishes to subordinate his own needs to those of others. He wants the other to have enough freedom and space. As a result, he thinks his contacts are more intense. The room he wants to maintain in his contacts would not be in keeping with an exclusive relationship, for an exclusive relationship would involve ownership instincts and imply that one claims another person to a certain extent. He consciously renounces having a love relation with a woman, because he does not want to be completely guided by his own needs.

For Paul, celibacy has a lot to do with his religiosity. Being celibate he always keeps the space between him and the other open. Should he have an exclusive relationship, then the most important place where he can find God would be gone for him.

ANALYSING THE TWO CASES FOLLOWING GROUNDED THEORY

We can see that the above are two completely different cases: John experienced his celibacy more and more as something that estranged him from his fellow people. It hindered his contacts with others and made him less open and available to them. For Paul, however, detachment became the essence of his religious experience; he enjoys his celibate life and feels that it intensifies his relations with others.

Before discussing the results of an analysis according to the method of Glaser and Strauss, we want to have a look at the possible results when trying to understand the data by means of earlier research concepts. These concepts were: mother-fixation, giving a religious meaning to celibacy, seminary training, age of choice and lack of the possibility of correction.

In the case of John, we notice that although the bond with his mother was close, she was not a dominating person. His father was literally absent: he died when John was 8 years old. We also see that at the seminary he was hardly talked into any feelings of guilt about sexuality. He was, however, taught to become more detached in his contacts with people: he became more contrained and closed. This detachment was expressed especially in his contacts with women. John chose priesthood - and not so much for celibacy - at quite an early age. He also discovered that he really liked getting feedback from his girl-friend. He did not succeed in giving a religious meaning to his celibate life.

Using these factors, we can understand why, in the beginning years of his work, John had a rather detached attitude towards people and why he was unhappy with it. He needed that relation with his parishioner and apparently the relationship with his girl-friend later in order to get rid of his emotional aloofness.

In Paul's case, there was a warm and patient mother who remained in the background, whereas the father asserted himself and quite often vented his rage upon the children. Paul only visited a minor seminary and never a major seminary. He hardly had any feelings of guilt about his sexuality. He was supervised well during his divinity training course. There he learned to face his own imperfections. At the seminary, there was also room to experience conflicts: falling in love, doubting one's faith, etc. Not until the age of 30 was he ordained a priest. He is still enthusiastic about being celibate, and gives a religious meaning to his celibate life: exactly there he meets God. Paul has developed himself well in the field of sexuality and affectivity and even enjoys celibacy. He does not seem to have an abnormally strong mother fixation and he never repressed his sexuality. He studied theology in an open atmosphere, where he was well supervised. At the age of thirty, he made a well-considered choice of celibacy and he is able to give a religious meaning to it.

Do these factors give us a fully adequate understanding of the cases? Upon further consideration it appears that a number of important questions remain unanswered. This becomes clear when we analyse the material using the grounded theory of Glaser and Strauss. For this purpose, we will compare the two cases with each other on differences and similarities. We will not discuss the results of this comparison exhaustively. As the reader may remember, at this point we mainly want to establish the usefulness of the method of Glaser and Strauss.

Let us compare John with Paul. The most important difference between them is that John, although he got rid of his detachment later on, was not happy in his celibate life. When looking at Paul we see the same detachment in his contacts, but he is not unhappy with it at all. On the contrary, he is so attached to his celibate life, that he could imagine giving up his profession, but he can hardly conceive of himself as giving up his celibacy. In short, John was unhappy being detached from others and withdrew from the celibate life in the strict sense, whereas Paul was happy with it and remained celibate.

The question then, of course, is how this difference can be explained. It could be that it has something to do with childhood experiences of both respondents. It is striking that John, talking about his mother, was so pleased to be with his mother when they had to collect money: "Just the two of us, together (...), that you were together then (...); it was real physical with your mother's arm hooked into yours as a child". Nearness and physical contact already appealed to John when he was a child. Paul on the contrary talks about the fact that his father often sent him upstairs as a punishment and how he enjoyed staying upstairs longer than the required hour. Thus, in a way Paul enjoyed being set apart from others when he was a child. This would mean that an early childhood relation with a (significant other like the) parent plays an important role in the experience of being celibate. Therefore, here we may have discovered an important concept for explaining their different experiences of celibacy.

A second question related to this difference in experiencing their detachment reads: is a detachment like Paul's a necessary condition for maintaining a strict celibacy? To answer this question, we would have to look at other, similar cases.

Another question that arises from this comparison between John and Paul is: why was it sufficient for Paul but not for John to have friends and family to satisfy his affective needs? Does this have something to do with the fact that Paul was capable of giving a religious meaning to celibacy and John was not? Or is there perhaps a connection with their early childhood relations with the mother or the father?

If the explanation lies in giving a religious meaning to celibacy, then the question here is also how the difference between John and Paul can be explained. Why is it that Paul was capable of ascribing a religious meaning to celibacy? Also striking in this comparison is that in Paul's life several people have played a rather important role. For him they probably were important identification figures. What exactly is the importance of these identification figures?

This concludes our first application of the grounded theory method. It shows that with the questions that arise from this comparison we traced a number of important themes. Implicitly, several theoretical concepts come to the fore, such as (the experience of) detachment, early childhood relationships, identification figures, the role of friends and family and the religious meaning of celibacy.

On the basis of these results, we decided to settle for the grounded theory method of Glaser and Strauss. Below, I will discuss some of the problems we came across in our further analysis of the material.

SOME PROBLEMS IN THE FURTHER ANALYSIS

As we know, grounded theory is based on the systematic generating of theory from data. However, in their publication *The discovery of grounded theory* Glaser and Strauss (1967) are quite vague as to the exact procedures to be followed.

Our procedure has been as follows. We started the analysis of the data by discussing each case in a group of four: the two interviewers and two members of the advisory committee. One of the first problems we came across was disagreement in the group on the amount of rationalization on the part of some respondents. Some of us had serious doubts about the authenticity of Paul's experience with being celibate. His statement that celibacy makes him happy was considered either a rationalization of his incapacity to lose himself in intimate relationships or as a reduction of cognitive dissonance, stemming from his desire to be a priest. Here we disagreed on a vital point: the experience of being celibate itself. Also in some other cases, differences of opinion showed up. One respondent, for example, was considered by some to exhibit an extreme avoidance of conflict, whereas the other members of the group thought him reasonably normal in his dislike of conflicts.

Because of the complexity of the material, it was not easy to work out our differences. The overall picture one had formed of the respondent seemed to be important in interpreting his behaviour. We therefore decided to continue our discussion on the level of this overall picture itself. Central themes in this overall picture seemed to be: 'self-esteem', 'ability to make contacts' (empathy in combination with a proper distance) and 'capacity to handle conflicts'.

Although in this way our differences became smaller, they did not really vanish. Our discussions did not so much lead to the discovery and development of new categories and concepts, but unwillingly became more like clinical case conferences. Apparently it was difficult for us to leave the clinical perspective.

Since our differences tended to ask too much of our time and energy, we considered two possible ways out of this deadlock. The first possibility was to make explicit all the dimensions, criteria, aspects etc. of the themes 'self-esteem', 'interpersonal abilities' and 'conflict handling', in order to make them more objectively measurable. To do so, however, seemed to require a time consuming study of the literature on identity formation, affective development and conflict management. A potentially better alternative seemed to be a careful line by line coding of one summary of an interview. This was expected to yield a number of themes and questions on the basis of which the rest of the interviews could be handled.

These extensive coding activities resulted in about 200 different categories. On the one hand, according to Glaser and Strauss (1967), the codes have to be sensitizing, that is as concrete and specific as possible. On the other hand, they have to be analytic, that is sufficiently generalized to designate characteristics of concrete entities, not the entities themselves. Partly because of this, the coding activities did not have the result we hoped for. We also learned that this type of coding was too extensive and was not guided enough by theoretical insights and concepts.

How do matters stand at present? Although the problems have not been solved completely and new problems undoubtedly will arise in the future, we certainly have moved in the right direction. Thanks to a greater understanding of grounded theory - a more recent publication by Glaser (1978) was very helpful in this, as was Wester (1984) - we were able to discover the flaws in the way we proceeded until now. For example, we came to realize that both the concept of 'rationalization' and the concept of 'overall picture' were on too high a theoretical level. The two concepts may very well turn out to be part of the developing theory, but for now, discussions about them are premature.

Furthermore, we became convinced that our discussions about respondents definitely should not have the character of clinical case conferences. Discussions sometimes centered around whether or not a specific behavioural pattern was indicative of narcissism, extreme avoidance of conflicts etc. These discussions were by themselves not very helpful in improving our understanding as to the why and how of the celibatarian experience of the person. It is important to stick to a comparison between cases in order to trace important categories. Concepts from clinical psychology may become part of these categories, but not exclusively.

Let me give an example to clarify this. In one case, we tried to answer the question as to why respondent X became stuck in his doubts about starting a relationship. Among other things, the lack of a warm mother figure and a resulting basic mistrust appeared to have something to do with it. Before, we tended to leave our discussions at that. Now, we continue by asking how the experience of another respondent with a similar mother figure, Y, can be so different from X's. Then, for example, the discovery is made that although both became priests out of love for this work, X in his time did not have a choice between becoming a priest or becoming a pastoral worker. Moreover, X underwent a long psychotherapy, which in his perception was aimed at helping him to live a good celibatarian life. Thus the potentially important concepts of 'having a choice between priest or pastoral worker' and 'influence of psychotherapy' are discovered. They may become key categories in our developing theory.

Another problem concerned making categories explicit in order to improve their measurability. We initially supposed that for this it was necessary to leave the empirical field and turn to existing theories, for example theories on 'self-concept' of 'self-esteem'. Meanwhile we have come to realize that in grounded theory, the data themselves are the best means for developing a theory on, for example, 'self-concept' (see also Dijkstra, 1984). For that purpose, all passages pertaining to self-concept or self-esteem in the interviews are being compared with each other. In this constant comparison within and especially between interviews, the concepts become more specific and better defined. By doing so, different aspects, dimensions, characteristics and even variants of the category 'self-esteem' can be discovered.

Such a precise elaboration of important concepts is also necessary in view of future coding activities. First, all potentially important concepts must be traced, like the previously discussed concepts of 'choice between priest or pastoral worker' and 'influence of psychotherapy'. Then the characteristics of these concepts must be well defined in order to allow for a more or less objective coding of the cases. The concept 'choice between priest or pastoral worker', for example, seems to have only two variants: present or absent. 'Influence of psychotherapy' probably has several variants, one of them being 'therapy lasting as long as five years and having the purpose of adapting the respondent to celibacy'. Further comparisons with other respondents who underwent psychotherapy will undoubtedly lead to a more precise description of this subcategory.

So much for some practical problems in the application of the grounded theory approach[3].

I will conclude this paper with a short presentation of some preliminary results of our research.

SOME RESULTS OF THE PROJECT

The first conspicuous result of our research concerns the sexual morals of the respondents, which shows a remarkable change from some decades ago. With two exceptions (interestingly enough the oldest - 67 years of age - and the youngest - 30 years-old priest in the group), all our respondents consider sexuality to be a normal human need, just like eating, drinking and sleeping. We hardly found any feelings of guilt about masturbation among them.

A second surprising fact about the interviewees is the relatively great amount of homosexuals among them: 8 out of 25. They are between 30 and 44 years of age, so most of them have never been to a seminary. This would indicate that seminary training is not as crucial in causing homosexuality among priests as is often assumed.[2]

A third interesting result concerns the role played by the duty to remain celibate in the lives of these 25 priests. Here we can distinguish between roughly four types.

The first group consists of those who have more or less accepted the obligation to remain celibate. Then, there is the group of those who have already been struggling with it for quite some time. A third group of priests consists of those who have an intimate relationship with someone. And finally, there is the group of convinced celibatarians.

The group of those who have accepted the demand to remain celibate consists of 8 persons. Half of them are homosexuals.

The second group of five persons who struggle painfully with their celibacy is quite heterogeneous. One respondent, for example, became involved with women several times - more or less against his own will. These were usually women who were about to disappear from his life - through removal or through impending death. Another one had great problems with loneliness. He did have a girl-friend for some time - even lived with her, but put an end to this relationship because he could not reconcile it with his being a priest. Yet another one had several nervous break-downs and many short relationships with women. With the help of a psychotherapist, he finally found some peace of mind, though he remains fundamentally unhappy with his situation.

The third group consists of respondents who are all having a steady intimate relationship. All 6 persons in this group feel they still live a celibate life, because their work and their religious life is more important for them than their partner. For the sake of their priesthood, they gave up some of their desires. Thus, for example, all except one would not want to marry or live together with their partner, not even should the official celibacy demand be abolished.

The last group consists of 6 persons who are celibatarians from conviction. This group is remarkably homogeneous in a number of aspects. First of all, these convinced celibatarians are quite young. Four out of six are younger than 35 years; the other two are 40 and 44 years old. All except one chose celibacy at a relatively late age, i.e. around their thirties. This is connected with the fact that all except one had been doing pastoral work for some time prior to their ordination. Although they are very positive about their own celibacy, 5 out of 6 are definitely against the official demand for celibacy, just as, by the way, all the rest of our respondents are.

All emphasize the fact that not everybody is fit for the celibate life. As for themselves, they feel that they just happen to have a character that goes well with celibacy. For example, most of them are quite capable of being alone and even like it.

Friendships are most important to them. They definitely need people with whom they can be wholly themselves.

Another remarkable similarity among the priests in this group is that all seriously considered becoming a monk once. They still pay regular visits to abbeys. A last point worthy of mention here is their sober lifestyle. Without forgetting about their own happiness in life, they want to serve as much as possible the needs and wants of other people. This sobriety, which is indissolubly connected with their celibacy, also shows in their renunciation of having a partner.

SUMMARY

This article describes the plan and methodology of an ongoing qualitative research project on priests' experience of being celibate. The usefulness of the grounded theory approach of Glaser and Strauss (1967) is demonstrated on case material. Problems concerning the reliability of the results and some practical difficulties in using the grounded theory method are discussed. Finally, some results of the project are presented.

NOTES

[1] Literature studies by Kerssemakers (1984) and by Godin (1983) were helpful in this.
[2] A more detailed description may be found in Hoenkamp-Bisschops (1984).
[3] See, for a possible explanation of this high amount of homosexuals in our research sample, Hoenkamp-Bisschops (1985).

REFERENCES

Bovenkerk, F. (1977). Geen woorden maar daden. Het levensechte experiment als methode van sociaal onderzoek. (The real-life experiment as a method of social research). In: L. Brunt (Ed.), *Anders bekeken, wet en werkelijkheid in sociaal onderzoek,* 127-143. Meppel: Boom.
Bogdan, R., & Taylor, S.J. (1975). *Introduction to qualitative research methods.* New York: Wiley.

Bowers, M. (1963). *Conflicts of the Clergy.* New York: Nelson.

Calon, P.J.A. (1956). *Priesterschap en celibaat* (Priesthood and celibacy). Nijmegen: Brochure van Katholiek Leven.

Christensen, C.W. (1969). The occurrence of mental illness in the ministry. In E.M. Pattison (Ed.), *Clinical Psychiatry and Religion,* 191-200. Boston: Little.

Dijkstra, C. (1984). Een 'client-centered' gevalsbeschrijving: enkele praktische suggesties (A client-centered case description; some practical suggestions). *De Psycholoog,* XIX, 11, 670-677.

Giorgi, A. (1976). Phenomenology and the foundations of psychology. In J. Cole & W.J. Arnold (Eds.), *Nebraska symposium on motivation: conceptual foundations of psychology,* vol. 2. Lincoln: University of Nebraska Press.

Glaser, B.G. & Strauss, A.L. (1967). *The discovery of grounded theory.* Chicago: Aldine.

Glaser, B.G. (1978). *Theoretical sensitivity. Advances in the methodology of grounded theory.* California: The Sociology Press.

Godin, A. (1983). *The psychology of religious vocations.* Washington: University Press of America.

Hoenkamp-Bisschops, A.M. (1984). Priesters en het celibaat, drie case-studies. (Priests and celibacy; three case studies). *Praktische Theologie,* 5, 522-544.

Hoenkamp-Bisschops, A.M. (1986). De ontwikkeling van een 'gefundeerde theorie'. (The development of a grounded theory). *Psychologie en Maatschappij,* 36, 276-288.

Hoenkamp-Bisschops, A.M. (1987). Die gegenwärtigen Zölibatserfahrungen katholischer Priester in den Niederlanden (The contemporary experience of celibacy of Dutch catholic priests). *Archiv für Religionspsychologie und Religionswissenschaft.* Göttingen: Vandenhoeck & Ruprecht.

Kerssemakers, J. (1984). Het ambtscelibaat. Een overzicht van de sociaal-wetenschappelijke literatuur. (Celibacy of the priest. A survey of social scientific literature). *Praktische Theologie,* 5, 502-521.

Mitchell, K.R. (1970). Priestly celibacy from a psychological perspective. *Journal of Pastoral Care.* 24, 216-226.

Plé, A. (1969). La vie affective du célibataire consacré (The affective life of the ordained priest). *Supplement de la Vie Spirituelle.* 22, 217-234.

Potvin, R.H. & Suziedelis, A. (1969). *Seminarians of the sixties: a national survey.* Washington: CARA Publ.

Rey, K.G. (1969). *Das Mutterbild des Priesters* (The mother image of priests). Einsideln und Köln: Benziger.

Trimbos, C.J.B.J. (1955). Het priesterlijk celibaat. Enige psycho-hygiënische beschouwingen. (Priestly celibacy. Some psycho-hygienic considerations). *Nederlandse Katholieke Stemmen.* 51, 320-337.

Vergote, A. (1967). Das Werden des Priesters als Mensch und Christ in psychologischer Sicht. (Becoming a priest from a psychological perspective). In: *Der Priester in einer säkularisierten Welt,* 54-75. Luzern: Akten des 3. internationalen Kongresses zu Luzern, 18-22 Sept.

Wester, F. (1984). *De gefundeerde theorie-benadering. Een strategie voor kwalitatief onderzoek.* (Grounded theory approach. A strategy for qualitative research). Nijmegen: Sociologisch Instituut.

Chapter 10

PHENOMENOLOGY AND FAMILY THERAPY

Bertha Mook

In the young, creative field of family therapy, rapid advances have been made in the progressive formalization of various core models or orientations which all aim to apply the systemic paradigm to theory and clinical practice. Sluzki (1983) has identified three such core models, i.e. the process-, structure-, and world-view orientations around which most of the thinking in the field is organized. However, the prevailing conceptual diversity in family therapy still leads to many contradictions and confusions. This condition has given rise to a recent trend of metatheoretical inquiry with a particular focus on epistemological issues.

In the spirit of the present climate of metatheoretical inquiry in family therapy, I want to challenge the heuristic value of an exclusive focus on the systemic paradigm for the theory and practice of family therapy. Such a focus is at least incomplete and at most dangerous because it does not take the uniquely human dimension sufficiently into account, and may ultimately sacrifice the individual subject to an anonymous pattern. The present enthusiasm in the systemic viewpoint has relegated family experiencing to the background, viewing it as incidental or at most anecdotal. The formal, relational and systemic features of the family system, on the other hand, are regarded as of the utmost importance. Systemic family therapists tend to overlook that the individual family members give meaning to their own and to each other's behaviours and experiences and are continuously creating their own personal and interpersonal structures. Although the systemic viewpoint acknowledges the complexity of interrelationships, it ignores the uniquely human dialectic of reflection as exemplified in Kierkergaard's idea of the self being a relationship relating to the relationship (Nordentoft, 1978). In a comprehensive theory of family therapy, the family members will have to be acknowledged to be conscious, intentional and meaning-creating subjects who relate dialectically to themselves and to each other and who foster their own self-differentiation within the family group through reflection upon their own and each other's experiences.

To my thinking, the key metatheoretical problem in family therapy lies in how to bridge the gap between the abstract-theoretical concepts of systems and structures, and the concrete existential-phenomenological world of lived family experiences. In search of an answer, I propose a phenomenological approach to the theory and eventually the practice of family therapy which aims to simultaneously address the experiential, structural and systemic dimensions in family life. Starting with the family's lived experiential world, it aims to elucidate the situated structures embedded in systemic family phenomena.

A social phenomenological approach to family therapy has of course been proposed and demonstrated by Laing and Esterson (1964) in their outstanding pioneering work with schizophrenic families. However, an acknowledged limitation of their work is their focus on the identified patient within the family rather than on the living family system itself. Since their early work, a phenomenological approach to family therapy has been neglected in favor of developing various systemic models.

In a previous paper (Mook, 1985), I have discussed the relationships between phenomenology and system theory in terms of basic characteristics, formal similarities and fundamental differences. I have pointed out that a key similarity exists in their mutual emphasis on man's contextual and relational reality and in their search for structural patterns in human life. However, fundamental differences prevail in system theory being a natural science model interested in formal structures which provide explanatory principles for the cybernetic and regulatory features of closed and open systems. Phenomenological psychology on the other hand is a descriptive human science that seeks to understand and explicate the nature of human structures present in the phenomenal world of lived experiences.

In proposing a phenomenological approach to family therapy, the different meanings of the concept of structure in phenomenology and in family therapy need to be addressed. The next section seeks to clarify these meanings. This will be followed by the application of a phenomenological method to the analysis of an actual structural family therapy interview in order to illustrate its possible heuristic value in understanding systemic family functioning.

THE CONCEPT OF STRUCTURE

Structure is a key concept both in phenomenology and in systemic family therapy. Amongst the various orientations in the field of family therapy, the structural model is the one which explicitly focuses on family structures and their modification (Minuchin, 1981). This approach is therefore of particular relevance to phenomenological psychologists interested in the nature of human structures embedded in family life. However, the different philosophical orientations underlying the concept of structure in phenomenology and in structural family therapy have to be kept in mind.

In phenomenology, Merleau-Ponty is the philosopher of structure par excellence. In his classical work, *The Structure of Behaviour* (1963), he distinguished on philosophical grounds between physical, vital and human structures which are shown to be autonomous and thus irreducible to each other. Merleau-Ponty endorsed the general concept of structure as denoting a complex or totality of relationships between parts within a whole. For him, the formation of vital and human structures differs fundamentally from physical structures and depends on the nature of the task in which the organism finds itself engaged. He wrote: "...the organism itself measures the action of things upon it and itself delimits its milieu by a circular process which is without analogy in the physical world" (p. 148). The relationship between the organism and its milieu is not mechanical but dialectical with both poles participating in the same structure. Merleau-Ponty further reasoned and demonstrated that the autonomy of vital and human structures can be accounted for by the idea of signification. Vital acts are intentional and have a significance, a meaning for the subject. Between the organism and its milieu exist intrinsic relations of meaning, and the response of the organism will depend on the significance of the occasion for him.

What distinguishes the human from the vital order, is the fact that humans do not simply delineate but intentionally create new socio-cultural milieus. Through the dialectical relationship of their perception of situations and their actions upon them, they are in principle capable of transforming these situations and at the same time they transform themselves. In general terms, the most fundamental character of the human order is this continual movement of transcendance: this capacity to orient oneself towards the possible and move beyond created structures in order to create new ones.

In view of Merleau-Ponty's phenomenological understanding of structures, we need to acknowledge that structures in families and in family therapy belong distinctively and irreducibly to the human order. Between the family members and their socio-cultural context exist intrinsic relations of meaning which are dialectical in nature. The response of individual family members to one another will depend on how they perceive their particular situation and on its vital significance for them. The behaviour of family members as individuals and as a group is structured according to the intended meanings attributed to their own and to each other's experiences. Through their intentional behaviour, the family has in principal the capacity to create, transform and transcend their own structures.

The concept of structure in structural family therapy is fundamentally different from the phenomenological understanding of Merleau-Ponty. Structural family therapy represents a theoretical and methodological model consistent with the thrust of general system and structuralist thinking (Aponte, 1981). Its concept of structure is drawn from a natural science perspective in which Merleau-Ponty's crucial distinction between physical, vital and human structures is not taken into account. In general, structuralists define structures as a totality of relationships in which the elements can vary but remain dependent upon an autonomous whole. They are further characterized by the properties of self-regulation and transformation (Piaget, 1970). Structuralists assume that there are innate, determined mechanisms in man which act as structuring forces and which strongly influence the rules that govern human relationships (Lane, 1970). Departing from this assumption, structuralists approach all human phenomena by seeking to identify the codes which regulate human behaviour. These codes are formalized into structures which in turn provide explanatory principles for the functioning of open systems. According to Piaget (1970), all structuralists postulate structures to be self-sufficient and intrinsically intelligible.

In structural family therapy, Minuchin (1974) views the family as a system that operates through transactional patterns. The family's structures are seen as formed by the organizing and regulating codes through which the members relate to one another. Minuchin writes: "Family structure is the invisible set of functional demands that organizes the ways in which family members interact" (p. 51). Minuchin (1974) and Aponte (1981) further conceptualize the structural dimensions of family interactions in terms of boundaries, alignments and power. The central concept of boundaries of systems and subsystems refers to the rules defining interactional participation. Alignment indicates the joining or opposition of family members to one another in their mutual interactions. Power is seen as the relative influence each member exerts on the outcome of an activity.

Minuchin views well functioning families as approximating a normative developmental model. They are characterized by a hierarchical structural organization with clear boundaries between the subsystems and flexible alignments between the various members. Dysfunctional families, on the other hand, show a faulty organization with poor boundary power. Various dysfunctional structural patterns have been identified depending on the nature of the presenting symptomatology (Minuchin, 1978).

In practice, the structural family therapist seeks to identify dysfunctional family structures. Through observation and participation, he searches for the codes and rules which regulate the family's transactions and maintain the identified problem. Through joining, creating and modifying existing patterns of interactions, he aims to change the structural and organizational features of dysfunctional family systems.

It is of particular importance for our discussion to note that in the systemic and structuralist perspective applied to family therapy, attention is directed primarily to the formal, extrinsic and observable aspects of family transactions. The nature of each family member's lived experiences is regarded as incidental and of no particular relevance.

Minuchin (1981) explicitly assumes that changes in family structure produce changes in the experience of individual members. The individual subjects themselves are viewed as decentralized, subordinate parts which derive their significance only from the family as a totality.

For the phenomenologist, on the other hand, the nature of the individual's and the family's lived experiences is of paramount importance. He seeks to understand and describe the family members' perceptions of themselves and of each other as well as the dialectical relations and patterns of intentional meanings embedded in their experiences and behaviours. He further aims to explicate the nature of the particularly human structures intrinsically and implicitly present in their phenomenal world.

A PHENOMENOLOGICAL STUDY

The major aim of the present study is to illustrate the nature and the possible heuristic value of a phenomenological method of analysis applied to a life structural family therapy interview. Such a method seeks to address simultaneously the experiential, structural and systemic dimensions of family functioning as revealed through the course of the family therapy interview. More specifically, the phenomenon I sought to explicate was the phenomenological nature of the family structure that sustained the problematic behaviour of the identified patient as it gradually emerged within the family therapeutic system.

Ideally, a phenomenological method of analysis should be applied to a family therapy interview conducted by a phenomenological family therapist who is attuned to the family members' perceptions and experiences of themselves and of each other and who seeks to reveal the lived meanings and the human structures relevant to the particular family's problems. However, this kind of material is hardly available at the present time. I therefore decided to apply a phenomenological method of analysis to a single consulting interview conducted by a master therapist in structural family therapy. The latter approach was chosen because it is systemic and seeks to identify the dominant family structure(s) relevant to the family's presenting problem albeit from a structural family therapist's point of view. A consulting interview was selected because it formed a relative unity in itself within the course of an ongoing family therapy. The master therapist was Harry Aponte who is an internationally known expert in structural family therapy. His consulting interview is both diagnostic and therapeutic in his successful exposition of initially obscured family conflicts. His penetrating search for an evaluation of the family's problems offered a relatively rich source of material for a phenomenological study.

Phenomenological research is basically descriptive in nature and seeks to articulate the psychological acts and the meanings of lived experiences as they appear to consciousness (Husserl, 1977). The phenomenological method originally developed by Husserl, has been successfully systematized and applied to the analyses of various psychological phenomena by Giorgi and his co-workers in various publications (e.g. 1979, 1985). The phenomenological method used in the present study is based on the work of Giorgi but significantly modified in the light of an analysis of a transcribed family therapy interview.

In Giorgi's method, the researcher starts by eliciting individual subject's descriptions of certain experienced phenomena. Through the delineation of "meaning units" within the original description and their subsequent transformation in terms relevant to the researched phenomenon, he arrives at the structure of the subject's experience of the particular phenomenon. In the present study, I followed a similar course of phenomenological analysis with the important difference that I applied it to a group of subjects in the form of a family, and started with a description of a life family therapeutic interview. The latter was perceived as a specific life situation expressive of human meanings revealed through personal and interpersonal perceptions, actions and experiences. In addition, my particular interest was to explicate the investigated phenomenon in terms of its experiental, structural and systemic dimensions.

The raw material used consisted of a one hour audio-video recorded family therapy interview. The interviewed Knight family is white, middle-class Canadian and consists of four members: the spouses in their early forties, Anne aged thirteen and Tom aged eleven. Tom is the identified patient and clinically diagnosed as manifesting mute, withdrawn and depressed behaviour. The family therapy tape was repeatedly viewed and accurately transcribed to include all verbal and most non-verbal behaviours.

The study was further conducted in three phases. First a detailed description was made of the whole family therapy interview reflecting its lived character by staying as close as possible to the expressed verbal and non-verbal perceptions, experiences and actions of all participants. Secondly, the personal, interpersonal and structural constituents of the description were expressed in terms relevant to the investigated phenomenon. The third phase focused directly on the investigated phenomenon and resulted in a specific description of the situated structure in the family system that embeds and sustains the problem behaviour of the identified patient. The three phases of the phenomenological method employed can be seen as representing three hierarchical levels of abstraction which are interrelated and interdependent on each other. The third level culminates in an explication of the researched phenomenon and incorporates its experiential, structural and systemic dimensions. Only the results of the second and the third phase will be presented in detail.

THE CONSTITUENTS OF THE FAMILY INTERVIEW

In the first brief phase of the interview, the therapist joins with each member of the family. Mr. Knight takes the initiative and presents himself as controlled, direct and very verbal. Mrs. Knight appears sad and quiet in leaning over to her son and looking down most of the time. Anne who is seated between her parents, manifests a light and bright manner of communicating and succeeds in relieving tension by evoking family laughter from all except Tom. He in turn appears exceedingly sullen, withdrawn, motionless and very reluctant to communicate.

In response to the therapist's question as to how they see their problems, the family verbalizes a distinct communication problem which they see as originating in one member. The parents are in full agreement that their son is generally uncommunicative and withdraws into total silence when upset. His refusal to communicate leads his parents to express great concern and feelings of frustration, failure and helplessness. The relationships between the spouses themselves and their daughter appear close, agreeing and positive. The daughter plays a mediating role between her parents and her brother maintaining positive relationships to both, which inevitably puts her in a stressful position.

From a structural family therapist's point of view, the family's perception of their problems seems to indicate a dysfunctional structure and leads to the hypothesis that the identified patient is used by the parents to obscure or deflect parental conflict. The family therapist aims to break into this dysfunctional family pattern. He decides to explore the nature of disagreements amongst the various family dyads and their ways of coping with them in the hope of exposing implicit family conflicts.

The therapist's exploration of disagreements in the mother-daughter dyad reveals a very close relationship between them in which disagreements and arguments are avoided. However, father brings forth a problematic issue in which Anne refuses to comply with her mother's rules and expectations regarding family meals. The therapist's questioning on how mother and daughter deal with it, brings to light that Anne avoids an open confrontation with her mother as well as her own personal responsibility by excusing her behaviour in terms of forgetfulness and bad habits. Her mother in turn underplays the importance of the issue and resorts at last to unconvincing, authoritative control. When father's view is called upon, he reveals an ambiguous attitude in blaming and excusing both his wife and daughter. In response to the therapist's probing questions, he blames Anne but immediately protects her by saying that she behaves unknowingly and without intent. He also indicates that the issue between mother and daughter is implicitly kept alive in the family by mother's occasional temper outbursts. The parents and their daughter seem to avoid facing up to problematic issues and are instead mutually protective for the sake of preserving close relationships.

The apparent family pattern of avoiding disagreements emerges again when the therapist explores disagreements in the father-daughter dyad. Only the therapist's challenging questions lead father to expose a disciplinary problem in the family. It appears that he sets the rules and is overtly supported by his wife but both fail in consistent disciplining. Mr. Knight repeatedly attributes both his own and his wife's failure to follow through on their rules to forgetfulness followed by passive acceptance. This apparent weakness in the parental subsystem leaves both children in a powerful position in which they successfully defy parental authority.

The emotional tone of the family changes from relative lightness interspersed with laughter to a tense seriousness when the therapist directs attention to the father-son dyad. Father openly and directly expresses his disagreements and a sense of total frustration with his son for not communicating with him, and for refusing to engage in organized team sports despite all joined parental efforts. The son's minimal self-defence is quickly put down and his efforts degraded by his father's criticisms in which he is non-verbally supported by his wife.

In the therapist's exploration of disagreements in the mother-son dyad, mother perceives Tom's lack of communication as their biggest problem underlying all other concerns about him. In response to the therapist's sympathetic probing into the nature of her distress, she tearfully reveals her belief that Tom is suffering from unresolved inner conflicts and that he has expressed negative self-perceptions and a wish to be dead. The parents support each other in their perceptions and concern for their son's problems. However, their relationships to him are distinctively different, with father openly expressive of his frustrations and criticisms where his son fails to meet his expectations, and mother emotionally overinvolved and very despondent in finding no solutions to her son's problems. Both parents tend to avoid arguments or open confrontations with him.

Upon the therapist's inquiry into the family's avoidance of arguments and disagreements, Mrs. Knight reveals that her husband sets the leading tone by his belief and attitude that nothing is accomplished through arguing. Her concerns lead to occasional emotional outbursts towards him which he accepts superficially without personal involvement. When the therapist confronts Mr. Knight with the issue, he significantly admits that disagreements have upsetting effects on him which lead him to withdraw into long silences. Herewith he implicitly acknowledges that he is strikingly similar to his son in his response to emotional stress. Anne, on the contrary, is defined by him as "a complete opposite" in letting everyone know how she feels. In expressing his affection for her through loving words and gestures, he underscores his polarized attitude towards his children.

In response to the therapist's searching questions, Mr. Knight further reveals a personal dislike for disciplining others because it evokes upsetting, negative feelings in him. Upon reflection, he realizes that this problem may be linked to the fact that he tends not to show or express his dislikes and disapproval of others. However, he contradicts and justifies himself by rationalizing that he does not have to express his dislikes because he can live with it. He does admit that he hides his upsets from others for a long time which his wife and daughter affirm to be true.

When the therapist empathizes with Mrs. Knight that it must be difficult to be angry with an emotionally unresponsive husband, she expressively voices her frustrated feelings but quickly retracts when he protests. When Anne light-heartedly states about herself that she is a lover and not a fighter, Mrs. Knight temporarily endorses her daughter's attitude which shows her ambivalence in dealing with negative feelings. However, when the therapist comments that they can be better lovers if they can also fight, he speaks to her heart and she complains that she has repeatedly told her husband but that he does not believe her. Mr. Knight responds with puzzlement that he leaves her alone when she is upset which she has indicated to be the opposite of what she wants. With clarifying support from the therapist, Mrs. Knight pointedly and accurately remarks that her husband fails to get involved.

In support of Mrs. Knight, the therapist contrasts the mutual attitudes in the family where her husband and son stay uninvolved while she wants to be involved with both of them, which places her in a very painful position. With her husband and son at a distance, her daughter stays close and supports her in saying that one should express all one's feelings which evokes a spontaneous, relieving expression of affection from her mother. Mr. Knight acknowledges the unresolved problem between him and his wife and defines it as "very obscure".

In a systemic fashion, the therapist links the problems between the spouses and their son, with both father and son not knowing how to express their negative feelings, and sees the solutions as mutually interdependent. A lack of differentiation between Mr. Knight and his son's problem surfaces when Mr. Knight does not know who of the two his wife refers to when she states that he does not even verbalize his upsets and rarely ever a disapproval or disagreement. In a low and painful tone, Mrs. Knight dramatically reveals that her husband hardly ever expresses his feelings and would give her a minimal response only after prolonged prodding with the implicit message not to get involved based on fear to get hurt, which he admits to be true. His behaviour forces her to "play dead" most of the time.

The therapist points to the consequences of Mr. Knight's uninvolvement for himself: if he refuses to share his feelings, he will not be consoled either and ends up suffering in silence like his son. Attempting to sidestep the emphasis on himself and his marriage, Mr. Knight blames the external source of work for his frustrations but the therapist's confrontation leads him to admit that he avoids facing frustrations and unhappiness in his marital relationship. In tears, Mrs. Knight reveals that they never communicate despite her repeated efforts which has led to a great distance between them. He only allows her to touch him superficially despite all her loving efforts to bring him close. The weight of unresolved issues and loneliness has become unbearable for her and can no longer be endured. The therapist correctly senses that the spouses do care for each other and emphasizes the need for more openness and sharing between them. Encouraged by the therapist and by her husband's affectionate and receptive attitude, Mrs. Knight expresses her pain and her need to be nurtured and pleads with her husband to let her know him after twenty years of marriage.

When Mr. Knight again blames external sources for the family's burdens, the therapist stresses the first and foremost need for personal change. He further calls Tom the victim of the spouses' problem and sees change in him dependent on change in his father and in the couple's relationship. The therapist indicates the need for self-reflection in Mr. Knight on his own pain when he gets upset, which will help him to understand a similar pain in his son. He could only reach his son if he could reach himself, and only then could his son learn to reach out and touch others. The therapist emphasizes the urgent necessity for Tom to be reached and drawn out of himself in order to learn to express his upsets, anger and unhappiness by other means than mute withdrawal. Through self-reference, he encourages Mr. Knight to be emotionally expressive with his son in his efforts to reach him, and adds that he should ask his wife to help him. He stresses the need for the couple to work on their own relationship towards greater emotional sharing and mutual support.

FAMILY STRUCTURE IN RELATION TO PROBLEM BEHAVIOUR

The above-mentioned structure can be seen in terms of its surface and deeper level of appearance. The surface structure is manifested by the family's presentation of their problems. The deeper nature of the structure becomes visible when the family therapist within the therapeutic system breaks through the surface structure and exposes the implicit personal and relational problems in the familiy. He thereby facilitates the possibility for change and meaningful restructuring of the family.

In the surface structure manifested through the family's view of their problems, the son is clearly defined as the symptom-bearer. He is the only one seen as uncommunicative and distant in an otherwise communicative and close family. Relationships between the spouses and with their daughter are presented as positive, close, agreeable and mutually supportive. Only their son's unintelligible behaviour leads the parents to be greatly concerned and evokes feelings of failure, frustration and helplessness. By his sulking behaviour and mute withdrawal, he embodies and expresses the family's unhappiness. The dialectical balance of relationships between the parents and their son seem strongly polarized in a negative direction where the interrelations between themselves and their daughter show a positive polarized character. Such a skewed balance of interrelationships in the family interferes with an open, dialectical intercourse and tends to be lived repetitively (Lovlie, 1982). It leads to an overstabilization of the systemic family structure which in turn serves to resist change and to sustain the problem behaviour of the identified patient.

The nature of the deeper family structure in which the problem behaviour is embedded, gradually emerges in the course of the family interview. The therapist's exploration of disagreements in both parents' relationship with their children throws light on the nature of these distinctly different triangular patterns of interrelationships. In their relationship to their daughter, all three tend to avoid disagreements, arguments, open confrontations and negative feelings in order to maintain overall close, positive and mutually protective relationships. Problematic issues are not resolved but covered up and personal responsibility is avoided by attributing failures in problem resolution to forgetfulness. In their mutually overly close relationships, the intergenerational distance is minimized and the parental authority is weakened.

In their relationship to their son, on the contrary, both parents openly express communication problems and disagreements with him as well as negative feelings of failure, frustration and helplessness. At the same time, both of them tend to avoid arguments or open confrontations with him. However, the individual nature of each parent's lived relationship with their son differs greatly. Father experiences total frustration with his son for not communicating with him, and indirect anger through his critical and degrading comments for not meeting his expectations regarding participation in organized team sports. Mother directly expresses great sadness and despondency in seeing him suffer from a negative self-perception, unresolved conflicts and a wish to be dead. She paradoxically seems emotionally overinvolved with her distant son.

Therapeutic penetration of the manifest close spouse relationship, reveals a great personal and emotional distance between them. The wife's persistent but unsuccessful efforts to reach and involve her husband in sharing and resolving significant family issues, has led to great unhappiness and frustration between them, which he in turn avoids. Mr. Knight's refusal to become emotionally involved, has forced his responsive wife to stay uninvolved as well. This leaves her in a lonely and burdened position, leading to occasional outbursts from accumulated feelings of frustration, anger and desperation. In a world devoid of personal involvement with each other, their son has emerged as the locus of their attentive involvement and mutual concern.

Further therapeutic exploration revealed that Mr. Knight hardly ever verbalizes his feelings, dislikes, disapprovals or disagreements and withdraws into long silences when emotionally upset. A striking resemblance is thus uncovered between father and son who both avoid involvement in potentially conflictual and painful interpersonal situations, not knowing how to express their anger and hurt except by silent withdrawal. A similarity is also apparent between mother and son who seem emotionally overinvolved with each other. Both find themselves for different reasons in a lonely and unbearable position and both experience great sadness and despondency. It seems that the spouses, in the absence of a personal relationship with each other, partially live their personal and relational problems through their son. He in turn dramatically expresses a fused state of his own and his family's emotional distress.

It can thus be said that in this family system, the parents' overt distant relationship to their son paradoxically hides a covert degree of fusion between their respective, problematic life situations which prevent open dialogical relationships between them. Instead, it locks them together in repetitive interactions curtailing mutual self-differentiation and growth. The parents' positive polarized attitude to their daughter further accentuates the victimization process. The family can be seen as caught in a frozen dialectical balance of interrelationships leading to repetitive patterns of dysfunctional interactions. This particular situated family structure serves to overtly maintain a one-sided, positive, agreeable and mutually supportive relationship between the spouses and with their daughter, in order to avoid involvement in disagreeable and painful personal and relational issues between them. In the covert interpersonal distance between the spouses, their son emerges as the focus of their attentive involvement and is victimized to carry, in addition to his own problems, the family's collective burden of frustrations and discontent.

A STRUCTURAL FAMILY THERAPY VIEWPOINT

The question arises as to how a structural family therapist would view the dysfunctional structure that sustains the problem of the identified patient in the Knight family. Although a detailed comparative analysis between a phenomenological and a structural family therapy point of view is beyond the scope of this chapter, the posed question should be briefly addressed.

The theory of structural family therapy provides a conceptual framework that explains individual and family dysfunction in terms of structures and indicates the general direction in which the system should change. Guided by his theory, the therapist searches for the already formed present structures manifest in the family's operational transactions.

In the Knight family, Aponte most likely hypothesized the existence of a conflict-detouring triangular structure in which the identified patient is used to obscure a parental conflict. In terms of Minuchin's (1978) typology of "rigid triads", it could be specified as a detouring, supportive structure in which the parents mask their differences by focussing on their problem child with an overprotective concern. The family structure further appears to be "emmeshed" in view of the overly close and mutually protective relationships, and the avoidance of arguments and disagreements. In addition to these alignment and boundary problems, the therapist discovers a failure in the "functional power" of the family system (e.g. the parents fail in consistent disciplining and leave too much power to the children).

The structural goal of the therapist is to break through this dysfunctional structure and to search for other possible family problems. By means of divisive techniques (e.g. exploring disagreements, developing implicit conflicts), he succeeds in his goal. He finds that Mr. Knight is actually "disengaged" from his wife in their marital relationship, and also from his son which has led to serious communication problem with both of them. Aponte thus found support for the hypothesis of the presence of a detouring-supportive dysfunctional structure sustaining the problem behaviour of the identified patient.

In the last part of the consulting interview, Aponte moves beyond the typical position of a structural family therapist when he explores the family's emotional and relational problems. His emphasis on the importance of self-understanding and personal change to Mr. Knight as a prerequisite for understanding his son, has an existential flavour. It seems that this family needed therapeutic intervention on a personal, experiential level in addition to systemic structural change. The fact that Aponte departed from a typical structural approach shows his responsiveness to this particular family's problems as well as his openness to other therapeutic orientations.

CONCLUSION

It has been pointed out that the theory of structural family therapy guides the therapist in recognizing and identifying the dysfunctional structures present in various families. Basically, the theory of structural family therapy assumes the primacy of structures which are seen as innate forces that structure and organize the family system's functioning. These structures are regulated by family codes and rules which are in term observable from the family's transactional operations. Consequently, the therapist does not pay much attention to the family's own perception of their reality. In this context, Kantor and Neal (1985, p. 19) remark: "The structural therapist does not allow his or her personal perspective about the family or the therapy to be questioned from the perspective of the family's reality". The structural family therapist is interested in formal, extrinsic and observable structures.

The phenomenologist, on the other hand, assumes the primacy of the family's lived experiential reality. He sees structures as created out of this lived reality by the intentional meanings which the individual and the family attribute to their personal and collective experiences. The phenomenologist brackets all theoretical considerations and opens himself to the family members' perceptions, behaviours and experiences in order to discover the meaning structures embedded in their shared familial world.

In the present study, I adopted a phenomenological attitude and applied a phenomenological method of analysis to a single structural family therapy interview. I departed from a description of the family's lived experiences of themselves and of each other. The description was analyzed in view of the researched phenomenon and revealed the meanings of the behaviours of the family members within the family system. These meanings were subsequently articulated within a systemic structure. This analysis resulted in a distinctly different view of the dysfunctional structure that systained the problematic behaviour of the identified patient, in comparison to the theoretical formulations of structural family therapy.

The reported study remains exploratory in nature. Many metatheoretical and methodological problems will need to be addressed. The use of more extensive raw material, e.g. a series of therapeutic interviews, and additional interviews with individuals, dyads and triads in the family will undoubtedly enrich and deepen our understanding of the phenomenal world of lived family experiences. Nevertheless, our phenomenological study undercuts the various core models which have been formulated and illustrates how the experiential, structural and systemic dimensions in family therapy can be integrated into a comprehensive understanding of family phenomena.

SUMMARY

This chapter proposes a phenomenological approach to family therapy which addresses simultaneously the experiential, structural and systemic dimensions involved in family therapy phenomena. An in-depth phenomenological analysis of a structural family therapy interview reveals the situated structure which sustains the identified patient's problems. This study illustrates the meaningfulness and potential richness of a phenomenological approach to the theory of family therapy.

REFERENCES

Aponte, H.J., & Van Deusen, J.M. (1981). Structural family therapy. In Gurman, A.S., & Kniskern, D.P. *Handbook of Family Therapy.* New York: Brunner/Mazel.

Giorgi, A. (Ed.). (1985). *Phenomenology and psychological research.* Pittsburgh: Duquesne University Press.

Giorgi, A., Knowles, R., & Smith, D.L. (1979). *Duquesne studies in phenomenological psychology.* Vol. III. Pittsburgh: Duquesne University Press.

Husserl, E. (1977). *Phenomenological psychology.* The Hague: Nijhoff.

Kantor, D., & Neal, J.H. (1985). Integrative shifts for the theory and practice of family systems therapy. *Family Process,* 24. 13-30.

Laing, R.D., & Esterson, A. (1964). *Sanity, madness and the family.* London: Penguin Books.

Lane, M. (1970). *Introduction to structuralism.* New York: Basic Books.

Lovlie, Anne-Lise (1982). *The Self: yours, mine or ours?* Oslo: Universitetsforlaget.

Merleau-Ponty, M. (1963). *The structure of behaviour.* Boston: Beacon.

Minuchin, S. (1974). *Families and family therapy.* Cambridge: Harvard University Press.

Minuchin, S., & Fishman, H.C. (1981). *Family therapy techniques.* Cambridge: Harvard University Press.

Minuchin, S., & Rosman, B.L., & Baker, L. (1978). *Psychosomatic families.* Cambridge: Harvard University Press.

Mook, B. (1985). Phenomenology, system theory and family therapy. *Journal of Phenomenological Psychology, 16.* 1-12.

Nordentoft, K. (1978). *Kierkegaard's Psychology.* Pittsburgh: Duquesne University Press.

Piaget, J. (1970). *Structuralism.* New York: Basic Books.

Sluzki, C.E. (1983). Process, structure and world views: toward an integrated view of systemic models in family therapy. *Family Process, 22.* 469-476.

Chapter 11

VERBAL DISPUTE AND TOPIC ANALYSIS: A METHODOLOGICAL COMMENTARY ON A DRAMA CASE STUDY

Karin Aronsson

Recent studies of discourse analysis have, for the most part, dealt with rational discourse, e.g. lessons, news-reporting or decision-making situations such as medical consultations. Therefore, analysis of discourse coherence has in many ways been fraught with what I would call a cognitive bias. Emotional determination has been bracketed as if it would be possible to analyse all discourse in terms of singular intentions and logical coherence.

This cognitive bias may in fact conceal important phenomena concerning discourse structure. For instance, the cognitive bias is also related to a consensus perspective in discourse analysis. In the conversational maxims of Grice (1975), cooperation is discussed as one of several important prerequisites for human dialogue. However, Grice refers to cooperation in a philosophical sense, and not in a prescriptive or descriptive sense as a condition which would hold true for any specific conversation. In spite of this, a great number of discourse analyses have dealt with conversations characterized by consensus, as if the Gricean abstract maxims would be valid for any specific concrete dialogue.

During the last ten years, the field of discourse analysis has expanded greatly. There are at least three different theoretical foundations: ethnomethodology, text linguistics and artificial intelligence simulation of dialogues. Within linguistics there has been a growing interest not only in larger linguistic units (texts rather than words and sentences in vacuo), but also a growing interest in spoken rather than written language. Therefore, the field of text linguistics has more and more turned its attention to discourse studies. Researchers with a background in text linguistics or artificial intelligence have tried to spell out rules for discourse structure, so-called *turn-taking* rules (distribution of the discourse space) and rules for *topic coherence* and *topic boundaries* (cf. Brown & Yule 1983; Coulthard 1977; Van Dijk 1977). These endeavours have often been based on premises of rationality and order, and what has here been referred to as a cognitive bias.

Ethnomethodology is influenced by phenomenological thinking and more specifically the writings of Alfred Schutz (1945). However, within ethnomethodological explorations of the everyday world, the emphasis has been on communicative cooperation. Thus, ethnomethodological studies have also been restricted by a consensus bias (cf. Heritage 1984).

The present point of departure is that if conflict and ambiguity are, more often than not, encountered in human communication, then models of spoken discourse need to take this into account. One important way of exploring conflict and ambiguity would therefore be to study prototypical conflict situations, such as argueing.

Some questions I hope to answer are: what are the essential constituents of verbal dispute and what are the prototypical actor and turn-taking characteristics? What are the typical manifest and latent goals, and what determines topic boundaries? Related to these questions, the present paper also addresses some questions to discourse theory. Is it possible to reliably establish topic boundaries? What are the complications of topic analysis in a world of multiple realities?

METHOD

Recently there has been a growing concern for natural dialogues.[1] However, transcripts of real-life disputes are quite rare, and persons who would volunteer such tapes or transcripts would not be representative of the population at large. For practical as well as ethical reasons, I have therefore chosen to apply discourse analytical procedures to a drama case material. The play chosen is "Long day's journey into night" by the Nobel Prize winner Eugene O'Neill. This drama was chosen because it is as close to 'real life' as possible in that it is based on autobiographical material. Also, it is chosen for its richness. O'Neill is, in my opinion, an insightful observer of human conflicts, and the play in question contains a series of covert and open disagreements, covering the whole emotional range from mild reprobation to unrestrained fury. The script does not offer a direct recording of real disputes, yet it echoes authentic struggles once fought. In the dedication, O'Neill refers to it as a recording of "old sorrow, written in tears and blood".

In O'Neill's four act "Journey into the past", he recounts past dialogues of the tormented Tyrone household, torn apart by guilt and by mutual mistrust. There are four principal characters: James Tyrone senior (a well-known actor), his wife Mary (a former beauty who has serious drug problems) and their two grown-up sons: Jamie (an alcoholic, second-rate actor) and tubercular Edmund (alter-ego of the author). Both sons express contempt of their father on many accounts: for his close-fisted approach to life, for his romantic ethnic pride in the Tyrone Irish catholic heritage and for his shying away from conflicts. For each point of accusation, he has countercriticism against his sons, for parasitic reliance on family resources, for an atheistic lack of respect for traditional values and for 'morbid' dwelling on sordid aspects of life. Tyrone struggles to uphold his self-esteem against guilt and fears, actualized by Edmund's tuberculosis (first held secret from Mary) and by Mary's drug problem and all the concomitant shadows from the past. In the process of disputing, the family's past history is interpreted and reinterpreted again and again, and the family's members all argue about each others' versions. Mary has been free from drugs for two months at the beginning of the day which sets the scene of the drama, but she resumes taking her injections in that long day of pain which eventually turns into night.

Primarily, the data have been analysed with the research goal of assessing the reliability and validity of discourse analytical concepts. To what extent is it possible to make topic analyses of verbal disputes (analyses of topic boundaries, of local and global coherence, etc.), and to what extent is it profitable to analyse dispute in terms of turn-taking patterns? Secondarily, the purpose has been to identify important communicative strategies in verbal disputes.

First, I read the play a couple of times as openly as possible, only to get a global sense of the main characters and their mutual conflicts. Thereafter, I did several close readings, filtering the play through different discourse analytical perspectives (topic- and turn-taking analyses). Lastly, I tried to identify important dispute strategies which had not been captured through the close readings. Methodologically, the last step is perhaps the most important one in that it reflects the present attempt to ground theory on the actual data and not on pre-set hypotheses (cf. Glaser & Strauss 1967).

TOPIC ANALYSIS

Not every disagreement qualifies as a dispute. For instance, a superior may strongly criticize his subordinate. Such an exchange is a matter of 'scolding' or 'discussion' rather than a matter of 'verbal dispute'. In a dispute proper, the prototypical relationship between the two contestants is one of symmetry, and not asymmetry. The prototypical dispute is thus always one between relative equals, such as long-time partners, man and wife, or between parents and grown-up children, or between grown-up siblings. In the present drama, all the family types of symmetrical disputes are well represented.

Also, a verbal dispute requires a minimal degree of discourse coherence. Thus, the quarrels of many young children are disqualified, not only on account of childrens' assymetrical positions but also because of their more limited conversational repertoire. Coherence can be defined as local coherence (connectedness between individual statements) or as global coherence (connectedness pertaining to a conversation as a whole). In children's discourse, conversational leaps are more frequent, and there are less restrictions in terms of coherence requirements. In the following, we will examine the Tyrone family dialogues in terms of coherence patterns.

Reference, in the dialogues, is often vague or misleading and there is thus not seldom poor local coherence. For instance, Jamie at one point comments about the fact that Mary has been alone in her room for some time "...And now you tell me she got you to leave her alone upstairs all morning". Edmund then replies, "She didn't! You're crazy!" (O'Neill 1966, p. 49). Edmund's reply evidently does not refer to the fact that she was left alone, but to the more crucial fact (not voiced here) that she may have started to take drugs again. Thus, in terms of local coherence, Edmund's reply makes little sense (why should he violently deny that she had been alone, after first having mentioned it casually himself). However, within the full (including implicit) domain of his reference, the response makes perfect sense. What is known but not said - implicit common knowledge - has to be taken into account for a proper evaluation of both local and global coherence.

One of the basic characteristics of the prototypical verbal dispute concerns participants' framing of the conversation in terms of different communicative intentions. On the surface, the overt goals of one or both contestants may be to change or modify a specific set of ideas or actions. Rational impersonal aspects of discourse are therefore foregrounded in the overt formulations of divergence. However, such divergence on a purely intellectual level (differences in thinking or planning) does not account for dispute structure or dispute emergence. On a latent level, verbal disputing involves interpersonal goals on the part of one or both contestants. Also, in the prototypical disagreement, the actors describe their own intentions in terms of rational exchange of ideas, whilst others are attributed with interpersonal goals of disparagement.

In the Tyrones' interactions, many contested opinions and actions are perfectly innocuous on a surface plane; e.g. Tyrone's concern for the careers and the future of his sons or Jamie's concern for the medical care of his brother. However, at a deeper level, such concerns are inextricably tied to old family conceptions of neglect and self-interest. When Jamie worries about the health of Edmund, he is simultaneously accusing their father of miserly conduct (in that Tyrone has consistently advocated the services of an allegedly incompetent doctor - with inexpensive fees). Jamie thus criticizes Tyrone's choice of doctor - "the cheap old quack", Dr. Hardy, who is also held responsible for Edmund's consumption ("it might never have happened if you'd sent him to a real doctor when he first got sick" (O'Neill 1966, p. 26)). Thus, his criticism also contains bitter resentment against Tyrone for jeopardizing his family's health out of sheer stinginess. The course of action under debate (the employment of Dr. Hardy's services) is thus at the same time a discussion of Tyrone's personal credibility, as a father and as a husband. It should perhaps be noted that Mary's initial contacts with morphine occurred when she was treated by a different but also allegedly incompetent and inexpensive doctor.

Because the discrediting of Dr. Hardy is thus basically also a discrediting of Tyrone himself, it is perfectly logical that Tyrone also counters by challenging Jamie on personal grounds. After a brief initial defense of Dr. Hardy, Tyrone attacks Jamie *ad hominem*, and as a matter of logical elegance, on economical grounds, though for quite different reasons:

> TYRONE. That's a lie! And your sneers against Doctor Hardy are lies! He doesn't put on frills, or have an office in a fashionable location, or drive around in an expensive automobile. That's what you pay for with those other five-dollars-to-look-at-your-tongue fellows, not their skill.
>
> JAMIE (with a scornful shrug of his shoulders). Oh, all right. I'm a fool to argue. You can't change the leopard's spots.
>
> TYRONE (with rising anger). No, you can't. You've taught me that lesson only too well. I've lost all hope you will ever change yours. You dare tell me what I can afford? You've never known the value of a dollar and never will! You've never saved a dollar in your life! At the end of each season you're penniless! You've thrown your salary away every week on whores and whisky!
>
> JAMIE. My salary! Christ!
>
> TYRONE. It's more than you're worth, and you couldn't get that if it wasn't for me. If you weren't my son, there isn't a manager in the business who would give you a part, your reputation stinks so. As it is, I have to humble my pride and beg for you, saying you've turned over a new leaf, although I know it's a lie!
>
> JAMIE. I never wanted to be an actor. You forced me on the stage.
>
> TYRONE. That's a lie! You made no effort to find anything else to do. You left it to me to get you a job and I have no influence except in the theatre. Forced you! You never wanted to do anything except loaf in bar-rooms! You'd have been content to sit back like a lazy lunk and sponge on me for the rest of your life! After all the money I'd wasted on your education, and all you did was get fired in disgrace from every college you went to!
>
> JAMIE. Oh, for God's sake, don't drag up that ancient history!
>
> TYRONE. It's not ancient history that you have come home every summer to live on me. (O'Neill 1966, p. 27-28).

As can be seen, there need not be any internal consistency between argument and counter-argument in a more classical philosophical sense. Rather, blows to the self-esteem of one contestant are returned in terms of counter-blows.

Similarly, in an argument about Mary's past, Tyrone reminds her of when she, half crazy, once tried to throw herself off the dock (ibid, p. 74). Mary responds first by pleading with Tyrone not to remember, then immediately thereafter by denying the facts: "It doesn't matter. Nothing like that ever happened". Lastly, she responds by actualizing other shadows from the past - how Tyrone made her live in cheap hotels with cheap "quack" doctors. The logic is here not that of argument and counter-argument, but rather one of humiliation against humiliation. In this specific case, one painful event of the past is balanced against another painful past event. Emotional retaliation rather than logical conclusions is at stake. It is the person, not the topic which is the target of the speech acts.

Emotional retaliation is often quite isomorphic - accusations are often countered by related counter-accusations (rather than by defensive argumentation). When Tyrone at one point (implicitly) accuses Edmund of having triggered Mary's relapse through his tuberculosis (ibid, p. 121), Edmund responds by talking about Tyrone's past role in Mary's drug addiction, his unwillingness to hire good (expensive) doctors, etc. . Emotionally loaded accusations are thus often not met by defensive argumentation but rather by counter-accusations.

Topic incoherence thus gives way for an emotional and interpersonal coherence of battling. The rationality of dispute is one of what we will call here *emotional trading*   rather than one of logic. It is the emotional loading of a given topic that is measured against other loadings, and attacks against the person that are compared to equivalent attacks.

Who is sensible, and who is miserly? Or who is paranoid and who is well-tempered and mature? The intersubjective differences with respect to attribution and self-attribution (of communicative goals) seem to form quite important parameters in dispute exchanges. The contestation of thoughts or actions at the same time forms a contestation of values and preferences. From the perspective of the speaker, his contribution may be about ideas only (discourse construed as 'discussion') or about actions and outcomes of actions (discourse construed as 'negotiations'). Yet, from the contestant's perspective, the person and not the explicit topic is at stake (and the discourse is construed as a 'dispute'). Ultimately, the value dimension concerns esteem and self-esteem. What is at stake in a dispute is always to some degree a matter of disparagement. Directly or indirectly, disputes challenge the esteem of the interlocutor, typecast as less worthy (on a temporary or more permanent basis). It is thus the value of the speaker which is the overriding implicit topic other things being equal, if the person is the implicit 'topic', then the conflict will be more complex, the lengthier the common past of two contestants. A more extended common past will produce more mutual associations to past grievances, which in turn complicate any topic analysis. As has been seen in the Tyrone family, the theme of Mary's relapse blends into that of Edmund's tuberculosis and/or Tyrone's miserliness, which in turn brings to the fore Jamie's wastefulness and then Jamie's professional reputation etc. (in a recursive fashion). Quite often the 'initial' dispute topic is thus obliterated into related ones.

DISPUTE AS A SPECIAL PROVINCE OF MEANING

As has been shown, past actions are held against other past actions; ad hominem arguments are often met by other ad hominem arguments, and blows and counter-blows tend to be quite isomorphic. Emotional justice is thus often meeted out in terms of blows of matched strength. In terms of logical coherence, these retaliation patterns are quite shaky. However, in terms of overall emotional structure, such patterns are meaningful and effective. The more global analysis thus shows a different type of coherence than an analysis of the argumentation sequences per se. One or both parties may be aware of the true state of events, but the battling as such may require denials, exaggerations or other distortions of reality as part of the dispute rhetorics.

In the terminology of Schutz (1945), verbal disputes would form a special province of meaning. The emotional trading, as discussed above, would be one special feature in this province of meaning. Also, truth seems to be handled differently from what is the case in natural everyday discussions. We would like to talk about a type of *rhetorical truth* or defensive distortions of reality, geared to saving face and to standing up in disputes.

It has here been shown how Mary responded to Tyrone's accusations with accusations of her own on the one hand, and with flat denial on the other. In the Tyrone context, lots of facts are associated with severe guilt, which means that allusions to illness or drug addiction also trigger feelings of humiliation. On several occasions in the dialogues, facts are denied which one party knows that the other person knows about. Such stubborn denials occur again and again all through the play: Mary denies her relapse when disputing with Tyrone and so does Edmund (deny Mary's relapse) when disputing with Jamie, and then there are disputes between Jamie and Tyrone who take turns in denying the seriousness of Edmund's illness. In discourse analysis, *mutual knowledge* refers to situations where speaker A knows that B knows X, and B knows that A knows, etc. In the Tyrone family, denials often occur in a context of mutual knowledge; both parties in fact know the true state of events.

Such denials are not to be interpreted as regular lies. Rather, there seems to be a latent logic which equates each accusation with an attack on the other person "you are bad, because X". In denying X, the accused thus refutes the first proposition ("you are bad"). In the emotional context of an argument, such flat denials therefore seem to form consistent forms of self-defense.

Obviously, many psychodynamic defense mechanisms - projection, rationalization, intellectualization, denial - should be at work in verbal disputes. The more anxiety provoking the dispute, the more there will be dramatic switches between aggression and intro-aggression, between denial and projection and so on. Since the present paper does not purport to present a psychoanalytic reading of O'Neill, no specific analyses will be attempted. Rather, it suffices to point out that verbal disputes contain all types of distortions of reality, which means that topic coherence can never be analysed from one single perspective.

Distortions of reality also seem to operate quite overtly on a lexical level. One person may talk about events which *never* or *always* happen when it is obviously the case that these events - at best - occur *seldom* or *often*. For instance, Mary will talk of her home in such absolute terms and Tyrone will answer in the same vein.

> MARY.... It's unreasonable to expect Bridget or Cathleen to act as if this was a home. They know it isn't as well as we know it. It NEVER has been and it NEVER will be.
> TYRONE (bitterly without turning around): No, it NEVER can be now. But it was once, before you - (O'Neill 1966, p. 62; capitals added).

Such a 'language of absolutes' is typical for disputes, and the emotional trading pattern is also quite characteristic. One person will talk about "you *never....*" and the contestant will answer using the same or similar terms. Again, this has to do with 'rhetorical truth' in that both persons (most likely) know at some level that they do not exactly mean *never* or *always*. However, within the dispute province of meaning, such categorical positions are quite consistent (again if interpreted within the more global context of the family dynamics rather than within a traditional model of precise reference).

TOPIC BOUNDARIES

Analysis of discourse coherence is, for practical reasons, often done on local coherence and on stereotyped materials, such as news discourse. In spoken language between equals of long standing, local coherence is often of little relevance except for the most ritualized of everyday events. Sentences connect to form organized discourse units, but the more important coherence is rather that of whole segments of speech. Furthermore, if we consider spoken language, global coherence is a matter of coherence over time, of being familiar with the antecedants of a specific discussion.

Other things being equal, dispute topics with a long history would tend to become more infected, as do topics embedded in other topics of debate. Superficially innocuous topics, such as Tyrone's tight-fisted saving, may thus acquire distinct dispute qualities. Also, evidently, the dispute qualities of a specific topic should be related to the type of potential narcissistic injury involved, whether it is unspecific in its focus or more specific in terms of distinct personal failings on the part of the interlocutor. Integration is important in that well-integrated dispute topics acquire *overdetermined* qualities analogous to the overdetermination of dream symbols in the psychoanalytical sense (a given symbol representing several different things at the same time). Overdetermination in disputes, for one thing, implies that the emotional loading of a given topic will be high. Thus, convergent forces render strength to the narcissistic injuries involved. Such overdetermination may be illustrated through a dispute between Tyrone and Edmund. At night, in the Tyrones' household, Edmund does not accept his father's admonition to turn out the lights. The explosive undertones of the exchange that ensues are better understood within the context of the family's history of miserliness.

TYRONE. I'm not going to argue with you. I asked you to turn out the lights in the hall.
EDMUND. I heard you, and as far as I'm concerned it stays on.
TYRONE. None of your damned insolence! Are you going to obey me or not?
EDMUND. Not! If you want to be a crazy miser put it out yourself!
TYRONE (with threatening anger): Listen to me! I've put up with a lot from you because from the mad things you've done at times I've thought you weren't quite right in your head. I've excused you and never lifted my hand to you. But there's a straw that breaks the camel's back. You'll obey me and put out that light or, big as you are, I'll give you a thrashing that'll teach you - ! (Suddenly he remembers Edmund's illness and instantly becomes guilty and shamefaced). Forgive me, lad. I forgot - You shouldn't goad me into losing my temper.
EDMUND (ashamed himself now): Forget it, Papa. I apologize too. I had no right being nasty anout nothing. I am a bit soused, I guess. I'll put out the damned light. (He starts to get up).
TYRONE. No, stay where you are. Let it burn. (He stands up abruptly - and a bit drunkenly - and begins turning on the three bulbs in the chandelier, with a childish, bitterly, dramatic self-pity). We'll have them all on! Let them burn! To hell with them! The poorhouse is the end of the road, and it might as well be sooner as later! (He finishes turning on the lights).
EDMUND (has watched this proceeding with an awakened sense of humour - now he grins, teasing affectionately). That's a grand curtain. (He laughs). You're a wonder, Papa. (O'Neill 1966, p. 110-111).

One other phenomenon with respect to integration in time is what will here be called *fossilization* of conflict. A topic of dispute which has been repeated over and over again may finally become fossilized. This means that it, although integrated in the history of the contestants, has lost something of its initial potency. Furthermore, the exposure of something like a family secret may bring about strong reactions the first time it is brought out into the open, and only weak reactions after more exposure. For instance, in the Tyrone household, Edmund's consumption is at first a well-guarded family secret and taboo subject (purportedly not to upset Mary into a relapse). However, the taboo was broken, first by Jamie and then by Tyrone, in a heated discussion. Once broken, the subject looses some of its initial potency. As can be seen in the above excerpt from act four, Tyrone even refers indirectly to the consumption when talking to Edmund himself ("Forgive me, lad. I forgot"). Yet, related topics (such as the accompanying costs for medical care) are still infected with old forlorn mistrust.

In accordance with the time perspective adopted here, it is difficult to assess when a verbal dispute starts or closes. Somewhat schematized, it would be possible to outline the course of dispute as follows:

pre-history + (triggers) + opening + argumentation sequence + (climax) + (resolution)

The minimal requirement of a verbal dispute is, as postulated, an argumentation sequence. This also implies that there are one or more points which mark the opening of such a sequence. Within ethnomethodology, the concept of *pre-sequences* can be applied to pre-openings, pre-announcements, pre-requests etc. (for a useful discussion, see Levinson 1985). However, the greater the dynamic integration of a given topic, the more difficult it will be to discern when a dispute is opened or pre-announced since a great number of disputes form parts of old patterns.

Aside from nonverbal signals (raised tone of voice etc.), how are we then to determine when a specific disagreement opens and closes? The most important signals of emerging disagreement probably pertain to topic choice and to topic avoidance. By bringing up (or avoiding) specific topics loaded with dispute potential, participants trigger off or initiate verbal disputes. Disputes reveal several problems concerning topic identification in discourse analysis. Does a disagreement start when a specific topic is first brought up (maybe innocuously) by one of the participants, or when he/she is challenged by the contestant? Is it legitimate to define the disagreement in terms of topic as identified in terms of latent structure (from a third party perspective) or should topic analysis be restricted to topics as identified by the participants themselves? Evidently, problems of this type are also relevant for identifying those discourse passages that should be included in a disagreement sequence.

If the opening and continuation of a dispute is difficult to define, its resolution is even more difficult to identify. One partner may explicitly propose that the argument should be brought to a close, e.g.:

Oh, all right. I'm a fool to argue. You can't change the leopard's spots (Jamie to Tyrone, ibid, p. 27).

All right, Papa. I'm a bum. Anything you like, so long as it stops the argument. (Jamie to Tyrone, ibid, p. 28).

(Boredly): Let's forget me. I'm not interested in the subject. Neither are you. (Jamie to Tyrone, ibid, p. 28).

Don't start jumping down my throat! God, Papa, this ought to be the one thing we can talk over frankly without a battle. (Jamie to Tyrone, ibid, p. 32).

(Placatingly): All right, Kid. Don't start a battle with me. I hope as much as you do I'm crazy. I've been as happy as hell because I'd really began to believe that this time.... (Jamie to Edmund, ibid, p. 50).

Mama! For God's sake, stop talking. (Edmund to Mary, ibid, p. 64).

Shut up, both of you! (Tyrone to Jamie and Edmund, ibid, p. 66).

Mary, hold your tongue! (Tyrone to Mary, ibid, p. 78).

(Stammers pleadingly): Please, don't talk about things you don't understand! (Mary to Edmund, ibid, p. 81).

....Well, well, let's not argue... (Tyrone to Edmund, ibid, p. 111).

Shut up! I'll be God-damned if I'll listen to you any more (Tyrone to Jamie, ibid, p. 147).

However, the interactive nature of dispute implies that one person alone cannot decide that an argument should be closed. Even if the contestant accepts a termination of the dispute, the speaker himself may decide to continue, albeit often with a somewhat different line of argumentation. This means that "let's not argue" may often work as a marker of topic boundary (but not dispute boundary). The dispute continues, though in terms of one of several other related topics. For instance, in most of the Tyrone disagreements (where an attempt is made to come to an end - as above), the dispute continues, though often in terms of a slightly different topic. Hence, disputes are not resolved on demand.

More effective resolutions are sometimes to be found in different types of more or less dramatic action; in laughter, crying, acting out, physical fighting, departure from the scene of dispute, symbolic break-ups, reconciliation (sex, exhaustion). However, what may appear to be a dispute resolution may merely be one out of several climaxes in an argument or series of arguments.

REAL-LIFE AND DRAMA DISPUTES

In everyday language, the typical dispute has a distinct opening and resolution, and we talk about quarreling *about* something (topic x). However, this seems to be an idealized version of dispute structure. On the contrary, disputes highlight problems of topic identification in discourse analysis. What is the topic of a specific dispute? The first one (as alleged by the initiator) or a different one (as proposed by the contestant) or a third topic (identified by a therapist or third party)? In a world of multiple meaning, topic identification is necessarily a matter of perspective. Furthermore, the time dimension complicates the identification of dispute topics. In the terminology of the present discussion, either overdetermination or fossilization may be at work; lending different types of potency to conflicts of the past.

The issues of topic identification and topic boundaries simultaneously raise problems for the praxis and theory of discourse analysis. In conversational analysis, the whole concept of topic and topic coherence is intimately linked to notions such as mutual knowledge and shared or divergent presuppositions (cf. Levinson 1985). Delineation problems in topic analysis are, of course, highlighted by complex disputes between persons with a long common past and with violent internal conflicts as in the Tyrones' case. A sceptical reader would possibly object that everyday disputes are quite different. However, I would claim that these differences concern differences in intensity and differences in quantity (e.g. time spent disputing) rather than differences in kind. The theoretical and methodological issues of boundary establishment and topic identification would be relevant also for less fervent and less complex disputes.

If we accept the premise that disagreement is present in much of human discourse (to some extent), the present reasoning will raise reliability and validity problems for any discourse study that attempts to analyse topic boundaries in real life conversations between persons with a common past. In the analysis of rhetorical truths, it was suggested that dispute truth conditions pertain to the person (as topic) rather than to the overt topic. Two contestants may therefore operate with empty threats, blatant denials, exaggerations, and what has here been called the language of absolutes, and yet both feel that they act in good faith. This is so, since it is the person as implicit 'topic' which overrides the overt dispute topic as such. Incoherence in the overt topic gives way for coherence by means of emotional trading.

Obviously, it will be most difficult to identify topic boundaries in the case of two people who have disputed many times before and where many associations link innocuous topics to infected ones, increasing the dispute potential of any given topic. Conversely, problems in identifying topics and topic boundaries will be less in types of discourse where there is little disagreement and where there is not a long pre-history (of battling) between the two speakers.

Lastly, we may ask if problems with topic boundaries also raise problems for disputes as such - as lived by men. Verbal disputes may at times function as safety-valves or cathartic outlets. In verbal disputes, evil spirits may be exorcised and terminated when brought out into the open. We may thus ask - what are the conditions for successful exorcism? As implied, one important condition seems to pertain to dispute boundaries. Catharsis or exorcism implies a termination, i.e. that the dispute is resolved. *Pro primo,* the felicity conditions for dispute would thus require dispute termination. According to the foregoing analysis, this would be quite difficult in such cases as when the discourse topic is overdetermined or deeply embedded in other related conflict topics. With a pre-history of battling, it is difficult to argue about any one singular topic, since each dispute actualizes old injuries and emotional counter-accusations. Theoretically, we thus conclude that the art of felicitous dispute management is a most demanding one, since it is reasonable to assume that a great many real-life disputes are of an aborted type, with no clear opening and no clear resolution, the mute revelation of old sorrow and discontent.

SUMMARY

Much recent research on discourse structure has been fraught with two biases; a cognitive bias on the one hand (emphasis on rational dialogue) and a consensus bias on the other hand. Certain methodological problems in discourse analysis were elucidated through the application of key concepts such as *topic coherence (local/global coherence)* to verbal dispute dialogues.

Eugene O'Neill's drama "Long day's journey into night" was chosen for its richness of such material and for the fact that it is close to real life (being based on autobiographical material). A close reading of the drama - from a phenomenological perspective - revealed several problems pertaining to topic boundaries and to topic identification. Apparent incoherence on a local level would be dissolved if thematic content was analysed in terms of global content structure. In turn, such global structures could only be inferred through a holistic reading, and if the drama disputes were analysed as taking place within a specific province of meaning, where implicit rules regulate the framing of content, truth conditions and type of lexicon.

NOTES

[1] The author is engaged in a larger research undertaking on authentic discourse - such as medical interviews, courtroom examinations (cf. Adelswärd, Aronsson & Linell 1986; Aronsson & Sätterlund-Larsson 1986).

REFERENCES

Adelswärd, V., Aronsson, K., & Linnell, P. (1987). Discourse of blame. Courtroom construction of social identity from the perspective of the defendent. *Semiotica* (accepted for publication).

Aronsson, K., & Sätterlund-Larsson, U. (1986). On the social choreography of doctor-patient communication. Linköping University: Department of Communication Studies. Manuscript.

Brown, G., & Yule, G. (1983). *Discourse analysis.* Cambridge: Cambridge University Press.

Coulthard, M. (1977). *An introduction to discourse analysis.* London: Longman.

Dijk, T. van (1977). *Text and context. Explorations in the semantics and pragmatics of discourse.* London: Longman.

Glaser, B.G., & Strauss, A.L. (1967). *The discovery of grounded theory.* Chicago: Aldine.

Grice, H.P. (1975). Logic and conversation. In P. Cole & J. Morgan (Eds.), *Syntax and semantics 3. Speech acts.* New York: Academic Press.

Heritage, J. (1984). *Garfinkel and ethnomethodology.* Cambridge: Polity Press.

Levinson, S.C. (1985). *Pragmatics.* Cambridge: Cambridge University Press.

O'Neill, E. (1966). *Long day's journey into night.* London: Cape.

Schutz, A. (1945). On multiple realities. *Philosophy and Phenomenological Research, 5,* 533-576.

ABOUT THE AUTHORS

Christopher M. Aanstoos is an Associate Professor and a member of the graduate faculty at West Georgia College. His research interests are in cognitive, developmental and social psychology, as well as the historical, methodological and philosophical foundations of phenomenological psychology. He has edited the book *Exploring the Lived World: Readings in Phenomenological Psychology* and he is editor of the journal *The Humanistic Psychologist*.
Address: Psychology Department, West Georgia College, Carrollton,
GA 30118, U.S.A.; phone: (404)836-6510.

Mike (Myron) M. Arons is Professor and Chairman of the Psychology Department, West Georgia College. His doctoral thesis completed in 1965 under Paul Ricoeur centered on creativity and methodological concerns in psychology. Many of his numerous papers and publications since have re-examined basic assumptions inherent to the relationship between psychology's subject and method. Since 1968, after assisting Abraham Maslow, at Brandeis, he helped to establish one of the first programs in the U.S.A. with a focus on an existential-humanistic orientation.
Address: Department of Psychology, West Georgia College, Carrollton,
GA 30118, U.S.A.; phone: (404)836-6510.

Karin Aronsson is lecturer at the Department of Psychology, Lund University (1976-1981) and Associate Professor (Linköping University since 1981 and presently). She has done research on the psychology of language. Her more recent work is on language and socialization, including bilingual acquisition, and on understanding and control in authentic discourse such as pediatric interviews and courtroom trials.
Address: Department of Communication Studies, Linköping University,
S-581 83 Linköping, Sweden; phone: 013-281000.

P. Erik Craig is a licensed psychotherapist in private practice and the director of the Center for Existential Studies and Human Services in Worcester and Cambridge, Massachusetts. He has also served as a graduate psychology professor at Assumption College for the past sixteen years. His primary ongoing fascinations are with the study of dreams and consciousness and with articulating the existential-phenomenological essences of psychoanalytic thinking. Other research interests include the experiences of identity, alienation and intimacy.
Address: Center for Existential Studies and Human Services,
          57 Cedar Street, Worcester, MA 01609, U.S.A.;
          phone: (617) 791-0755; 347-9548 (residence).

Amedeo Giorgi is currently Director of Research at Saybrook Institute in San Francisco, California. He is interested in applying phenomenological thought to problems of research in psychology and in developing the theory and practice of psychology as a human science. He tests these methodical and theoretical ideas primarily in the areas of adult cognitive processes.
Address: Saybrook Institute, 1772 Vallejo Street,
          San Francisco, CA 94123, U.S.A.; phone: 415-441-5034.

Mariane Hedegaard is Assistant Professor at the Institute of Psychology (Aarhus) since 1970. She has published on concept learning, on the methodological basis of research in teaching and learning and on the way in which children become related to the world. Her main research theme is concept learning within general, developmental and educational psychology.
Address: Institute of Psychology, University of Aarhus, Asylvej 4,
          DK-8240 Risskov, Denmark; phone: 6-175511.

Anke Hoenkamp-Bisschops works at the Social Science Department of the Theological Faculty of the University of Heerlen, The Netherlands. She teaches psychology of religion and conducts courses in interview training and client-centered counseling. At present she is writing her Ph.D.-thesis on the experience of celibacy of Roman catholic priests.
Address: Past. van Soevershemstraat 18, 6525 SW Nijmegen,
          The Netherlands; phone: 080-550234.

Steinar Kvale is Professor of Educational Psychology at the University of Aarhus. His research interests are: evaluation in education, in particular with regard to social functions, and the issues of authority, legitimacy and validity. And also, the practical and theoretical development of the qualitative interview into a research method within a phenomenological and a hermeneutical conception of psychological science.
Address: University of Aarhus, Psykologisk Institut, Asylvej 4,
          DK-8240 Risskov, Denmark; phone: 06-175511.

Bertha Mook received her Ph.D. in Clinical Psychology from the University of Ottawa, Canada, in 1968. She held academic and clinical positions at the Universities of Cape Town and Johannesburg before returning to the University of Ottawa in 1975. At present, she is Professor in Clinical Psychology and in Child and Family Psychotherapy in particular. She has published books, book chapters and articles in the fields of child psychopathology, child psychotherapy, family history and family therapy. Her main interest is in a phenomenological and hermeneutical approach to childhood, families and psychotherapy.
Address: Child Study Centre, University of Ottawa, 10 McDougall Lane,
Ottawa, Ontario K1N 6N5, Canada; phone: 1613-7460035.

Diane Reed Barnett obtained her bachelors degree from the University of Virginia and her masters degree from the Duquesne University in Pittsburgh; at present she is a doctoral candidate in clinical psychology at Duquesne and a practising psychotherapist.
Address: 4592 Bucktail Drive, Allisons Park, PA 15101, U.S.A.,
phone: (412) 452-4453.

Frederick J. Wertz received his Ph.D. in Phenomenological Psychology at Duquesne University. Holds the position of Assistant Professor of Psychology at Fordham University. Serves as Chief Editor of *Theoretical and Philosophical Psychology,* Bulletin of Division 24 of the American Psychological Association. Practices psychotherapy privately in New York City. Has written in the areas of human perception, development, abnormality, criminal victimization, phenomenological research methodology, psychoanalysis, and the philosophical and cultural foundations of psychology.
Address: L.L.916, Division of Social Sciences, Fordham University,
New York, NY 10023, U.S.A.; phone: (212) 841-5444, 5115.

Florence J. van Zuuren is Assistant Professor of Clinical Psychology, University of Amsterdam, and a licensed psychotherapist. Her 1982 dissertation on phobias was based on therapeutic insights combined with quantitative research. It was followed by articles and book chapters on personality traits, symptomatology and social roles. In recent years she became interested in qualitative methods, investigating such topics as the breaking of implicit rules, the experience of being in psychotherapy, and coping with threatening (medical) information.
Address: Psychological Laboratory, Department of Clinical Psychology,
P.O. Box 20218, 1000 HE Amsterdam, The Netherlands;
phone: (0)20-5253142.